At the Edge of the World

Also by Jean-Vincent Blanchard

Éminence: Cardinal Richelieu and the Rise of France

At the Edge of the World

World

The Heroic Century of the French Foreign Legion

JEAN-VINCENT BLANCHARD

BLOOMSBURY PRESS

NEW YORK · LONDON · OXFORD · NEW DELHI · SYDNEY

Bloomsbury Press
An imprint of Bloomsbury Publishing Plc

1385 Broadway	50 Bedford Square
New York	London
NY 10018	WC1B 3DP
USA	UK

www.bloomsbury.com

BLOOMSBURY and the Diana logo are trademarks of Bloomsbury Publishing Plc

First published 2017

© Jean-Vincent Blanchard, 2017

Maps created by Gary Antonetti

ISBN: HB: 978-0-8027-4387-9
         ePub: 978-0-8027-4388-6

33614080189128

LIBRARY OF CONGRESS CATALOGING-IN-PUBLICATION DATA IS AVAILABLE.

2 4 6 8 10 9 7 5 3 1

Typeset by RefineCatch Limited, Bungay, Suffolk
Printed and bound in the U.S.A. by Berryville Graphics Inc., Berryville, Virginia

To find out more about our authors and books visit www.bloomsbury.com.
Here you will find extracts, author interviews, details of forthcoming events and the option to sign up for our newsletters.

Bloomsbury books may be purchased for business or promotional use. For information on bulk purchases please contact Macmillan Corporate and Premium Sales Department at specialmarkets@macmillan.com.

Contents

Contents

Introduction

Fes took early twentieth-century European travelers by surprise. Approaching the Moroccan city from the west, from Meknes, they saw Fes rise like a citadel in the midst of a wide rocky valley, with nothing outside its fierce defenses but barren land punctuated here and there by a prickly pear cactus, a palm tree, or a wild geranium. The city's nine miles of ramparts and a belt of lush gardens enclosed a tangle of narrow streets, the medina, where ninety thousand people lived in a fascinating concentration of humanity. At dusk, when a low sun gave the city's walls, towers, and bastions a soft golden glow, Fes shone as the ancient, vibrant heart of Morocco.

May 28, 1912, was Fes's most dangerous day and one of its most memorable. After the Sultan of Morocco, Abdelhafid, and France's diplomatic representative, Eugène Regnault, declared Morocco to be a French protectorate on March 30, 1912, the sultan elite guard revolted and, together with the poorest of the population, massacred sixty-three French officers and civilians. French reprisals were equally ferocious. Resentment simmered in Fes over the following weeks, and it spread through the entire city. By the end of May, tensions between the Moroccans and the French reached their nadir. Fifteen thousand warriors coming from the surrounding mountains attacked the city to take it back from the foreigners who still occupied it. After four days of fighting, on May 28, the warriors stood ready to descend again to deal the final blow. European civilians and French personnel were trapped in the labyrinth of the medina, unable to evacuate given the number of wounded that lay sheltered in the hospital.

Right outside the walls of Fes, the Foreign Legion, an essential asset of the city's French military forces, was positioned to bear the brunt of this last attack. Companies of legionnaires were assembled to the north, on a ridge overlooking the city, by the sixteenth-century ruined tombs of the Marinids, an old dynasty of sultans. More legionnaires stood ready for action at the camp of Dar Dbibagh, to the southwest of the city walls.

The Europeans trapped inside, as well as many citizens of Fes, put their last hopes on these legionnaires, who had trained in sweltering Algeria to be fearless. As an all-volunteer corps of the French army, founded in 1831 with a special right to hire foreign-born recruits, the Legion had distinguished itself in France's colonial conquests, building an empire from Algeria to Indochina, from Madagascar to Morocco. From the 1830s until well after World War I, the Foreign Legion were essential troops in a colonial expansion in the professed name of civilization and racial superiority, at a time of rising nationalism and murderous rivalries between European powers.

In one of Fes's palaces with a shaded courtyard, a veteran of the French colonial wars, Louis Hubert Gonzalve Lyautey, oversaw the defense of the siege as the appointed resident-general of Morocco, entrusted with both civil and military powers. Resident-General Lyautey had entered Fes four days earlier to find himself in the thorniest situation. Sultan Abdelhafid, whom he had met upon his arrival, wished to abdicate. The ulemas, Fes's highest clergy, told Lyautey that nothing they or the sultan could do would avert a disaster. The wealthy elite merchants, the *chorfas*, were said to be negotiating with the Amazigh (Berber; plural Imazighen) chiefs to facilitate their assault on the city. News came that the attackers had removed the saintly robes kept in the shrine of Moulay Idriss II, Fes's founder and patron saint.

The last attack on Fes began at four o'clock in the afternoon of May 28. Thousands of warriors poured down on Fes in a clamor of cries and rifle shots. In no time they were massing at the gates, or climbing the crumbling parts of the walls, and quickly disappearing in the maze of the medina.

On the roof terrace of his headquarters, Lyautey smoked cigarette after cigarette. The wave of fighting rolled toward the palace. Shots were fired. Lyautey and his officers understood that they were now cut off from any communication with the outside. The resident-general pointed his spyglass toward the Maranids site on the mountain and saw the legionnaires advancing.

The roots of Lyautey's admiration and confidence in the colonial army corps of the Legion ran deep. He had first become acquainted with the Legion as a French army officer, when he was dispatched successively in 1894 and 1897 to Southeast Asia and the African island of Madagascar, to solidify recent French colonial conquests. There, among the different corps of the

French colonial army, was the Legion. Lyautey steadily rose in rank, giving orders to the legionnaires as they conquered western Algeria, and then Morocco. Afterwards, as the resident-general in that kingdom from 1912 to 1925, a colonial viceroy who had acquired an international reputation, he demonstrated political, administrative, and military talents, relying again on the Legion to accomplish his mission. He would write on the centennial anniversary of the Legion, in 1931:

> You all know that I am a legionnaire both in body and soul. Since 1894, in the Tonkin, I constantly marched with the Legion, in Madagascar, in the South Oranais, at the head of the Oran military division, at the border between Algeria and Morocco, and then in Morocco. All that without respite until 1925, for thirty-one years in a row.[1]

Crucial to the Legion's aims and missions was Lyautey's project of conquering "by winning hearts and minds." As an architect of French colonial expansion, Lyautey wanted to build roads, market places, and schools to show the benefits of the French occupation and slowly gain the people's trust in what the French viewed as a civilizing mission. With sincere declarations of respect for Moroccan culture and Islam in general, he protected the cultural heritage by encouraging traditional arts and preserving the urban fabric of Moroccan cities. The Legion played a key role in realizing these projects thanks to the astounding variety of skills—engineering and otherwise— that the legionnaires brought to the corps. This is why Lyautey saw the corps as the quintessential troop in his vision of a colonization. The Legion would help spread French civilization like an "oil slick," a *tache d'huile*—the metaphor used by Lyautey himself and his colonial mentor, Joseph Gallieni.

In the courtyard of Mnebhi Palace, on May 28, 1912, Lyautey's aides-de-camp were gathering crates of papers with cans of gasoline nearby, should these papers need to be burned. Lyautey had not slept for two days, yet three hours into the attack, he remained remarkably calm, confident that the Foreign Legion and the other corps of the army would prevail. He ordered dinner to be served on the terrace of his palace, overlooking the medina and the war scene. Days later, the resident-general recounted the night in a letter to a friend:

> I had in my company a charming little poet, Lieutenant Droin . . .
> We took his book to the dinner table so that we could read

the most successful verses, just as the skirmishers were firing from the terrace and other officers were taking their tour of duty. The night, I must say, was beautiful, and the moonlight perfectly lit those white-robed Moroccans tumbling down towards the city. The moment had to be lived.[2]

Twenty-two years after claiming Morocco for themselves, the French were still fighting courageous Amazigh resistance fighters in the Atlas Mountains, to the point where they had to resort to extraordinary force and weaponry, and accept mass casualties. When the Moroccans objected to their country's being led by the French, troublemakers had to be put down by force. The Legion was the perfect troop for that, too. "The Maréchal attacked his problem with unfailing energy, using tact when tact was needed, and the Foreign Legion when things had gone beyond the limits of mere talk," wrote Prince Aage of Denmark, one of the most popular soldiers to ever join the corps, in the early 1920s.[3]

The Legion showed appreciation for the marshal. As a group of foreign-born soldiers, legionnaires did not have a country, but they had a corps to rely on, and exceptional officers who fostered much of that relationship. Lyautey embodied this empathy and leadership. He was the strategist who led his troops to victory, but he was also their protector outside of the war theater, treating the soldiers with humanity. When the rowdy behavior of the legionnaires came under criticism, he replied that one "did not build empires with virgins."[4] Sensitive to the hardships the legionnaires endured in the field, Lyautey built rest houses for them to use when they were on leave or in retirement (Salé, Oran). Conversely, many legionnaires sent to Lyautey remembrances and expressions of respect.

The legionnaire as a colonial soldier created an archetype in an epic of conquest, and that is key to understanding the kinship between the military leader Lyautey and the Foreign Legion. The Legion became the stuff of legend when news from the colonies became of interest to more than foreign affairs politicians and commercial lobbies. During the first decades of the twentieth century, newspaper articles, memoirs, novels, movies, and songs featured the Legion's exploits. By the time of the 1912 siege of Fes, the soldiers of the corps already had an enviable reputation for sustaining fire with much panache. One of the most famous works that spread the romance of the Legion was Percival C. Wren's *Beau Geste*, published in 1924. Wren's novel established some typical images of the legionnaire's life: a figure standing at edge of the Sahara, wearing a blue coat and a white kepi, a flat-topped cap in the shape of an elliptic cylinder, with a visor and a white cloth flap to protect the neck from the sun; guarding a mud-brick fort against attacks from Algerian and Moroccan warriors; stomaching the sadistic impulses of an all-powerful officer who wants to push his soldiers to the limit of their human capacities; finding redemption and an existential purpose through camaraderie and abnegation. The legionnaires were featured in several films such as *Morocco,* in 1930, starring Gary Cooper and Marlene Dietrich.

Not only did the public eagerly consume these images of fit, alert men, but generations of young men entertained the thought of joining the French Foreign Legion. The phrase ". . . or else I'm going to join the Legion!" was a token expression of dissatisfaction at the deepest level, an uncompromising stance toward life, and perhaps a penchant for melodrama. To become a legionnaire was an alternative option, and many felt its allure. Englishman Brian Stuart explained what happened after he took time off at a movie theater in London, one fateful afternoon:

> I forget the title of the film being shown at the cinema, but it was of the blood, bullets, bayonets, and brutality variety—with a few luscious Arab maidens here and there—dealing with the French Foreign Legion. The blue smoke of a Balkan Sobranie curled above my head as I descended the marble staircase and out into Charing Cross Road. I made up my mind to join the Foreign Legion.[5]

Blood, bullets, bayonets, and women in an Arab land: How and why did the Legion come to exert such a mysterious attraction, embodying both the violence of war and the lure of exoticism? Who were these men, and how did these "dogs of war" fight so efficiently?

Edith Piaf's popular "Mon légionnaire" defined the nature of the mythical colonial soldier. French singers had been celebrating the Legion with popular songs for years, but this memorable piece, its lyrics written by Raymond Asso to a tune composed by Marguerite Monnot in 1936, struck a chord with the public.[6] Piaf sang of her longing after a night of lovemaking with one of the blond and tattooed recruits of the Legion—at the time, a substantial majority of them were Germans or Northern Europeans:

He had very light eyes / *Il avait de grands yeux très clairs*
That flashed brightly at times / *Où parfois passaient des éclairs*

Like a thunderstorm though the sky.	*Comme au ciel passent des orages.*
He was covered in tattoos	*Il était plein de tatouages*
That I never fully understood.	*Que j'ai jamais très bien compris.*
On his neck: "Never seen, never taken."	*Son cou portait: "Pas vu, pas pris."*
Over his heart one could read: "No one."	*Sur son cœur on lisait: "Personne."*
On his right arm, one word: "Think."	*Sur son bras droit un mot:*
	"Raisonne."

This is the legionnaire: moody, marginal, and uncompromising. In the song Piaf regretted not having asked the name of her lover, and he did not volunteer information either, because the figure of the legionnaire is characteristically that of a mysterious man who speaks little. He is a man without a past, since his past is likely the reason he had to join the ranks of the Legion in the first place. The Legion had a reputation for harboring political refugees, ex-convicts, scions of aristocratic families leaving behind gambling debts, plain adventurers attracted by the prospect of life in warm countries, and many more with broken hearts or other lamentations. The Foreign Legion asked few questions. It took all those who were physically fit to join, and then made sure that their pay was well earned over their five-year contract.

The training of the legionnaire was infamous for its long, exhausting marches in the desert during which trainees were burdened by unbearably heavy backpacks. Discipline could be iron-fisted. A culture of hard boozing and sex with prostitutes provided distraction for the disgruntled moments of release called *partir en bombe*. Officers regularly closed their eyes on this behavior, because they knew that a peculiar depressive affliction of the legionnaire known as *le cafard*—the "cockroach"—might set even more heavily on their troops, bringing the deepest funk and loathing of the world, with consequences often tragic. Georges d'Esparbès, whose *Les Mystères de la Légion étrangère* played a key role in popularizing the image of the incurably moody legionnaire in the year of the siege of Fes, described the ailment with these words: "The cafard gains entry in the cerebral matter, there it drags its thin legs, slips into a crevice, trots along, crawls, noses about, and thus corrupts all comprehension."[7] Nowhere was the deleterious effect of *le cafard* felt more strongly than at those outposts at the edge of the desert, or in the wilderness of the Atlas Mountains, where solitude and the barren landscape would often return the legionnaire's thoughts to his lonesome destiny.

Still, the "Legion of the Damned" offered hope for redemption. Out of so many differences in nationalities, creeds, and tormented pasts emerged a sense of togetherness that could make a battalion of legionnaires a superior force. First and foremost, legionnaires fought for the Legion itself. They fought under the mottos, "Legio Patria Nostra" ("The Legion is our only country") and "Honneur et Fidélite" ("Honor and Fidelity"), which eloquently captured the goal of forming a steel-clad esprit de corps. After bouts of *le cafard* and episodes of *la bombe*, a newly found solidarity, backed with the lingering notion that there is not much to this earthly life, gave the legionnaires discipline. Hence this striking description of combat:

> Grimly, silently, swiftly, the Legion advanced, Major Büschenschütz at the head. There was no cheering, no waving of banners; just a line of khaki-clad, lean-jawed soldiers setting out to accomplish a professional task. Here and there a man stumbled, pitched forward on his face, to twitch a bit and then lie still. Automatically the gap was filled, and in less time than it takes to tell it here, the battalion closed with the enemy and got to work with the bayonet.[8]

Legion solidarity instilled desperate courage under fire, and in man-to-man combat. Aage remarked in his memoirs, "At the moment of death, wherever they are, legionnaires vomit and blaspheme their disgust for life and for men."[9] Beyond the battlefield, the value of loyalty permeated the whole existence of the legionnaire. When a soldier shouted "Come to me, Legion!" in glorious action, but also during a brawl, from the depths of the seediest joint of a Moroccan medina, his fellow men pounced to the rescue without asking any question, as described by the legionnaire Frederic Martyn, soon to arrive in Indochina:

> Outside, before anything that was not legionnaire, the Legion clustered together and presented a united front. *'Oh! La Légion!'* Upon that cry legionnaires would come out from everywhere, they did not question the motives of the one who called. Without any discussion, they united against others.[10]

The tradition of unswerving loyalty apparently originated at the Siege of Constantine in 1837, when Captain Achille Leroy de Saint-Arnaud pronounced the words in the midst of an epic assault and rallied his platoon.

The French government used these soldiers for their most difficult missions, especially since their deaths were much less costly politically than those of French citizens. The legionnaires took it in stride, determined as they were to perform their destiny as a band of outcasts. Such was the dark ethos that brought solidarity to the Foreign Legion. They were known to toast one another in the most desperate moments, or break out singing, showing a touch of artistry that was at the core of the legionnaire's stance on life—and death.

Like the legionnaires, Lyautey had a taste for adventure and the exotic, and a resolutely anticonformist attitude. Lyautey had an artist's soul, with talents as master of ceremonies and as a fine writer elected to the Académie Française the year he became resident-general. He cut a dandyish figure, wearing a burnous and living in a tent decorated with the finest rugs. He had the physique to play the part.

Just like his cherished soldiers, Lyautey hated civilian life and what it had come to represent in a rapidly modernizing Europe: bureaucracy, the banality of existence, and manufactured life and leisure. Lyautey, too, swung from feelings of exhilaration to bouts of deep depression during which, in spite of his immense achievements, he proclaimed that he was wasting his life. This expression of disenchantment became even more acute after World War I, when all the illusions of a morally superior civilization collapsed.

To understand the Legion is to appreciate the paradoxes it embodied. On pages and pages of memoirs, otherwise redolent of pessimism and a drive toward self-destruction, a spiritual trajectory appeared. In Antoine Sylvère's autobiographical novel, *Le Légionnaire Flutsch*, Sylvère, a seventeen-year-old post office clerk caught fabricating fake money orders, flees the French authorities in 1905 and joins the Legion under the following credentials: "Gabriel Flutsch, Luxembourgeois, 1m77 and 76kg" (five feet ten inches, 168 pounds), service number 16674. His story not only provided a vivid testimony of life in the Legion in turn-of-the-century colonial Algeria but also delineated a typical itinerary, that of a youngster in need of structure and experience who grew into a responsible man through the experience of the regiment's hardship. The day Flutsch realized that he was now free in the most existential sense of the word, he decided to surrender to French justice, which forgave him and dropped all charges. Enlisting in the Legion was understood as entering an ersatz religious order. Flutsch explained:

> One enters here as one enters a convent when overtaken by the faith. The first novitiate lasts five years. After that, the legionnaire realizes that he does not belong to that world outside the Legion and that he cannot live in it anymore. What happens next is

exactly what would happen to a drunkard who is sent back to his own after five years [of willful sobriety]. In general, he only aspires to return to the bonds of the community that formed him, that liberated him from needing any rule.[11]

Georges d'Esparbès, in his *Les Mystères de la Légion étrangère*, describes the corps as a "monastery of action" that one joined as others chose to become Carthusian monks. Legionnaire Flutsch called it a cloister, the "monastery of unbelievers."[12] The commemorative book that the Legion published in the wake of its centennial celebrations, in 1931, echoed that particular trope of religious engagement, disillusion, and personal quest: "Along with monasteries, the Legion is the last refuge of all those who bear in themselves the nostalgia of what they would want to be, of what they could be."[13] "One does not join the Legion for the billy," went an old saying, meaning that life entailed a renunciation of certain worldly comforts for the sake of enlightenment. When he suffered from his most acute bouts of *le cafard* in his youth, Lyautey had retreated into a Carthusian monastery located deep in the solitude of the French Alps. In Morocco, he nicknamed his closest circle of officers his *zawiya*, an Islamic religious fraternity.[14] Major Zinovy Peshkov, another famous officer of Prince Aage's generation, observed, as he stood in the solitude of an outpost in the middle of Morocco, "Yes, I like these nights when I am on the rounds, even if the weather is terrible. The depth of my heart is opened, and I hear strange calls. I do not know from whence they come. I cannot define them. They come from some obscure source."[15]

At the edge of the world, self-loathing and estrangement could lead to revelation. The desert, the colonies, were a mirror in which soldiers such as the legionnaires and their high officers like Lyautey fought their own demons. A riveting contradiction appears: How could men both challenge the modernization of Western society and carry out one of its core projects, colonization? Attraction and destruction, narcissism and self-loathing, are key elements of the Legion's story.

Through memoirs and testimonies, many of which remain unpublished; through the material the Legion put out to shape the image of its corps; or through some infamous anti-Legion propaganda (mostly German) that sought to counter the fascination exerted by this corps, the myth of the Legion emerged. The Legion's "Heroic Age" ran from the early 1880s to the 1930s, largely under the command of Lyautey, and accompanied the formative time of the French Third Republic's political regime. This was also a time of rising nationalism, of modernization, and of globalization. Exotic

images circulated ever more rapidly and widely in the artistic effervescence of the Belle Époque, a crucial factor in the emergence of the Legion's myth. In the end, the archetype of the legionnaire set the standard of what a man ought to be, defining an ideal of masculinity for generations.

"Non, je ne regrette rien," sang Piaf in another world-famous song that few know she dedicated to the Foreign Legion in the midst of the Algerian War—she recorded it in 1960. Life's contradictions resolved—the good, the bad, both the pleasures and the chagrins forgotten—a new life started with time spent at the Legion. "With my memories, I lit a fire," added Piaf in her song. For the legionnaire, it could happen right away, or years after joining. Many never made it to that point of absolution so eagerly sought.

CHAPTER I

An Early History of the Legion

Ernst Jünger, famous German fighter in World War I and writer, joined
the French Foreign Legion in 1913. Born to a well-to-do family of
Heidelberg, the eldest of seven children, he dreamed of seeing Africa.
He showed up at the Legion's office in Verdun, where the recruitment officer
welcome him:

> "Young man, I hear that you want to go to Africa. Have you
> thought it over carefully? There is fighting every day down there."
>
> This was naturally music to my ears. And I hastened to
> answer that I was looking for a life of adventure.
>
> "Not bad. You will do well. I shall now give you an enlist-
> ment paper to sign."
>
> And taking a printed form from a pile of papers, he added:
> "You can choose a new name if you like, if you don't like your old
> one anymore. We don't ask for documents."[1]

Although the Legion allowed recruits to enlist under a borrowed name, it
did demand that they disclose their true identity. Thus Jünger enlisted as Herbert
Berger, service number 15308.[2] He took a train to Marseilles and soon found
himself performing drills under the hot Algerian sun, in Sidi Bel Abbès, where
the main base of the Legion stood. Some twenty years earlier, the Briton George
Mannington had faced a more dubious welcome when he showed up at the
Legion's recruiting office, armed with equal determination to live adventures on
other shores: "No! No! A good dinner at the Moulin Rouge and tomorrow you
will be cured, *sacré bleu!*" said the recruiter as he swatted Mannington away.[3]

This attraction that pulled young men toward the Foreign Legion in the last decades of the eighteen hundreds and until after World War I, with enough resolution to brave one of those surly recruiters of the French army bureaus, and constitute of force of approximately 11,500 men by 1900, is a complex phenomenon to approach. It must first be understood in the context of France's intricate political history and equally turbulent foreign relations and colonial policy and adventures.[4]

Out of political mayhem was the Foreign Legion created in 1831.* The French Bourbon kings, restored after the abdication and exile of Napoléon in 1814, hardly reinstated the people's faith in the old monarchy. Louis XVIII died in 1824 and King Charles X succeeded him on the throne to face an economic and political crisis, which, after a series of authoritarian measures aimed at propping up his regime, led to a revolution in July 1830. Paris rioted and barricades blocked the streets of the capital. Charles X's flight from France allowed the Orléans branch of the dynasty to inaugurate a constitutional, more liberal monarchy, and King Louis-Philippe, who would reign until 1848 in this "July Monarchy," incarnated for a while France's deep desire for calm.

Louis-Philippe, in the first months of his reign, faced an unsettled France. European refugees—Italians, Poles, Germans, Spanish—had converged on France in a year when many other capitals were being shaken by political unrest. Other foreigners roamed aimless: the Swiss soldiers of the old monarch's traditional guards who had been disbanded after they defended the king during the July revolution, leftover fighters from regiments that Napoléon had raised abroad—France had had a long history of using foreign-born soldiers for hire. Then there were immigrants, with no work. What to do with a substantial population that could fuel yet more trouble out of misery and boredom? On March 9, 1831, the French legislative assembly voted a law allowing the creation of new army regiments, where foreign-born men between the ages of eighteen and forty could enlist: The French Foreign Legion was born.

Authorities had conceived of the Legion as a temporary solution to a threat to public order. But there was another reason to create the corps: Algeria, where France had launched an uncertain colonial endeavor just a year before, needed an army corps that could face danger and human losses

---

* For clarity's sake and ease, I refer to the Legion as the Foreign Legion (Légion étrangère) throughout this book, although it existed under the name Régiments Étrangers (Foreign Regiments) between 1856 and 1875.

without drawing the political backlash that French-born victims would elicit.

Hence, the Legion's destiny was tied with France's most important colonial venture. Charles X, the monarch chased away in 1830, had thought that he would boost his political fortunes with a resounding foreign coup. On July 5, 1830, after landing in Algeria with a force of twenty-seven thousand men, the French took Algiers. They seized the major ports of the coast, causing destruction and death. The justifications for this occupation appeared as trivial as they turned out to be catastrophic. The representative of the Sultan in Algiers, the dey, had had a quarrel with the French consul over a long-standing commercial dispute. On April 29, 1827, three years before the expedition, tempers had flared and the dey used his fly swatter to strike the Frenchman in the face during an audience. Martial temperaments won out in Paris, and the expedition sailed from the French military port of Toulon. When the news of the landing and taking of Algiers reached Paris, the revolution of July 1830 was already under way, and the reign of Charles X was already irreversibly compromised.

Charles's successor, Louis-Philippe, who created the Legion, inherited an unwieldy situation, and in the turmoil of his first years in power, he could not decide on a firm policy on Algeria. Economic interests in Marseilles were for keeping French control over the main coastal cities, such as Algiers and Oran, and they prevailed against a public opinion that saw nothing of interest in Algeria. In 1832, a year after the creation of their corps, the legionnaires landed in Algeria to fight their first battle on April 7, 1832, south of Algiers, a scuffle during which the corps lost its first officer, Lieutenant Cham. The Legion went at work on infrastructural projects, while disease exacted a terrible toll on its members. Eventually, Joseph Bernelle, the commander of the Legion in 1833, decided to mix soldiers of different nationalities within the battalions; until then recruits had been grouped by region of origin.

What had been planned by Charles X's and his army leaders as a punitive excursion and a takeover of Algeria's ports became an unplanned full colonial invasion. Often in European wars, taking the capital of a country signaled victory for the invaders. In Algeria, however, this did not apply. Even though the dey had been removed, the French found a population determined to resist their advance and send them back to their shores on the other side of the Mediterranean.

Algeria at that time can hardly be characterized as a body of people united by a national sentiment, but it was not a mere patchwork of populations, either: Many texts refer to it as the Country of Algeria, and that country existed under one religion. After Roman legions had settled the land during the first two centuries of the Christian era, a fact not lost on the French legionnaires who would fight there, the Arabs had swept through North Africa during the second half of the seventh century and the eighth century, bringing their religion to the indigenous Amazigh populations. Centuries later, in the early sixteenth century, Algeria remained a land of Islam under the domination of the Ottomans, known as the Regency of Algiers. Although to most French people the name Algeria evoked the pirates who used Algiers as a base to attack their vessels, seize the goods they transported, and sell their passengers into slavery, most Algerians supported themselves through agriculture and herding, in groups that viewed themselves first and foremost as belonging to a village of tents, a *douar*, and then identified by tribe. This population numbered about three million at the time of the French landing.

The Emir Abdelkader is remembered as a national hero by Algerians for organizing the Algerian people's resistance against the French. Other local potentates also played important parts. The hostility shown the French by Ahmed, the bey of Constantine, led to a French expedition in October 1837 to take over his city. Thanks to a bold rush through a breach opened through the fortifications (when the rallying cry *Oh! La Légion!* would have been first heard), the legionnaires, led by Achille de Saint-Arnaud, at great cost, forged at Constantine an important link in a history of brave, resolutely cool charges under extreme fire. Still, the name that stands out in the history of the Algerian resistance remains that of Abdelkader. A learned, pious young man from a prestigious family of religious figures, this leader was also an excellent warrior.

Abdelkader fought the French in a holy war until 1837. Then, the Algerian leader struck a compromise with the invaders. By the Treaty of Tafna, he received the right to rule over large parts of Algeria, while the French retained sovereignty over Algiers and other regions of the coast. Abdelkader used the peace times to create a federation of Algerian tribes, with its own army, fiscal system, and religious authority. In short, a state took shape alongside the colonial establishment of French Algeria. By then, French settlers were already arriving to occupy the country. By 1839 it had become apparent that colonization would extend much farther than was originally agreed, and Abdelkader repudiated the treaty and relentlessly attacked French settlements, as well as the military outposts and the convoys that moved between them.

This is when the Legion found more opportunities to strike and further reinforce an emerging esprit de corps. Governor-General Thomas Robert Bugeaud arrived in 1841 to strike back at Abdelkader's forces. Bugeaud, who stemmed from the lesser nobility of the Périgord region and had risen as a politician, was also a seasoned military man, already a veteran of Algeria (1836–1837) and a lieutenant-general at the time of his appointment as governor-general. German legionnaire Clemens Lamping, who served under Bugeaud, described him this way:

> He appears to be fifty, and has an air of great determination and coolness. He is of middle size and strongly built; his face is much sunburnt, but pleasing; and he would be taken for a younger man than he is, did not his snow-white hair betray his age. Bugeaud is a man of restless activity, and keeps everyone alert by his continued presence.[5]

Blunt authoritarianism and resourcefulness thrived under Bugeaud's determination and coolness.

When Bugeaud arrived he found a relatively small array of corps, composing the Armée d'Afrique. Throughout the history of their corps the legionnaires fought alongside soldiers from other formations, especially in the wars of colonial conquest. Some of these corps were first raised in Algeria for the needs of the colonial occupation. The Zouaves, a unit founded in 1830, was recruited first from the Berber Zwawa tribes of Algeria (hence their name), and eventually from the French and European settler population. The Algerians also contributed to the Skirmishers, an infantry troop, and the Spahis, a cavalry unit known for its flamboyant uniform with a cape. Present on the colonial war theaters, alongside the Armée d'Afrique, were the Troupes de Marine belonging to the navy. Nicknamed Marsouins, they took the name Troupes Coloniales in 1900. After Bugeaud's arrival in 1841, the Legion troops forming five battalions split into two regiments— the Second Regiment went to Saïda in western Algeria. By 1847, the Armée d'Afrique under Bugeaud had grown to one hundred thousand soldiers.

The sheer number of troops was less important to Bugeaud than the method of warfare, however. For Bugeaud, military success against Abdelkader depended on rejecting the war methods of an army that still wanted to relive the epic of the great Napoleonic campaigns: all swaggering attacks and French fury. The urgent question that the French faced at that juncture was how to wage war in extremely hostile terrain such as the arid mountains and the desert. The tribesmen of Abdelkader had a decisive advantage against columns weighed by artillery, water, and forage for their mounts. "We must forget those orchestrated and dramatic battles that civilized people fight against one another, and realize that unconventional tactics are the soul of this war," Bugeaud wrote.[6]

The Legion entered here in a redefined role. Aiming to create mobile units that could survive on their own with few resources and rapidly reach Abdelkader's bands, notably in the mountains of Kabylia, Bugeaud gave the troops an opportunity to test their mettle. The Legion of those years had first failed to impress Bugeaud: He found it to be quite a ragged lot, and even considered dissolving the corps in 1842. Political refugees, coming from Spain in the wake of the Carlist wars, filled the ranks in the early 1840s. Desertion, even to Abdelkader army, was endemic, stoked by poor leadership. The dangers of drinking the water made wine a preferable choice, enabling alcoholism.

Legionnaire training under Bugeaud strained the men to their maximum capacity. Under the relentless North African sun, soldiers marched on for hours. Lamping describes a march dreadful enough to push a man to suicide.[7] At last they would reach an enemy position, usually a remote village. What followed was ugly. There was another, much less savory aspect to Bugeaud's strategy for establishing permanent French colonial order over the Algerian territory, an aspect that also gave the Legion troops a ruthless reputation among the local populations.

Bugeaud was convinced that, since the Arab and Amazigh fighters did not fear death, his best chances of getting both psychological and concrete advantage was to destroy their property and make livelihood impossible over his enemy's ancestral lands. On and on, during raids called by their Arab name, razzias, villages were devastated, crops burned, palm trees and orchards felled, herds seized or destroyed.[8]

Alexis de Tocqueville, commenting on French colonialism, justified these tragedies as those "unfortunate necessities" of waging war with Arabs.[9] Among soldiers, rationalizations of this kind are harder to discern. For those indigenous elements who had joined the French army, and who had often been at war themselves against Abdelkader troops, looting was in the order of things. Soldiers from Europe, enraged by the indigenous customs of torturing and mutilating the bodies of fallen, responded in kind. In France, there was a growing awareness of how Bugeaud's techniques contrasted with the self-declared civilization of its culture.

Abdelkader's forces ceded terrain from the beginning of the resolute campaign led by Bugeaud. In 1843, the French captured the encampment of

Abdelkader, his *smala*, while he was absent—this *smala* must have numbered twenty thousand people, and several thousand fighters. When the Algerian emir sought and received the help of the Moroccan sultan against the French, Bugeaud won the Battle of Isly against the Moroccans, on August 14, 1844. On March 18, 1845, the peace treaty of Lalla Maghnia was signed between France and what would eventually become another of its colonies, in 1912. The Sultan of Morocco and France, in the treaty, agreed on a set border between the kingdom and French Algeria.

At long last, on December 23, 1847, Abdelkader surrendered, marking the end of a decisive phase of Algeria's colonial conquest and an era during which the Foreign Legion emerged as a most useful asset of colonial warfare. There was to be more sporadic violence in Algeria in the following years and decades. In 1849, for example, legionnaires from the First and Second Regiments besieged the oasis of Zaatcha, a costly operation for the French forces. Another battle involving Legion troops took place at Ischeriden, in 1857, against Kabyle warriors of Amazigh origin.

Lamping had noticed that although legionnaires appeared "brutal and undisciplined," they "formed a band, who, under an energetic leader, might do great things."[10] Until Bugeaud, French military leadership had manifested damaging neglect. Inspectors from Paris "know nothing about the soldiers, and care nothing about them."[11] With a leader such as Bugeaud and much opportunity for action, the performance of the corps improved significantly, as did solidarity created by a shared history. One Belgian legionnaire, Louis Lamborelle, commented: "Courage is also a bit of a matter of habit, and often one does not find it in itself on the first day. One must not forget either that courage has an older sibling called: the sentiment of honor and duty."[12]

The colonization of Algeria proceeded at a steady pace beyond the coast and the rich Tell region that runs parallel to it. Bugeaud left an interesting legacy in the perspective of colonial settlement, for there was even more to his philosophy of war in a colonial context. In Burgeaud's view, the Legion had a role to play. Colonial authorities had seized vast expanses of land, and yet Algerian land often proved to be particularly difficult to exploit for Europeans who came with dreams of rapid wealth in the colonies, and often no practical experience in agriculture. Native agriculture, essentially geared to the needs of the *douars*, hardly provided principles of efficiency and high yields.

Bugeaud, as it turns out, had a passion for farming, hence his idea that the soldiers of the colonial army could actually make excellent settlers: They were disciplined, hardy, capable of defending themselves, and they already formed communities that could easily constitute settlements. "Ense et Aratro," "By Sword and Plow," was the motto of Bugeaud's plan, and it was nothing new, considering how the Roman soldiers had often been the first settlers of the lands they occupied. In the case of colonial Algeria, this ideal of the military pioneer never came to fruition. Still, it is an interesting sidelight on how the idea that legionnaires perpetuated the legend of ancient conquerors came about and, most important, how the concept of an army as colonizers and settlers imposed itself.

In 1848, Algeria officially became a French territory, an extension of the fatherland divided into the three *départements* of Constantine, Algiers, and Oran. Across those *départements*, where settlers obtained concessions to develop their land, the legionnaires built roads, bridges, dams, and canals to drain areas too wet for agriculture. Cities rose from the ground. The most famous of those French cities, as far as the Legion is concerned, is Sidi Bel Abbès. From 1842 until Algerian independence in 1962, Sidi Bel Abbès harbored troops of the Foreign Legion, becoming the headquarters of the First Regiment and the entire corps in 1843 and 1933, respectively.

The city was near the eighteenth-century shrine of the holy man Sidi Bel Abbès and had been at first a fortified outpost between Oran, the inland towns of Tlemcen and Mascara, and the Sahara. Soldiers named these kinds of relay posts "*biscuitvilles*," in reference to those rations that their warehouses kept for passing troops. Sidi Bel Abbès lies in a fertile plain, against a backdrop of impressive mountain ranges. Cut off from the sea and the desert by the mountains, the town enjoys a climate that can be quite cold; it is, however, shielded from excessive humidity and heat. In 1847, a French royal decree elevated it to the status of a city, and later, due to its growth, it became a subprefecture.

The thousands of legionnaires that approached the city during all those decades of the Legion's presence in Algeria saw the fields of grain, olive groves, vineyards of large estates, and some carefully tended gardens forming a belt around the city. Bel Abbès was laid out rationally as a rectangle, in the style of an army camp, like the *castrum* of the Romans, with the two main streets dividing the town in four equal sections, leading to four gates guarded by soldiers. Barracks and hospitals stood out. The city also accommodated the barracks of the Spahis, the cavalry recruited in the native population of North Africa. Legionnaires did much of the construction, including the city walls, the roads leading to the town, the wells, and later the telephone lines.

As a military camp, Sidi Bel Abbès inevitably drew civilian settlers, mostly Spaniards, and fewer Frenchmen. The Beni Amer tribes, who lived in the region before the French military arrived, saw the seizure of their best ancestral land through dubious juridical arrangements. General hostility marked the relations with the native populations. Special dispositions of the law relegated Algerians to the status of second-class citizens. Famine and epidemics, notably in 1868, wreaked havoc.

While European migrants developed Algeria into an agricultural cornucopia, a few well-connected men benefitted the most from this colonization. One such landowner was Léon Bastide, the mayor of Bel Abbès at the turn of the century. Meanwhile, investments into roads, bridges, railroads, dams, and communications fattened the profits of great corporations.

If the conquest and colonization of Algeria largely determined the history of the Foreign Legion from the date of its founding in 1831 to the middle of the century, the next two decades' events of its history were molded primarily by the reign of Napoléon III and his foreign interventions. The year 1848, like 1830, was a year of deep turbulence in Europe, and in France especially. The authority of King Louis-Philippe was challenged by an economic and political crisis, made even worse by a bad harvest. Barricades rose up again in the capital. In February 1848, the king was ousted, and on December 10, elections gave France a new president who was the nephew of the emperor Napoléon. This Second Republic was short-lived: In 1851, by a coup d'état, Louis-Napoléon Bonaparte declared himself Emperor Napoléon III. The rural masses heartily supported this coup and the return of a strongman at the helm of France with a plebiscite. They had grown weary of republican or royalist political movements, which they associated with turmoil. The Second Empire ushered an era of prosperity for France. This is when Baron Georges-Eugène Haussmann redesigned the urban landscape of Paris, creating the wide avenues and the architectural homogeneity that make the capital of France a subject of wonder.

Napoléon III, after just a few years on the imperial throne, launched the Crimean War in 1854, fought by both French and British troops to hinder the Russian tsar, Nicholas I, in his designs on the weakening Ottoman Empire. Four battalions of Legion troops earned some important titles of glory in Crimea, a Russian peninsula on the Black Sea coast where Sebastopol, the Russian stronghold closest to Turkey, stood. The Crimean capital fell in September of 1855 after a long siege. It was the theater of daring attacks, one of which claimed the life of Colonel Raphaël Viénot. The Legion's barracks in Sidi Bel Abbès took his name, and when the Legion moved to Aubagne, near Marseilles, after Algeria's independence in 1962,

the Legion's quarters retained their name, Quartier Viénot. The assault of
the so-called Green Hill, the Mamelon Vert, is another feat remembered
from the Siege of Sebastopol. Harshest conditions marked that siege with
epidemics of cholera and typhoid fever causing many more deaths among
the military than the actual fighting. Of 95,000 French soldiers' deaths,
nearly three quarters were related to disease.[13]

Emboldened by his successful war in Crimea, Napoléon III embarked
on yet more conflicts destined to assert France's renewed status as a preemi-
nent power, and again the intervention of Legion troops allowed him to
wage wars without drawing from the regular French army and the French
population. Against Austria he supported Italy's movement for independence, leading the legionnaires to the battles of Magenta and Solferino, on
June 4 and 24 of 1859, respectively. When Mexico was engulfed in civil war
and Mexican expatriates in Paris clamored for a French intervention on
behalf of the monarchists and against the republicans of President Benito
Juárez, the emperor sent troops to prop up on the throne Maximilian, a
younger brother of the Austrian emperor. The United States, who would
have opposed French intervention, were then engulfed in their own civil war.

The French expedition in Mexico began in 1861. Landing at the port of
Veracruz under the command of Colonel Pierre Jeanningros in 1863, the
legionnaires escorted convoys from Veracruz to Puebla, through disease-
riddled swampy regions. They showed themselves to be a resourceful troop
on many counts, installing telegraphic lines along the road. Near the village
of Camarón, on April 30, 1863, Captain Jean Danjou, sixty-two legionnaires, and three other officers found themselves in a farmyard surrounded
by a force of the Mexican republican army. They refused to surrender and
fought until just a few were left standing, leading their adversary to exclaim
that these were not men but "demons." This episode soon was seen as the
Legion's emblematic battle, a symbol of extraordinary stubbornness in
combat, so much so that the Foreign Legion's annual celebration is named
Camerone Day in remembrance of this Mexican sacrifice.

Over the next year, the legionnaires were posted in small garrisons, or
found themselves in guerilla warfare against roaming bands of Juaristas.
They also maintained their reputation as a troop prone to severe lapses when
soldiers remained idle—cases of desertions multiplied. The general in charge
of the French force was François Bazaine, the former commander of the
Legion's First Regiment and a veteran of the Crimean and Italian wars.
Bazaine wrote: "I shall have some of them shot. It is quite clear that a good
many of them enrolled in [the Foreign Legion] to get a free trip, but it will

cost them dearly if they are caught."[14] Some of these deserters joined the very armed bands that they were fighting, or found refuge in the United States. In 1864, Maximilian arrived to claim his imperial throne, but, as the republicans gained both military and political ground, he was captured and executed after the French troops and officers had returned to Algeria.

Before the era when Britain, Germany, and France competed overseas and disputed their influence over vast regions of the world, Napoléon III was perhaps less aggressive in colonial expansion than he was against the other European powers. He showed some progressive understanding of colonialism. The Second Republic had officially designated Algeria as French territory, but after he visited the country in 1860, the emperor published a letter in which he called for the founding of an "Arab Kingdom," a kingdom where Algerians would enjoy more rights and protections under a French protectorate. The initiative never materialized. Eventually, the French offered their Muslim Algerian subjects citizenship, but to obtain it they had to renounce their religion. In the end, Napoléon III never questioned French presence in Algeria, only the nature of its rule.

That Napoléon III was less interested in colonial adventures is not to say that colonization had stopped. The emperor's reign witnessed events that were foundational for the future colonial expansion toward the end of the century, and for the Legion as a colonial troop. In Africa, the imperial government nominated Louis Faidherbe as governor of Senegal in 1854, while in Southeast Asia, religion became the justification for an increasingly aggressive assertion of French interests in the country.

Emperor Tu Duc, who reigned in Vietnam between 1847 and 1883, rejected Western influence and allowed the persecution of Vietnamese Christians.[15] There were anti-Catholic riots and massacres, as well as natural catastrophes, famine, and peasant revolts. France saw it as its duty to intervene on behalf of religious freedom. In 1858, Admiral Charles Rigault de Grenouilly led a fleet of fourteen ships to the port city of Da Nang in central Vietnam and bombarded its harbor.

Over the next few months the French settled in the area. Facing a steadfast refusal to negotiate from the Vietnamese authorities in the imperial capital of Hue, de Grenouilly led his troops to the south, where he seized Saigon, in 1859. Saigon then consisted of thatched-roof huts, a few larger houses for the local dignitaries, and pagodas. There was a citadel, which the French took. However, the site itself was enticing, because it was protected from typhoons and in a strategic place to benefit from commercial traffic between Europe and China.

In 1862 the Vietnamese emperor granted Saigon and some areas around it to the invaders. If he thought that this move would limit the ambitions of the French, he was terribly wrong. Five years later, and after extending their reach to Cambodia, the French gained control over the entire southern part of the empire, the Mekong Delta, which they referred to as Cochinchina. Saigon was the Paris of the Far East in the making. The palace of the governor rose from the ground in 1868, and a year later the streets were lit with gas lamps.

The colonization of Indochina made the construction of the Suez Canal a high priority. Europeans had dreamed for a long time of sparing themselves the long trip around the African continent by linking the Mediterranean with the Red Sea and the Indian Ocean. Ferdinand de Lesseps undertook the enterprise. After ten years of work, and at a terrible human cost of the tens of thousands of Egyptian fellahs (peasant laborers) who labored in the pharaonic enterprise, Empress Eugénie and throngs of dignitaries inaugurated the canal, which opened in 1869. It measured almost one hundred miles. Along with the construction of fast steamships and laying of undersea telegraph cables, the opening of the canal represented a high point in the history of colonialism in Asia and East Africa and Madagascar. Unfortunately for the French, the English soon snapped up the shares in the canal that were first owned by the Egyptian ruler, and secured for themselves easy access to their colonies in Asia.

Meanwhile, in Vietnam, a young navy officer and civil servant in Cochinchina named Francis Garnier dreamed of fulfilling the commercial promise of France's new colony in southern Vietnam by finding an easy route to China, in particular the province of Yunnan, which was reputed to be a land of mythical wealth. The Mekong River seemed to provide that access, so Garnier set out on an exploratory mission to navigate the river in 1866. He visited the extraordinary site of Angkor. A year after his departure he entered Vientiane, the capital of the Lao kingdom. Garnier realized at that moment that the Mekong route was nonfeasible, and that the most convenient route to the Yunnan lay in the Tonkin by the Red River, a region under direct control of Emperor Tu Duc.

Lawlessness was endemic in the Tonkin. There were armed bands that had once rebelled against the Chinese emperor and, defeated, had migrated south to the Tonkin, where they preyed on the countryside, sometimes as hires for local chiefs. Led by Liu Yongfu, they fought under a black banner, hence their name the Black Flags. Vietnamese dissidence against imperial authority also complicated the picture. The Chinese kept a keen eye on what they considered to be a vassal state, not hesitating to send their own regular troops, too. In a complex entanglement of shifting alliances, the French met aggressive, well-trained, and well-armed enemies, especially the Black Flags.

Undaunted, and given the lack of a central authority to further challenge him, in 1873 Garnier forced his way through the Red River by taking Hanoi's citadel. Garnier never had a chance to see his grand scheme toward China realized. He died that same year while pushing back against troops of renegade Chinese insurgents who roamed in the region. Thanks to Garnier, the French grip on Vietnam had grown stronger and had opened trade in Hanoi and Haiphong, setting events on a course that would end up pulling the Legion into some of the most tumultuous episodes of its history.

In his last war in Europe Napoléon III took on Prussia, long held to be a backwater province in the mosaic of Germanic states that was dominated by Bavaria and Württemberg. The conflict Napoléon III launched against Prussia in 1870, however, turned out to be a watershed event in France and Germany's history, for the French army in general, and for the fate of the Foreign Legion.

At the heart of the Franco-Prussian War of 1870 was Prussia's rise under the steady and ambitious guidance of Otto von Bismarck, the chancellor of King Wilhelm I (later, Kaiser Wilhelm). Prussia's rise disrupted the delicate balance of power that the Congress of Vienna had established between France, Britain, and Austria after Napoléon I's demise. German unification loomed large in Bismarck's schemes, but he also made several larger moves in Europe. In 1866, at Sadowa, the Prussian army had overcome Austrian forces, and this had given Bismarck the opportunity to control the throne of Spain through dynastic succession, which alarmed France. In a misjudgment of cataclysmic proportion, on July 19, 1870, Napoléon III declared war against Prussia, thinking he would quickly dispatch Prussia's army and further strengthen his hand in European affairs.

The French army had some modern equipment and weaponry, but it remained thoroughly unprepared for the challenge of this war with Prussia. Soldiers, recruited from the peasantry, were poorly trained and took too long to mobilize. Officers, including the former commander of the Legion, Achille Bazaine, who had returned from Mexico, had obsolete ideas about fighting. Many of them were still mired in the romantic ideals of the era when the first Napoléon had defeated Prussia decades earlier. Napoléon III was in poor health. Organization was dismal, and the generals were not even provided with good maps to design a strategy. After a series of brutal and murderous defeats before the Prussians' advance, France suffered the ultimate humiliation when the army of Wilhelm I captured Napoléon III at the battle of Sedan, on September 2, 1870, and took him prisoner.

Foreign Legion troops, although by definition mandated to fight abroad, were then called in. Sedan had not put an end to the war, but Napoléon III's Second Empire regime had fallen. On September 4, 1870, the French Republic was declared for a third time, while General Bazaine put out a futile resistance with leftovers from the imperial army, at the fortress of Metz. The Prussian army advanced and laid siege to Paris, bombing it from September 1870 to January 1871. Meanwhile, French army units constituted under the interim Government of National Defense moved about the country in an attempt to block the rest of the German invading forces. After Sedan, two battalions of legionnaires arrived from Algeria to join a battalion formed with volunteers in the Armée de la Loire.

On January 18, 1871, the German states elevated King Wilhelm to the title of emperor of Germany at the Palace of Versailles, which they had occupied. Some German states, especially those in the south, such as the kingdom of Bavaria, showed much reluctance regarding this advent of the emperor. They retained certain rights within the newly formed empire, because both in their Catholic religion and culture, they thought Prussia was as different from them as was France. This explains why the Legion would easily recruit German soldiers from southern Germany over the next decades.

At last, in February 1871, also at Versailles, the French interim government led by Adolphe Thiers signed a treaty with Otto von Bismarck, putting an end to the war in exchange for reparations and the loss of two provinces where many German speakers lived, Alsace and Lorraine. These people of France's easternmost regions, who until then had been French citizens, became Germans, and they would soon flock to the Legion's regiments, too. General proportions of nationalities represented in the Legion varied considerably depending on historical circumstances. Over the period spanning from the creation of the Legion in 1831 to 1941, 43 percent of the legionnaires enrolled were Germans and Italians, Belgians and French accounted for 10 percent each.[16] Frenchmen were allowed to join in 1881, once they had completed their service in the Metropolitan Army.

The population of Paris, especially those of the lower classes of workers who had lived the last few months of the siege under the most harrowing conditions, erupted in a revolt known as the Paris Commune, starting a civil war against the government of Thiers just as the peace treaty was signed with Germany. Thiers launched an army to retake the capital, and the legionnaires, in a less-than-heroic chapter of their history, entered the city on

May 25 as part of the Army of Versailles, to occupy the Buttes Chaumont and Belleville, in the east of the capital. By the end of the "Bloody Week," twenty-five thousand Parisians had been killed and many more arrested.

The defeat against Prussia in 1870 is an event crucial to an understanding of France in the Third Republic. Seared in French consciousness for decades to come, the *défaite* hovered until World War I as a memory place, structuring the French perception of themselves. Naturally, it affected how the army organized itself, how it viewed its mission, and its morale. Although it took a decade to consolidate the Third Republic, the consequences of the defeat had wider political, social, and cultural consequences. The outcome of the ill-fated war significantly informed attitudes toward colonialism.

The monarchists, both the Légitimistes, faithful to the main Bourbon branch of the monarchy, and the Orléanistes, who had taken power under Louis-Philippe's more liberal regime, held dreams of a restoration for years, and adamantly opposed the Republic. To many of the French, the Republic still evoked chaos. Until movements of nationalism and socialism emerged at the end of the nineteenth century, this opposition represented the traditional dyad of right and left politics. Catholicism still embodied opposition to progressive politics and remained associated with the right as a force under constant suspicion from the republicans. That did not prevent the general population from living its Catholic faith, but the French state adamantly declared itself to stand above beliefs deriving from religious revelation.

The constitution of the French Republic, which was formally defined in 1875, was a parliamentary regime that saw frequent change in the government. The French president hardly invoked his right to dissolve the Chamber of Deputies when he faced too strong a political opposition, and so his government, the Council of Ministers, often fell. Fallen governmental figures came back to power at remarkably close intervals, in a continuous recycling of political figures. Colonial events, such as the coming debacle at Lang Son in 1885, could trigger these changes, or be at the mercy of them.

To foster a national culture centered on republican principles, successive governments progressively asserted themselves over the monarchists by using many instruments: They elevated as national emblems the tricolor flag, the national anthem ("La Marseillaise"), and the figure of Marianne, the iconic figure of the Republic and its progressive values. They built a powerful, efficient state education system. The army represented another powerful means of national integration, although it was not without deep reservations from the republicans, especially concerning the officer class, which they viewed as beholden to Catholicism and the monarchic order.

Nevertheless, the French army grew. Its recruits first were drafted for five years, a duration that was shortened to three years in 1889. Throughout France, as barracks rose and military bands played in public, the metropolitan (homeland) army symbolized and created national unity. Since conscription had been used to fill its ranks, the army was not seen by the French as an instrument of colonization. The army existed to prevent another defeat such as in 1870, and to win back Alsace-Lorraine—not to fight mysterious populations overseas in malaria-ridden tropical swamps. Hence, a volunteer corps such as the Legion became much more indispensable in the age of colonization.

As the years passed after Sedan, France's Third Republic grew more confident in its cherished values of rational enlightenment, secularism, and scientific positivism. These were the progressive principles that would support colonialism. France, claiming that its glorious, oftentimes tragic, past, exemplified the universality of its values, would soon entrust itself with a civilizing mission that the troops of the Foreign Legion, and men such as Lyautey, would carry out in an adventure of epic scale.

Part One

CHAPTER 2

Algeria!

A s the Third Republic of France consolidated after the defeat at Sedan and the fall of Napoléon III, a young officer began a lasting relationship with North Africa. Algeria, so close and so far, fulfilled the promises that orientalist painters and novelists such as Eugène Fromentin and Eugène Delacroix had painted. Algeria produced a kaleidoscope of impressions:

> Thousands of palm trees bunched together, striking tones, the Arab village of El Kantara on fire, all the population under the sun, a vast highland of burnt sand, broken by pink marble blocks, the peaks of the Aurès Mountains, a horizon crenellated in blue; not one roof visible, not one tree; a mirage, with lakes that my driver spirits away at every turn of the car; camel herds in the distance, caravan after caravan, the red coat of a Spahi, an Arab horse riding far away, skeletons of camels; and then some red, some pink, some blue, all that in a blinding intensity; we shiver.[1]

At the edge of the desert, past the last outposts of French colonial rule, the Arab towns enchanted Louis Hubert Gonzalve Lyautey, in contrast to Algiers, which he found fake and shallow: "It's definitely not my kind of town. The Frenchman has a shady aspect, and the Arab looks too proper; one can tell that everything is too prime, one cannot find the Arab unawares there, his life, his color."[2] One thing was sure: "I am a lover of light, and I would give up any delineated landscape for a play of the sunlight."[3]

Lyautey was born on November 17, 1854, in Nancy, the industrial, commercial, and cultural capital of the eastern region of Lorraine. Standing straight and tall, with blond hair cropped short and a piercing stare, Lyautey was the image of a man raised in privilege and elite military training. He expressed nativist pride in his ancestry, which he described as devoid of "murky blood, blood of adventurers, of foreigners and business people."[4] On his father's side, with roots in the Franche-Comté, there were generations of military officers: His grandfather Hubert, a revered figure, lived long enough to tell him stories of the Napoleonic wars he had fought in; his father, Just, was an engineer and administrator in the army. Young Lyautey saw in his surname an emblem of the moral value that defined his patrilineage above all: *loyauté*.

Through his mother he belonged to old strains of the aristocracy, albeit of a more modest extraction, people from Lorraine who upheld tradition, in both their politics and the art of living in country châteaux. They were Légitimistes who lamented the demise of the French monarchy. A sense of the sacred nature of power was innate. Thus, Hubert and his siblings, Raoul and Blanche, grew up in a tightly knit, conservative, and Catholic environment. At the age of thirteen, he held firm opinions, which led to his producing one day a Légitimiste profession of faith.

As Lyautey's career advanced, ease and worldly assurance came to the fore, then something quite dandy. His relatives, and an increasing circle of friends in intellectual and literary circles, saw that an uncommon sensitivity animated this future figure of France's martial mythmaking. Such traits owed to difficult circumstances in his youth. After a bad fall, he had had to undergo spine surgery and had to remain completely immobilized for the next two years. As reading was the only activity permitted for so long, he developed an encyclopedic knowledge of and deep familiarity with France's literary and artistic traditions. When Lyautey was allowed to move again, at first he had to wear a leather girdle stiffened with a steel armature. Later he became an excellent horse rider in the French army's cavalry, overcoming with iron will the residual effects of the accident.

Given this paternal heritage and the natural inclination of the French nobility toward bearing arms, Lyautey prepared to take the exam for the prestigious military school of Saint-Cyr, where he was admitted in 1873 at the age of eighteen. Napoléon had created Saint-Cyr in 1802 to provide a general two-year training after which the students emerged as second lieutenants. On his first day at Saint-Cyr, Lyautey received an ill-fitting tunic. "'Does that jacket fit you all right?' asked a non-commissioned officer.— 'Yes, but the neck is too tight.'—and then he was told: 'When you're asked a question in the army, you begin by holding your tongue.'"[5] According to André Maurois, one of Lyautey's first biographers, this anecdote stuck with him as a constant reminder of the mindless atmosphere still afflicting the army after the Franco-Prussian War.

Lyautey was not impressed by what passed for an elite military education in those days. More than the mediocre curriculum, the promiscuity, brutish camaraderie, and tedious discipline he found at the school displeased him. He had an individualistic, anticonformist streak, a trait that would impact his future career. In Paris after Saint-Cyr, he finished military instruction at the École d'État-Major. While there, Lyautey found an outlet in the theatrics of life. He moved freely among good society, as a tall, attractive young man who handled the French language with dexterity and art.

Although his military training put him on a charmed trajectory, Lyautey was prone to somber moods, especially when he peered underneath the veneer of social niceties, and saw the deep rifts that still ran through the French society of his times after the defeat of 1870—rifts that an officer in the army, steeped in Catholicism and tradition, felt most acutely.

The French population in general respected the institution of the military, even after being defeated by Germany in 1870. The institution had failed to protect the country, but the fallen monarch, Emperor Napoléon III, and his cronies were held most accountable. Even after this defeat one could remain deeply patriotic, serve the nation, and support the army, since it had held the country together after the civil uprising of the Commune. In a country thrown into political disarray after decades of aristocratic rule, still riddled with anxieties toward the republican regime that had brought upheaval, for many the army represented stability and the permanence of tradition. As the republicans progressively secured their hold on power during the decades of the 1870s and 1880s, they envisioned the military as a force capable of representing the country and cementing national unity. Barracks towered high over towns throughout the territory.

The army's leadership, however, faced adverse political forces and public opinion. For many, the military leadership represented the conservative, traditionalist segment of French society, with a troubled history of collaboration with antidemocratic political regimes in French history and the possible specter of a monarchic restoration. This was especially true in the cavalry, where Lyautey eventually served and where, more than in any other army corps, a larger proportion of nobles could be found. When the Comte de Chambord, the direct Bourbon heir to the throne after the demise of Napoléon III, refused to guarantee that he would keep the tricolor flag over the white royalist standard, should he be restored to power as king of France, the possibility of a restored monarchy appeared politically much more unlikely (for many Frenchmen, the tricolor flag had to remain as a guarantee and symbol of inalienable rights). Aristocrats, particularly those from more provincial stock, conversely saw in the army one of the few avenues of social success that remained opened to them.

Regarding these higher-ranking officers with much suspicion, the republicans voted a law in 1872 that forbade officers from voting, because their dedication to the Republic and submission to civilian government required them to be apolitical, at least in theory. The prohibition lasted until after World War II, hence the nickname of the French army *"La Grande Muette,"* the Great Mute One. In the same spirit, another law of 1877 denied an officer the right to publish freely, unless superiors had authorized his writing. That said, officers at the highest echelons often participated in those very republican governments that boasted an anti-elitist rhetoric.

Officers still enjoyed social prestige, even more so as they were elected in national political contests, and their training eventually improved in schools such as Saint-Cyr. Their modest pay hardly matched this measure of recognition, however, and to rise through promotion was slow and rewarded time in service rather than talent. Eventually, a virulent antimilitarism specifically aimed at the officer class appeared in French literature, upbraiding with both satire or ferocious realism the officers' narrow-minded authority over troopers. Charles Leroy's *Colonel Ramollot* (1883) or Abel Hermant's *Le Cavalier Miserey* (1887) are examples of this literature. The latter work, because it contained transparent allusions to real characters in the military, caused a real scandal and strident protestations; Lyautey found that it also contained much truth concerning the poor understanding and respect that officers like him had for French conscripts.

Catholicism among the officers made them a favorite target of the republicans' anticlericalism. An establishment in Paris run by the Jesuit order on the Rue des Postes specialized in preparing the children of France's nobility for the exams leading to entrance to Saint-Cyr, the infantry's officers' school at Saint-Maixent, and the engineering school École Polytechnique. Lyautey was one of many officers who were products of the Jesuits' interest in influencing France's elites *ad maiorem Dei gloriam*— to the greater glory of God.

Lyautey not only represented this conservative and religious outlook on life and society by virtue of his upbringing and training with the Jesuits—he eagerly engaged with the militant religious philosophy of social Catholicism espoused by Albert de Mun. De Mun was a young captain in the army who, having witnessed with horror the civil war of the Commune, strived to breach the gap between the working class and political elites, including those of the armies. In 1874, the year after Lyautey entered Saint-Cyr, he met de Mun and heard him speak passionately and brilliantly. De Mun's ideas struck him, and the captain remained a mentor and a correspondent through whom Lyautey stayed abreast of France's socially progressive religious thought. Years later he confessed to de Mun that he still felt, "after so many years, the palpitation that your words, the mere sight of you, and the thought of what remained to be accomplished, stirred in me."[6] For such idealists, the military barracks of provincial France were far from being a platform to grand aspirations. Dreams required a profound renewal of an army that was drowsy with the routine and bureaucracy of prolonged peaceful times.

While he embraced enthusiastically de Mun's worldly outlook, Lyautey also yearned for a sense of the absolute. There was a spiritual side along with the action-bound Catholicism. He discovered a retreat at the convent of the Great Chartreuse, deep in the Alps of the Dauphiné, near Grenoble, and he visited the monastery in 1875 and 1876. The memory of this discovery remained with him all his life, too: "To contemplate my own image, to converse with myself, and possibly with God" were the high points of this encounter.[7] To his great surprise, he found former military officers among the men who lived in isolation by the mountain peaks. For the rest of his life, Lyautey would experience a pull between action and contemplation.

An idealistic French officer, receptive to the religious, elitist, and militant thinking of an Albert de Mun, necessarily lived a life of deep contradictions in those last decades of the 1800s. In the ranks of the French military, Lyautey contemplated a life spent in the ever-repeated exercises and rituals of an institution that could hardly reform.

Algeria offered itself to enthusiastic meditations under more colorful skies. The French army gave its graduating officers at Saint-Cyr an opportunity to travel, to perfect their education. In 1878, the twenty-three-year-old Lieutenant Lyautey made the fateful choice to go to North Africa for a month-long sojourn. Perhaps, in that meeting of earth and sky of Algeria's immense landscapes, he actually had the revelation that there were privileged places where the contradictions of life could be resolved.

By October of 1880, Lyautey had transfered to the Army's cavalry and he traveled to Algeria for a second time, with the Second Regiment of the Hussards.

Months later, his superiors promoted him to chief of staff of the military division of Algiers. At the same time, Lyautey took stock of what French colonization really meant, and showed a conscience toward the populations under French rule, realizing that his love for North Africa involved more than the landscapes: "I definitely feel more and more respectful toward these people," he wrote.[8] Lyautey also understood well why a population that was identified as barbaric, and described as such in the Algerian press targeted to the European settlers, could revolt:

> Since they are promised extermination or servitude in any case, instead of that famous participation in our prosperity, which the military at least wanted them to share to a certain extent, they risk everything, and would rather give a few pushes with their shoulder—provided they don't get beaten—rather than wait like lambs for the charming future that the French Republic promises them.[9]

Progressive inklings had their limits, however. In spite of Bugeaud's heritage of terror and the retrograde mentality of the colonial establishment, Lyautey still considered the military as much more capable of bringing peace than a civilian authority.

A look toward West Africa might have comforted him with the sight of rising talent in the French colonial staff, men such as Joseph Simon Gallieni. Tall, thin, with reddish hair and a chin that was "square, assertive," Gallieni had graduated from Saint-Cyr in 1870. He soon found himself fighting at Sedan and then a prisoner of the Germans. The defeat was a trauma, as it was for many of his peers. Later in his life he recalled: "To be twenty years old, having heard the sweet songs of the victories in Crimea and Italy, holding the firm belief that France was the greatest country in the world, and then all of a sudden to wake up in the disasters of the *année terrible* . . . what disillusion!"[10]

Gallieni arrived in Senegal in 1876 to pursue an outstanding career as a colonial officer and thinker, eventually becoming a close mentor of Lyautey when the latter was assigned to Indochina. The son of an Italian immigrant who had reached the rank of captain, Gallieni embodied the way the Third Republic could allow the rise of officers from humble origins. Gallieni was the kind of military man who came alive in the colonies: "It's towards other horizons, towards the colonies that we directed our efforts," he wrote, the infamy of 1870 in his mind.[11]

In Senegal, under the orders of Governor Louis Brière de L'Isle, Captain Gallieni helped to extend France's influence eastward along the Senegal River. For that he relied on the famous Tirailleurs Sénégalais (Senegalese Skirmishers), a corps constituted for the first time in 1857 because Governor Louis Faidherbe could not obtain sufficient men for the regular army. These Tirailleurs would often find themselves fighting next to legionnaires. In 1879 the government had approved a project to build a railway that would speed French expansion farther toward the Upper Niger, and so Gallieni set out to make alliances with local potentates and create an effective opposition to the powerful ruler of the Toucouleur Empire and Segou, Ahmadu Tall. The expeditions proved daunting: Many soldiers and officers died of tropical diseases. Gallieni, in his spare time, took detailed notes of what he observed, showing an interest in areas as varied as anthropology, linguistics, and biology.

Both in France and overseas, the time to admire colonial heroes had not yet arrived, in spite of Gallieni. Paradoxically, for a country that would soon hold even bolder dreams of a global empire, the army still had little to offer in terms of military leadership, because many more officers thought that venturing abroad deprived France of its talent and resources, including for the eagerly awaited revenge war against Germany. To serve abroad, in those first years of the 1880s, was a sure way to miss opportunities for a far-reaching career. It still only attracted curious, independent characters.

Thus, when an insurrection broke out in Algeria in those first years of the 1880s, providing evidence that peace in France's largest colony was far from assured and that Algerians hardly saw the French as benevolent conquerors, Lyautey could only lament France's general lack of interest in ruling its colony with equanimity and true military excellence.

Sheik Mohammed ben El Arbi (commonly referred to as Bouamama because of the turban he always wore) was a religious leader who brought unity to the scattered and oftentimes competing tribes from the southern regions of the French colony, between Algeria and Morocco. Bouamama's resistance to the French was caused by enduring economic hardship, religious antagonism, and arbitrary administrative rule. He also challenged further expansion. Now that colonization in the north and central parts of Algeria progressed at a fast pace, the French were sending reconnaissance missions toward the Saharan south, while audacious plans proposed a railway across the desert, reaching to regions the French saw as ripe for further economic exploitation and control. These were the very regions that Gallieni and his men labored to dominate.

Also crucial in the various motives for Bouamama's revolt was France's recent annexation of Tunisia, a country bordering Algeria to the west. Like Algeria before the French takeover, Tunisia was a province of the Ottoman Empire that enjoyed great autonomy under the authority of a ruler called a bey, and the bey had found himself bankrupt and with weak political authority. When Khroumire tribesmen living in the north of Tunisia crossed into Algeria, the French seized on the opportunity and sent an imposing army into Tunisia to restore order and assert their authority. The Treaty of Ksar Saïd, often referred to as the Treaty of Bardo, was signed on May 12, 1881, with Bey Muhammed as-Sadik. Under its terms, France expanded its empire across North Africa.

Facing the insurrection of Bouamama, the Armée d'Afrique fully deployed to the South Oranais region. The army included troops from the Foreign Legion, deployed first in a wide curve to protect French settlers of the Tell, the fertile region along the coast. Then, the legionnaires made up the spine of military columns that chased the insurgents. Two fine literary memoirs, by the legionnaire Chartrand des Écorres and by Jean-Louis Armengaud, a captain of the Foreign Legion who participated in several of these expeditions, offer a good view of life in the Legion during the years of Bouamama's uprising.

The Canadian legionnaire Chartrand des Écorres, a pseudonym for Joseph-Damase Chartrand, had first traveled in the United States. He served in the Texas Rangers for a brief period. Then, wishing to enlist under the French flag, he applied to take the exam at Saint-Cyr, but the French war ministry denied him the permission, given that his Canadian citizenship made him a British subject, but he was accepted in the Foreign Legion in 1878. His commanders recognized the stuff of a fine soldier, and Chartrand was promoted several times while marching through Algeria's remote regions just as Bouamama's revolt was about to boil over.

Shortly after fighting at the Battle of Mouallok, in 1881, Chartrand was naturalized a French citizen and entered the officer's school at Saint-Maixent. He settled in France following other tribulations, and then went back to Canada, all the while publishing extensively, including the story of his years in the Legion, *Au pays des étapes* (1892), a text written with personal irony, verve, and much color. The text details marches through Algeria's desert regions, portraits of shady characters, and the hardships of the legionnaire, including the plague of intestinal ailments, bugs, and, more serious, typhoid fever. Never discouraged by the icy demeanor of the women he meets, Chartrand weathers stoically a string of rejections: "We scare people, we

inspire fear and perhaps admiration, which is a little too thin a reward sometimes; but love, never."[12]

At the Battle of Mouallok (or Chellala) where Chartrand found himself on
May 19, 1881, a battalion of the Legion led a column, including some Zouaves
who covered the flanks and the Algerian Skirmishers who closed the column;
additional native horsemen guarded the flanks. The mission was to transfer
three thousand camels, stretching on a line measuring up to seven kilometers as
the column progressed. About to enter a valley, the legionnaires spotted
Bouamama's warriors and opened fire. A few kilometers back, the Zouaves then
made a crucial mistake: They moved forward, wanting their part of the action.
The bulk of Bouamama's horsemen, who had been hiding until now, rushed to
the flanks left defenseless by the Zouaves, and the confusion became chaos
when the Algerian horsemen fighting with the French rushed in to repel the
attack. They were indistinguishable from the attackers, and in the mayhem of
the battle, "cases of biscuit, barrels of wine, officer's baggage, trunks of medical
supplies, the whole kit (*saint-frusquin*) rolled on the ground in a perfect waste."[13]

On the front where Bouamama had first attacked the convoy, Chartrand
and his fellow legionnaires ravaged Bouamama's cavalry, oblivious to the
more significant attack in the back. They then discovered that all the camels
were gone. The legionnaires, enraged, jumped on the barrels of brandy and
drank heavily to forget. "It's a real disaster," concluded Chartrand as he took
stock of the death of fifty-two French soldiers, many wounded, and the loss
of baggage and supplies. The trip back finished off many of the wounded,
who had to be buried on the spot.

Colonel François-Oscar de Négrier, a veteran of 1870, became
commander of the Foreign Legion in July of 1881 and changed the course of
Bouamama's campaign. Under his leadership, lighter and faster military
columns finally inflicted losses on an enemy that had proved too fast and
much more adept at using the unfamiliar territory of the South Oranais
desert. De Négrier also blew up the tomb of a Muslim holy man that had
become an inspiration for resistance, after transferring the holy man's
remains to territory under full French control. "You see, we respect your
saints and your beliefs, but this mosque was an epicenter of revolt against
France. I destroyed it," declared de Négrier to the population massed to
witness the destruction of the shrine.[14] Bouamama had to retreat toward
Morocco, but combat continued. At Chott Tigri he tried to strike back,
against a column of legionnaires led by Captain Jean-Louis Armengaud.

On April 18, 1882, a topographical mission left Aïn Sefra for Chott
Tigri, protected by two companies of legionnaires. Following de Négrier's

efforts to create a swifter force, a company of legionnaires mounted mules. Captain Barbier of the Second Regiment led the force, and Armengaud served under him. As it returned with a good survey of the terrain and even the spoils of an engagement with Algerian resistants, on April 26, the column fell into a treacherous ambush of Bouamama partisans. The attack took place at dawn, in a narrow ravine. Hundreds of Algerian fighters, both mounted and on foot, descended from the hills surrounding the ill-fated convoy. What surprised Armengaud was how their enemies' women fought with them: "Some *mouquères* hanging from the saddles or from the horses' tails encouraged the warriors, their husbands or sons, with their cries of vengeance against the *roumi* dogs."[15]

Captain Barbier ordered the troops to reverse course, thus entrusting the advance guard of the convoy, the mounted company of the Legion, with the perilous mission of protecting the retreat. No bravery could help this detachment of mounted legionnaires caught in a swirl of howling riders; they were almost all put to the sword while they attempted to fight off the attack while still riding their mules.

Meanwhile, at what was now the forefront, other legionnaires fought their way to an elevated position that would allow them to protect the legionnaires and the convoy left behind: "*En avant, la Légion!*" shouted one Lieutenant Delacroix. Encouraged, the legionnaires reversed the dynamics of engagement and prevented a complete disaster. The assailants turned their attention to the baggage and took it away. What Armengaud called a "glorious defeat" had lasted three hours, and cost the French fifty-one casualties, a third of the forces present. A lesson had been learned: Mounted legionnaires brought an indispensable element of speed to French forces in the Algerian-Moroccan inter-regions, but as fighters they remained infantrymen whose superior fighting skills were hampered by their mules.

De Négrier forced Bouamama to negotiate despite the events at Chott Tigri, and he extracted quite an enormous amount of money in damages from the Algerians. They exiled another leader, the poet Mohammed Belkeir, and French rule in Algeria seemed definitively established.

From then on, detachments of legionnaires and other colonial troops used a newly established post at Aïn Sefra, which lay closer to Morocco. It was a relay used to store food and ammunitions, a "*biscuitville*," and it eventually became an important base for the region, out of which Lyautey and the Legion would radiate. As Armengaud's journal describes it, the soldiers operated in the atrocious heat of the desert's summer and on terrain at times rocky, at others sandy, and always a haven for scorpions to proliferate. Some of the missions aimed at topographical reconnaissance, and the search for potable water is an omnipresent theme in Armengaud's journal. Once in a while he and his men found enough of a rivulet to bathe. Armengaud describes how the legionnaires stood out, even at those moments of rest and leisure when the troops disbanded and no chief could keep a semblance of order:

> In those circumstances, after long marches for example, the chief and his comrades appreciate the resourceful trooper who relieves them. The services he provides are of the first order, because they relate to food, well-being, and produce excellent effects that influence morale, an important factor. He's the quintessential old soldier of Africa, his face well tanned. His soup is always cooked, and the first one at that, while the man next to him will let his fire die out, not knowing how to revive it because of the dampness of the wood: He will have taken his precautions beforehand, and his precaution will save him. He knows how to find straw, alfa grass that he will dry out if needed, in order to smooth out the ground that can be more or less bumpy and humid, and will always sleep on the dry ground.[16]

The South Oranais was held under close watch, but it would not be long before the people of the desert hinterlands of Algeria and Morocco would strike again at the invaders.

For Lyautey, the time to participate in this kind of heated engagement had not yet arrived. They kept him to his desk, administering the war machine that the colony required. He did participate in an expedition, although not in that column described by Armengaud. It was in early September 1882, on a reconnaissance mission toward Leghouat. There is no mention of the Foreign Legion yet in his text, except perhaps for a reference to "white kepis" in one of these tableaux that he fondly depicted. Very much pertinent to the raison d'être of the Legion, though, were his keen observations on the French military strategy. In spite of France's advantage, Lyautey remained unconvinced that the methods of Bugeaud were the last word in colonial warfare, and that his countrymen had the appropriate forces to continue their expansion, or conquer other territories:

> It's idiotic to let us be beaten in small formations by an enemy who has the advantage of mobility, of temperance, of convoy

simplicity, of physical vigor, of courage! And enthusiasm. We don't have older recruits; how then do you win over that quintessential warrior that is the Arab man, whose life is a daily training, with our poor little civilian recruits who count three years of service?[17]

In spite of de Négrier's improvements, much remained to be perfected in the methods of the Armée d'Afrique. It was up to Lyautey to find a definitive solution to these problems he perceived so acutely. He did not know at the time that this military solution would be bound with another preoccupation of his, a taste for culture and a keen awareness of how colonial politics were unfair: "Ah the relentless civilization!" In 1889, the *jus soli*, the right to French citizenship for those born on Algerian soil, would be extended to Europeans other than the French, but not to the indigenous population. One crucial factor in this discrimination was religion. The French Republic, by principle, was blind to matters of religion, but as one French politician put it, "anticlericalism does not get exported."

Lyautey had set himself up in a cozy villa overlooking the Bay of Algiers, in the chic area of Mustapha, near where the first quarters of the Legion had been established in the 1830s. An aesthete who loved good décor, he was fond of describing the villa in his always-voluminous correspondence: "With my *araberies*, carpets, mattress, and burnous, I really have a little study that is chic in excess: corridors, saddlery, all of that is ornamented and shining; there is not one harness, not one bit of leather that we have not used for the military decoration of the whole." From his office, decorated in a pure oriental style, he had quite a view to enjoy: "When I lift my nose off my desk, [I see] my little garden, my horses that are being bandaged right there in front of me; then, gardens, palm trees, villas, and finally Cape Matifou, the harbor, the port, all of Algiers in an amphitheater as a backdrop, the comings and goings of boats, always holding my spyglass to observe a boat that enters, another one that fishes."[18]

He studied Arabic two hours per day, read extensively on Islam, and frequented Moorish cafés. "The country interests me and fascinates me."

In 1882, Lyautey returned from Algeria to take a post in a small town in eastern France as a captain. The transition to bleak, gray provincial life was painful for the twenty-eight-year-old officer of the cavalry. He was depressed and took little interest in women, preferring to read Tolstoy or Turgenev. But once again, the army offered him a chance to travel, this time to Italy, to study his counterparts in the cavalry on the other side of the Alps. Unbeknownst to his superiors, he took the opportunity to visit the Comte de Chambord, the pretender to the French throne who lived in exile. Words nearly failed him: "I just left him. The emotion is such, the hold on me so strong that I cannot regain consciousness of my personality, abdicated in him, fused in him, during these hours of sheer grace—the King of France—I saw him, I touched him, I heard him."[19]

But shortly after, the Comte died without an heir, while the new pretender to the throne failed to rally the Légitimistes. In Rome, in 1883, Lyautey saw Pope Leo XIII, who recommended that the French accept the reality that France was a republic—this was a time of appeasement between the Church and her "eldest daughter," as France was often called.

Although Lyautey felt much fervor at meeting these figures, he did not relate to religion at such a deeply spiritual level. The early revelations he had experienced at the Great Chartreuse had only been a distant glimpse of spiritual truth, and in the end he never found in religion a remedy to his depressive temperament. The artistic wonders of Rome were the true source of satisfaction during this trip. He did, however, remain very much committed to Catholicism as a social movement, and his interest in the movement spearheaded by thinkers such as Albert de Mun continued. They still wished to bridge the gap that, in their opinion, the Third Republic had opened between the working classes whose welfare the political left claimed to serve and the elites, including those of the army to which Lyautey belonged. But given the dashed hope of a return to the monarchical regime, and the prospect of a *ralliement*, a rallying of the Catholic Church to the Republic, France would not be the theater of the kind of deep renewal that Lyautey had wished for in the past.

Back in France, Lyautey published the letters he had sent from Italy, while he served General Alexis L'Hotte, one of the most famous horsemen in the history of the French military. The time had come to take stock and face reality. It would still take many years for Lyautey to recognize that a career in the colonies would be key to his destiny, or that his destiny would include a Legion that was consolidating its own reputation. Colonialism was not yet the solution to his quandary, but it had opened a window into a dream world, and Lyautey would eventually push it wide open.

CHAPTER 3

1885

The Third Republic of France was founded on a belief in human reason and progress. Seeing itself as representing these values preeminently among other nations, the Republic became a fertile terrain for colonial ideology, and an era of colonization unparalleled in history opened up. In less than thirty years, beginning in the mid-1880s, the size of France's colonial possessions increased dramatically, as well as the size of the population under its domination.

In February 1883, Jules Ferry became president of the Council of Ministers for the second time. Most French citizens know Ferry primarily as the architect of the French national education system, but his role in expanding the *plus grande France* ("Greater France") has been underappreciated. Ferry's first government approved the annexation of Tunisia in 1881, and when Ferry held power again not only as president of the Council but also as minister of foreign affairs, the colonies finally found a true champion. Over the course of his political career, he acquired a reputation as the builder of an empire. Although Ferry's political beliefs placed him squarely in the camp of the so-called Opportunistes, the pragmatic left, French colonial interests spawned political fault lines. There was not, at the time, a specific colonial faction in Parliament, neither was there an explicitly formulated colonial doctrine. Nevertheless, many vectors of interest converged toward the idea, and necessity, of that Greater France.

In 1883, Ferry created the High Council of the Colonies, an advisory body that included civil servants, politicians, and some citizens of the colonies. Colonial thought also had deep roots in ideology. Out of strong sentiment of their political, philosophical, and cultural superiority, the French viewed the colonial conquest as a logical outcome to their history. Paul Leroy-Beaulieu, the author in 1874 of the influential *De la colonisation chez les peuples modernes*, explained:

> Colonization is the expansive force of a people, it's the power of reproduction, its dilation and multiplication through space; it subjects the universe, or at least a part of it, to its language, to its mores, to its ideas and laws. A people that colonizes throws the foundations of its grandeur in the future and of its forthcoming supremacy.[1]

Conquering foreign people allowed the French to fulfill their destiny, while rendering an immense service to the others, or so they thought. Reason, progress, science, culture, and freedom were seen as the gifts of French civilization, as paradoxical as it might seem, given the brutal nature of the conquests.

Geographical societies such as the Société de Géographie de Paris played a great role in the emergence of such a colonial mindset. These societies encouraged and financed explorers, distributed prizes, published travel narratives—in short, they created a taste for the exotic in the French public, including in children whose dreams of adventures led to many careers in the colonial army. When Joseph Gallieni came back from Senegal in 1882, for example, he frequently lectured on the wide circuit of these societies, and became a sort of a colonial hero and apologist. Literature also created a colonial conscience in the larger population. An entire generation read with excitement the novels of Jules Verne, the travel narratives of Francis Garnier in Indochina, up the Mekong River, or articles in the press. They felt the thrill of adventures in faraway exotic lands. At this point, colonial thinking in the late nineteenth century still represented the concerns of very specific interests and a small, albeit growing segment of the population.

Economic interests were another crucial motivation, or, at least, they made those exotic dreams of ideology and literature become a reality, as financial credits were voted by the deputies' assembly at the Chamber. The year 1875 had witnessed the creation of the Banque de l'Indochine. For Jules Ferry, colonial policy was the daughter of industrial policy, since France's economy had been stuck in a period of stagnation during the last three decades of the century, and industrialists and financiers were in need of new markets. Much of the great era of European colonialism is a consequence of the industrial revolution and capitalism's surge, as much as it was facilitated by transportation and communication technology—whether the investment was truly a good one in strict economic terms remains the subject of much debate among historians.

If economic interest fueled the appetite in the colonies, international rivalry created the conditions for the conquests. France had to protect its border with Germany, and possibly one day avenge the insult of 1870. The Ligue des Patriotes, an organization founded in 1882, was a staunch advocate for the revenge. Yet, for others, a wider perspective on international affairs imposed itself.

Great Britain had constituted the greatest colonial empire over the 1800s, an empire that would end up covering almost a quarter of the planet. That empire stretched from the Americas to South Africa; part of it, New France in Canada, had even been taken from the French in 1763. There was India, Ceylon, Burma. India certainly was the crown jewel of the empire. One had to reckon with that formidable British efficiency and spirit of entrepreneurship that seemed elusive to the French. The capital of the British Raj in India, Calcutta, showed the world grand avenues lined with monumental buildings and remarkable infrastructure. Administration was competent, recruited from the best schools to constitute the Indian Civil Service. This way, English products found a vast market overseas, while tax money from commerce and agriculture flowed back to the motherland. "What do you want? The English, initiative is in their blood," exclaimed Lyautey when he saw Singapore for the first time, on his way to the Tonkin.[2] Just as Jules Ferry governed in France, the English wrested control from Egypt's khedive, a major irritation for the French who were their rival in Egypt since Napoléon's campaign, launched in 1798. A French geography book titled *Le Monde pittoresque*, in view of such British achievements, refused to lose faith: "The duty of France, in tune with its most precious interests, is to not allow England to overcome her in the achievement of this peaceful revolution."[3]

From November 1884 to February 1885, European powers met at the Berlin Conference on colonization and exploitation of Africa, and the stakes were clear for France and Britain, but also for Belgium, Italy, or Portugal. All powers stood ready to carve up the rest of the African continent as it suited them, in what came to be known as the Scramble for Africa. Organized by First Chancellor von Bismarck, the conference also signaled the intervention of Germany as the newest player in the Scramble.

In both Senegal and Tunisia, France strove to consolidate its rule. Pierre de Brazza, as he explored more southern regions to the west of the African continent, established in 1880 a French trading post in what later became

Brazzaville, a starting point for what would become French Equatorial Africa. Madagascar, the large island to the southeast of the African continent, seemed like another attractive prize. Claiming that the Malagasy people were not respecting the terms of an arrangement they had signed with a French adventurer and developer, Pierre Laborde, the French landed on the island and occupied the port of Mahajanga and the capital, Antananarivo. On December 17, 1885, Queen Ranavalona III signed an alliance treaty whose equivocal terms eventually would give France another opportunity for an outright takeover of the island.

Would the French establishment in Indochina succeed in rivaling the English? It was thought that answers to that question still lay to the north of Indochina, in the Tonkin, where the wealth was presumed to be. Perhaps the Tonkin was not the land of geological riches that some had dreamed, and goldmines were not to be found there, but surely a prime position to trade with China represented enough of a reason to stand by. If the emperor of Vietnam thought that his cooperation with France would temper its designs, he was sorely mistaken again: His weakening dominance in the Tonkin, hidden dalliances with the Black Flags, and gestures toward the Chinese motivated further French takeover.

Captain Henri Rivière had developed a fascination with northern Vietnam. An officer of the navy with bold ideas and recklessness to match, Rivière fought the Chinese armies that penetrated the Tonkin, and then some armed bands that Emperor Tu Duc had resolved to employ. He took the citadel of Hanoi again in 1883 with five hundred men, but he fell on May 19, 1883, under the swords of the Black Flags, who chopped off the hands and head of Rivière's corpse. Colonial interests in Paris protested loudly. Emperor Tu Duc died, depriving the Vietnamese government of what authority it had left, and giving the French a freer hand in their colonial designs.

Guided by Jules Ferry, the Chamber of Deputies allocated three and a half million francs to shore up the final French takeover of Indochina. It was a job for the Legion. The first battalion of six hundred legionnaires sent to settle the Tonkin agitation left Algeria in September of 1883, led by Lieutenant-Colonel Jean-Frédéric Donnier.

It was a long journey to the Tonkin. In the days of steam-powered vessels, it could take up to forty-five days to reach the Tonkin from France. A fleet of modern ships, launched by the navy at the end of the 1870 and 1880s, served the French colonial conquests well. These boats could be fitted to transport hundreds of soldiers, and then easily converted to hospitals once at their destination. The *Mytho*, for example, measured one hundred and five meters (344 feet) and cruised at up to thirteen knots. A private enterprise, the Compagnie des Messageries Maritimes, also lent its services to the French army, transporting troops and officers.

Tonkin-bound troops left Sidi Bel Abbès with fanfare. Jean Pfirmann—a Bavarian who joined the First Regiment in 1887 and was the first in what would become an honorable dynasty of legionnaire recruits (his son Paul and grandson Claude were both born in Algeria and enlisted as legionnaires)— wrote in his notebooks that when his men headed out they first paid homage to the flag, and that as his battalion walked from the barracks of the Quartier Viénot to the train station, on October 23, 1888, the citizens of the town were out to salute them. Another legionnaire heard "the music being almost drowned by the rousing cheers of our comrades whom we were leaving behind."[4] Once in Oran they waited to board their ship on the docks. One Sergeant Bolis marveled at the beautiful martial air these soldiers displayed:

> I admired with pleasure those old soldiers among us, with their tanned faces, thinned out by hardships, looking rough, even a bit savage. They had that martial air, that beautifully belligerent air that characterizes our great army of Africa, under their worn-out kepis protecting their faces with large beards, their foreheads slashed by the menacing fold of brows used to frown under the sun. Their flaming eyes, as if they were full of some far-away mirage, seemed to have borrowed depth and glare from solitudes contemplated for so long.[5]

The boats carried legionnaires as well as many soldiers from other corps serving overseas. Seven hundred marine troops, the Marsouins, headed to Vietnam on one of those Tonkin-bound ships.

In little time the legionnaires were in sight of Port Said, gateway to one of the main attractions of the journey, the Suez Canal. For the legionnaires, it symbolized something different from French power and engineering—it represented the possibility of an escape, desertion, for those who had found life in the Legion too hard. Life on those ships was crowded, rations were poor and meager. Ships progressed slowly once in the canal, to prevent erosion of the canal's banks. That offered a prime chance to jump overboard and reach land. "Sentries, all of the Marine infantry, were posted round the ship's sides to stop any legionary who might take it into his head to desert."[6] Since this hardly deterred legionnaires who wanted to literally jump ship, recruits were ordered to remain in their quarters during the passage through the canal. Rising temperatures in the ship's hold and the proximity with the Marsouins, who were assigned the task to shoot at the legionnaires if necessary, led to epic brawls.

When the Red Sea appeared at the end of the canal, hopes of jumping overboard dwindled. There was a stop at the fortified British concession at Aden, and then the vast Indian Ocean. Life settled into a dull routine, in that queer existence suspended in the uncertain blue, gray, and green variations of the sea and the sky. Temperatures rose even further, as well as humidity. There was no wind to sweep away low cloud cover in the torpor of the tropics. Squalls came. For the troops stacked below in tight quarters, the journey became truly awful. Even those who had been spared seasickness suffered. Legionnaire George Mannington speaks of soldiers vomiting onto each other.[7] Water was in short supply, and poor body hygiene made life in the hot, crowded hauls intolerable. Most passing ships were English: vexing reminders of what France should aspire to be in the colonial race. Singapore, which the English acquired in 1819, more than two decades before it acquired Hong Kong, was the last port of call before French ships and their troops would reach Indochina and presented the last searing demonstration of English might.[8]

At last, the mouth of the slow-flowing, mighty Mekong River appeared, followed by Saigon, offering the better hopes for a *plus grande France* in Vietnam, and onward to the Southeast Asian peninsula. At the upper end of that thousand-mile-long elongated S that is Vietnam lay the land of Bac Ky or, as the French called it, the Tonkin. There, amid the emerald rice paddies and the strange shape of mountains from which the jungle cascades, would lie the nightmares of many legionnaires, and many of their dreams, too, for decades to come.

The wait in the famed Ha Long Bay was a striking introduction to the Tonkin for legionnaires and their officers. Tormented geological concretions emerge from the waters, forming shapes of animals, warriors, and architectural forms before dissolving in the misty tropical air. There were bands of lazy low clouds, their amorphous contours a manifestation of how time flowed at a new pace in this new world. Ha Long Bay is one of the most iconic natural wonders of Asia.

Moving to Hanoi citadel—Hanoi, still rather small, counted about forty thousand souls, and colonization had not yet transformed it—the soldiers got to enjoy more scenery. Enshrined in a wide circle of mountain ranges, the alluvial plain of the Red River and the rice fields of the Tonkin appeared both impressive and disconcerting. Aboard one of the steam-powered launches that, with the transoceanic steamers they had just disembarked from at Haiphong, were essential vehicles of Western exploration and conquest in tropical countries, Sergeant Pfirmann and his fellow soldiers of the First Regiment observed:

> My new detachment left Haiphong aboard a boat—it was the *Licorne*, I believe—on December 5, 1888. We had left Haiphong without any weapons, ammunitions, and food, and our stomachs tormented us with pangs of hunger. Still, we were already dreaming of encounters with tigers and pirates. An officer of the navy commanded the boat, which was equipped with a small cannon. We did not go fast, and had ample time to contemplate the banks of the river.[9]

That was the Tonkin of first impressions after Ha Long Bay, a seemingly infinite patchwork of rice paddies, mirroring the sun or bursting with the tender green of rice shoots, with the ubiquitous massive water buffalo chewing water lilies with a placid and indifferent air. After a while, the eye detected signs of life. Amid these rice fields, dense groves of bamboos and palm trees hid the villages that sheltered most of the population, tight gatherings of modest shacks, with "pagodas with quaintly sloping, red-tiled roofs and curved eaves, the crest of these being ornamented with gruesome looking dragons and griffins."[10] The population of Vietnam, mostly agrarian people united by Buddhism and Confucianism, numbered around ten million in 1875.[11]

Those soldiers of the first expeditionary corps of 1883 spent their first months protecting Hanoi and securing the strongholds around the city. Legionnaires fought the armed bands of Black Flags, or Chinese who would not let the new invaders settle in a region too close to their own. In December, troops including the battalion of legionnaires from the First Regiment took the fortified city of Son Tay, northwest of Hanoi on the Red River, from the Black Flags led by Liu Yongfu. Admiral Amédée Courbet was in charge of the entire French force. In March 1884, legionnaires newly arrived from Algeria played a leading role in taking Bac Ninh, this time against regular Chinese troops. Bac Ninh stood on the main road that connected Hanoi with the Gates of China, the main passageway between the Tonkin and the Chinese province of Guangxi.

A Belgian legionnaire, Polydore Minnaërt, a six-foot-tall daredevil, was one of the first to enter Son Tay and Bac Ninh. He made it his specialty to plant the French flag on the enemy's defense, just as the outcome of the battle became clearer, to give that final boost needed by the troops. More daring acts followed in his fifteen-year career. After the Tonkin campaign, he returned to Sidi Bel Abbès and became a *caporal-sappeur*, a military engineer and fireman, and saved two children in a dramatic show of courage and energy. In the Dahomey campaign of Africa, he rescued a fellow legionnaire from waters infested with crocodiles. Wounded twice in the taking of the village of Bossé in the Dahomey, he received the medal of the Légion d'Honneur. In Vietnam, thanks to men like this Minnaërt, the two brigades of the French army, led by General Louis Brière de L'Isle and François de Négrier, quickly progressed. De Négrier enjoyed the reputation of a victor, having fought Bouamama three years earlier in Algeria.

Vietnamese authorities in Hue and the Chinese both signed treaties with France, and the government of Jules Ferry announced in Paris that the French were masters of central Vietnam and the Tonkin. Nevertheless, China was not in a hurry to recall all of its troops from the Tonkin. In late May 1884, the Legion took an old fortress at Tuyen Quang, on the Lô River. The fortress commanded communications between the Yunnan and the Tonkin Delta. Tensions reached a tipping point when lingering Chinese troops ambushed a column led by Lieutenant Dugenne at Bac Le, leaving thirty-two dead and seventy wounded. The Sino-French War had begun despite the treaties, against a backdrop of Black Flag guerilla warfare and Vietnamese patriotic resistance.

It took time for the companies of the Legion, the infantrymen from the navy and the native corps, and some sappers and other civil personnel to settle in Tuyen Quang. Meanwhile, General Brière de L'Isle set his sight on eastern Tonkin, with a goal of pushing an army of forty thousand men from the Guangxi region back into China. Taking with him two more battalions of legionnaires commanded by Donnier, he marched victoriously until Lang Son, the main town near the Chinese border. He passed villages destroyed by the retreating army and took Lang Son on February 13, 1885. The Chinese, in a complete rout, abandoned strongholds and weapons.

One has to picture what leading a military column through the mountains of northern Vietnam represented. The uniform of those first campaigns, borrowed from the stocks of the navy infantry, was unsuitable for the tropics. It featured a dark blue coat of thick woolen cloth, with pale blue or red trousers, and leggings. Wearing the colonial helmet was mandatory, to prevent sunstroke. George Mannington, arriving at the end of April in the early 1890s, appreciated a climate "somewhat that of a warm spring day in

Europe." But he added: "We were soon to make acquaintance with the tropical summer of the Tonkin, which usually sets in about the middle of May,
when the terrible intensity of its heat is all the more appreciable owing to the
suddenness of its arrival."[12] A physician named Hocquard, who left a description of that campaign as he followed the French troops, elaborated:
"Humidity saturates the overheated air, so much so that skin evaporation is
blocked: one feels a constant, heavy sensation and an anguish similar to the
one in a steam bath; skin is covered with such constant and abundant sweat
that drops form even at the tip of fingers."[13] In other words, it was so hot for
a significant portion of the year that an officer had to change his shirt at least
three times a day. The legionnaires eventually obtained distinctive uniforms
in lightweight, pale fabrics.

Rather than taking what passed as the main thoroughfare to China,
General Brière de L'Isle had opted for a less obvious itinerary, hoping to
confound his enemies—the main road between Hanoi and the Gates of
China was at best three or four meters wide anyway. Tonkin mountains rise
slowly, but they reach high elevations, up to more than ten thousand feet,
forming, as in Halong Bay, the strangest, most abrupt shapes. Erosion has
fashioned the limestone into curiously rounded peaks, carved baroque orna-
ments, and grottoes. To cross those mountains and reach Vietnam's border
with China required navigating labyrinthine paths, many of which were
dead ends or circled in the jungle, involving risky crossings of torrents. A line
of one thousand soldiers and coolies, who were forced to carry supplies, food,
and weapons on their backs, stretched on the narrow muddy paths. The
journey went through the vertiginous mountain ranges, then dived into
suffocating, foggy valleys before reemerging under a blazing, lethal sun.
Given that it took from two to three hours to gather such a long line of
troops into a compact combat formation, it seems miraculous that the French
made it so easily without suffering too many mortal attacks.

In their haste, prompted by their success, the commanders did not let the
troops rest during the day's hottest hours. After walking knee-deep in rice
paddies and fighting the cutting tall grass that covered the bottom of the upper
valleys or the jungle of its abrupt slopes, troops already weakened started to
succumb to sunstroke, fever, and dysentery. "You are legionnaires meant to
die, so I'm sending you where one does," de Négrier is said to have declared.
Another danger was the ubiquitous Vietnamese tiger, known to snatch hapless
sentries who let their guard down while rolling a cigarette in the night.

As de Négrier settled in Lang Son, news came that Tuyen Quang, the
fortress taken earlier, was in great danger of falling into the hands of the

Chinese troops from the Yunnan and the Black Flags. De Négrier dispatched a relief operation, keeping with him three thousand men. When the soldiers of the relief corps arrived in Tuyen Quang later in the first days of March, they found a scene worthy of the Legion's gallery of heroism.

An old eighteenth-century Chinese fortress on a bend of the Lô River, Tuyen Quang offered at first a reassuring sight: Its brick walls, ten feet high and three hundred yards long, formed an imposing square. The garrison commanded by thirty-six-year-old Captain Marc-Edmond Dominé relied on other assets. Within the fortress rose a small mount on which stood some constructions. Then, there was a cannon boat aptly named *La Mitrailleuse*, *The Machine Gun*, moored to the east in the River Lô, beneath the walls.

Inside the walls were about six hundred men—two companies of legionnaires forming a total of 390 men, additional troops from the navy and native corps, eight sappers and civil servants, essentially cooks, but also a Protestant minister. Weapons were wanting. Dominé's men counted on six cannons. The rifles were not the best, either. The famous Lebel repeating rifle, which used smokeless powder, was not yet in use; it would be introduced in the Tonkin two years later. Dominé's legionnaires had spent the last weeks of 1884 in reconnaissance missions, preparing for a siege. They carved into the rock convenient stairs toward the central barracks while the Chinese presence in the surroundings grew. Beginning on December 11, they also built a blockhouse on a hill nearby. This smaller post offered the added protection of covering Tuyen Quang from an angle opposite that of the boat's firing range. One quickly noted, however, that the blockhouse was necessitated by the woody hills that surrounded Tuyen Quang to the west; these offered a dangerous vantage point over the fortress. The rest of the terrain was mostly rice paddies. The legionnaires completed the construction of the blockhouse in six days.

Meanwhile, more and more sightings and pursuit of Chinese troops in reconnaissance happened. Dominé learned from a deserter that the enemy numbered eighteen hundred soldiers. On December 24, the presence of Liu Yongfu, who now commanded an army of both Chinese regulars and Black Flags, was confirmed. His army had grown to thirty-two hundred. Hundreds of men appeared to be working on a trench line that stretched toward the blockhouse. The French were now locked in.

On January 26, 1885, Liu Yongfu mounted his first major attack against the citadel, the gunboat, and the blockhouse. The Chinese leader, too, had wasted no time, spending much energy organizing his troops, finding supplies, and conducting exercises. Eventually his soldiers numbered in excess of ten thousand, many times the number of legionnaires inside Tuyen Quang. While the attack on January 26 had been inconclusive, it offered Dominé an opportunity to measure what kind of serious enemy he faced. French historians and chroniclers of the siege found Liu Yongfu's methods so professional that they suspected he benefitted from the expertise of European officers; perhaps, but that assessment also spoke much of French colonial naïveté in general. Legionnaire Martyn, as he later faced a stubborn army in Dahomey, noticed this tendency "to find Englishmen or Germans at the bottom of every colonial difficulty that the French met with, and it was assumed that any natives who made a stand against the French forces were assisted by trained English or German soldiers—as far as I know without there being any foundation for such beliefs."[14]

Inside the fortress, the legionnaires resisted well at first, and most direct engagement outside the walls remained minor. By the end of the month, however, it became apparent that the blockhouse that oversaw the entire citadel had to be abandoned, so close the Chinese had been able to advance. Tuyen Quang was now dangerously exposed. This setback marked the beginning of what a soldier who lived through the siege, Captain Camps, described as a two-month-long hell of fire. February revealed an equally dangerous Chinese strategy: to dig tunnels and place mines at the base of the walls, to blow them up.

The French could distinctly hear the pick blows underground. The sappers and engineers led by Jules Bobillot, the stalwart of defensive engineering at the siege, went to work and deployed to counter the threat. They excavated galleries of their own to meet those of the Chinese, so that the force of their explosion would be blunted and redirected away from the foundations of the fortress. "This is the only way we can engage with the enemy, they are ten thousand, we have to fight underground."[15] From now on, the main events of the siege were the success and failures of the Chinese at blowing up and invading Tuyen Quang.

On February 11, at eight thirty in the morning, Legionnaire Maury had the surprise of his life: As he worked with his pickaxe in one of the underground tunnels, the wall of dirt crumbled before him and he came face to face with his Chinese counterpart, revolver in hand. After a furious fight with pistols and picks, Maury and his companions were able to patch the opening. That mine's explosion fizzled. Over the next two days, however, two mines exploded. The second one, which went off in the middle of the night, destroyed a wide section of the wall.

Thanks to Officer Moulinay, the ensuing attack faltered, albeit at the cost of six dead and six wounded. Ten meters outside the fortifications, however, lay the disfigured and mangled body of Legionnaire Schelbaum, blown up by the Chinese mine. Officer Camps wrote:

> Corporal Beulin of the Second Company appears before Commandant Dominé: "Mon Commandant, he says, one of ours is lying dead on the other side of the walls; give me four men, a stretcher and I swear I'll bring him back to you." The commander extends his hands and says: "Go!" Right away, about twenty soldiers stand at the fortifications to open a violent fire on the Chinese trench, while Beulin ventures out. This one leaves with four men of good will. In the middle of a hail of bullets, he gets the body of Schelbaum brought back.[16]

Life resumed its normal flow—so to speak—for a few more days of that February 1885. At six in the morning, the foes were at their posts, the French trying as best as they could to ignore the pestilence of the cadavers that rotted outside their walls or the trumpets and conchs blown by the attackers to get on their nerves. Good morale in such circumstances hung on maintaining a semblance of normalcy, and a few necessities. Officer Camps describes the moment of the day when all parties paused:

> That lull happens everyday around ten in the morning; it was the time when the Chinese eat their *tiou-tiou* and smoke opium. We take the opportunity to do just like them: soup replaces the *tiou-tiou*, and, unfortunately, tobacco hardly replaces the opium that we do not smoke: it's a shortage that's very hard on the men. Our stock could not be replenished, for lack of communication, and so the search for a pipe or a cigarette becomes a task harder to resolve by the day.[17]

Cigarettes or no, the situation worsened. Bobillot, leader of the sappers and engineers, was gravely wounded but survived to see the end of the siege. Dia, the leader of the Tonkinese Skirmishers that the French had recruited to fight along their own, died. To give him a decent funeral, the legionnaires built him a casket with biscuit box planks, which they ornamented with greenery plucked by the nearby riverbank while dodging bullets. Their own dead were buried in rudimentary shrouds made of woven straw, in graves that lined up at an alarming rate in a corner of Tuyen Quang.

Ten days after the loss that had motivated Beulin's heroism, a clamor coming from the assailants' ranks signaled imminent danger. A first mine struck at the southwest corner of the fortifications, creating an immense cloud of dust through which bricks shot like missiles. Moulinay and his men intervened again, running to the top of the walls to defend the opening, but this time a second mine exploded right away.

> Light disappears, the atmosphere becomes impossible to breathe, we swallow fire, one feels held, enveloped and crushed at the same time. Some think they are sinking in an abyss; others believe they've been thrown into the clouds. All would like to shout, because they all suffer, but there no voice left to shout with.[18]

When the dust settled, twelve soldiers, including Moulinay, lay dead; others wandered erratically, haggard, some so badly burned they were stripped of their skins. The Chinese launched a general assault, which failed. On February 24 yet another mine exploded, at four o'clock in the morning. The enemy rushed in. Forty-five minutes of blind fighting rage repelled them:

> Sergeant-Major Husband throws himself with his cohort before them: He is wounded, they step back; Sergeant Thévenet takes them back, it's his turn to be wounded, the legionnaires retreat again, just as Captain Cattelain arrives to charge with a section of the general reserve. We push back, bayonets held at the belt, the bold ones that have dared to step on our ground.[19]

Another hero of this expulsion was Thévenet, a soldier who had been decorated for bravery in the southern regions of Oran's prefecture during the Bouamama uprising. The Chinese left two flags behind them on that twenty-fourth of February 1885, flags that found a fitting destination in Sidi Bel Abbès. Symbols of uncompromising resistance formed the core of the Legion's culture, and visitors to the headquarters would not miss the memorabilia displayed in the Salle d'Honneur that Colonel Wattringue established three years later, in 1888. First, visitors saw the wooden prosthetic hand of Jean Danjou, which the captain had lost prior to Camarón in an accident. Then they saw the blue Chinese flags taken from the enemy at Tuyen Quang.

Liu Yongfu summoned Dominé to surrender, or else face annihilation. The French, however, had heard of the successful march to Lang Son and had heard through a spy that de Négrier was sending relief. More attacks and mines opened severe breaches in the walls; now Chinese forces could aim directly at the soldiers inside the fort. Moving from one structure to another inside the exposed citadel became a matter of life and death. On the evening of February 28, a mine killed a soldier whose head was found almost ninety yards away from his body. Any loss at that point could decide the outcome of the siege. There were one hundred and eighty guns to defend more than a kilometer of fortification. And yet, the legionnaires still were able to repel Chinese attempts at breaching the fort, piling up enemy bodies with each of these attempts.

At last, on March 2, 1885, shots heard from afar signaled that the rescue column was finally approaching Tuyen Quang after a journey of more than one hundred and eighty miles. A nasty battle at Hoa Moc was the Chinese commander's last effort to avert a defeat.[20] Dominé, widely lauded for his leadership, was promoted to the rank of lieutenant-colonel on the eleventh of that same month.

Meanwhile, in Lang Son, some startling events were unfolding, far less heroic than the siege of Tuyen Quang, but of greater political consequence. Dominé's men had been brave at Tuyen Quang, but this might have served more the reputation and history of the Legion than the strategic interest of the French colonial authorities. Was the fortress on the River Lô truly the key to securing the Tonkin? Much less disputable was the value of containing the Guangxi army to the east.

The strength of de Négrier's position seemed assured. Wine and coffee, those essential staples of life under the French flag, after cigarettes, were in short supply, but the troops in Lang Son were well fed. With a semblance of peace, villagers came back out of hiding and life returned to the markets, offering soldiers alternatives to the standard rations of biscuit and canned meat. Work on building a better road to the delta and Hanoi began. A Vietnamese official showed up, offering his services.

De Négrier decided to push his luck further, to the Chinese border and beyond. The French government hoped to pressure China into coming to terms with the French hold on northern Vietnam. On the twenty-third of March he reached the border and then destroyed the Gates of China, putting a placard on the construction rubble that said: "Respecting treaties protects a country more strongly than gates at its borders. The gate at Guangxi has vanished." To which the Chinese replied with a placard of their own: "We will rebuild our gate with the heads of Frenchmen."[21]

A few days later, at the end March, after a murderous engagement, de Négrier had to turn his army back toward Lang Son, with the Chinese at his heels. Dramatic rumors of an imminent arrival of massive reinforcements circulated. The enemy did show up, in numbers big enough to continue their challenge to the French, but Legion troops successfully fought back at the battle of Ky Lua, on March 28, and stopped the Chinese. Since de Négrier was wounded, command passed to his second-in-command, Paul-Gustave Herbinger. In circumstances that caused much controversy, and up to this day remain difficult to elucidate, Herbinger ordered his troops to abandon Lang Son. Panic and mayhem ensued. Men got drunk finishing the supplies. The artillery and transmission material was destroyed, a huge sum of money destined to pay the soldiers sank into the river. Once out of what they thought was Chinese reach, the stunning realization set in that the shame and waste of the retreat from Lang Son had been largely unwarranted.

When news of this disaster reached Paris, it stunned both the political establishment and public opinion. Crowds and press alike howled, "Ferry-Tonkin!" or "*Vendus!*" ("Sell-outs!"), and demanded the ouster of Jules Ferry. The unexplainable event in the Tonkin was a wound to French pride, some even called it a second Sedan, and those thought to be responsible had to pay. A vote of no confidence held under the august cupola of the Bourbon Palace took Ferry down. "He went to the tribune as one walks up to the scaffold."[22]

Important political debates held at the Chamber of Deputies followed, and they show how, in spite of the stunning reversal, ardent colonialists of the Third Republic remained undaunted, and how other deputies could also hold strikingly modern views on colonialism. The first one, in July 1885, concerned credits needed by the army in the wake of the expedition to Madagascar. Camille Pelletan derisively painted the opinions of the colonialists: "We were told that we had this imperious need, as men of a superior race, to go about civilizing the barbarians of the world with cannonballs. If we asked those barbarians, I think they'd be just fine being left alone. But precisely, they don't want us to ask these people."

Ferry, who remained as a deputy from the Vosges region, explained why France was justified when it conquered other countries; previously he had invoked Albert de Mun as a theorist of France's civilizing mission. His interlocutor, Jules Maigne, was a radical leftist who had distinguished himself in the revolution of 1848.

> JULES FERRY: It has to be said openly that superior races have a
> right with regard to inferior races.
> JULES MAIGNE: Oh! You dare say that in the country where the
> Rights of Man have been proclaimed!

. . .

FERRY: I'll say again that superior races have a right because they
are assigned a duty. They have the duty to civilize inferior
races.

To which Georges Clemenceau, another politician, responded with irony,
"Superior races! Superior races! That's easy to say. As far as I am concerned,
I've watered down this proposition since I heard scholars from Germany
demonstrate scientifically that France had to lose in the last Franco-German
war, because the Frenchman belongs to a more inferior race than the
German one."[23]

Clemenceau shone in 1885. Later in his career, however, he would
become more of a pragmatist in the face of a crisis in Morocco, playing a
decisive role in the invasion of that kingdom. Still, his declaration showed
how much colonialism was not the mindset of entire generations in French
history; it was subject to crisply worded positions in an informed debate.
There was much at stake in the august amphitheatre of the Chamber at the
Bourbon Palace: how the French colonial authorities would favor assimila-
tion between colonists and colonized populations, or rather imagine a form
of association, supposedly for the benefit of both. Contrary to expectations,
the debates established for many the idea that France's destiny was to be a
colonial power capable of rivaling the English.

CHAPTER 4

Le Cafard

Lyautey moved to a post near Tours in 1885, the year of Tuyen Quang, as the aide-de-camp of General Alexis L'Hotte. His superiors appreciated him: "Captain Lyautey always deserves the same praise, very hard at work, a learned mind; his general instruction as well as his professional instruction signal that he is an officer of great valor," wrote L'Hotte.[1] He spent his days on administrative tasks, or maintaining his horse riding skills. Yet again he spoke of dark thoughts: "Activity, no matter how hectic it is, does not exclude bitter *taedium*, when it originates from ruined hopes, the spectacle of a wasted life, of a panicked mind, a broken faith, a wounded heart."[2] Better to seek refuge in one's memories of happier times, spent under sunnier climates: "Wrapped up in white flannel, in the shade on my oriental smoking-room, I spend hours caressing the blue smoke of my Alexandria cigarettes, with an empty head, without a thought, looking vaguely at the trinkets that remind me of my warm years."[3]

On November 19, 1887, the thirty-three-year-old Lyautey received a significant promotion, putting him in command of a squadron of the cavalry. The promotion required moving to Saint-Germain-en-Laye, near Paris. At last, he closely frequented the social and intellectual circles that his writing talents had made his own, but at a distance. Well-clad in his uniform, he made dashing entrances around the capital, including in the aristocratic salons of the Left Bank. Gone was the tedious life of a provincial military scribe.

Captain Lyautey's interest in the life of the soldiers he commanded, from their recruitment to their progress in the military career, took a militant turn. A few years after his promotion, in November 1891, the *Revue des Deux Mondes* published an anonymous article. Titled "Le Rôle social de l'officier" ("The Officer's Social Role"), the slim essay landed on the desk of the French military hierarchy with a thump. It was a terse indictment of all the mediocrity and narrow-mindedness of the army. In the view of the author, the military had failed to respect its recruits and develop their potential, choosing instead pursuit of advancement, and, somewhere as a distant horizon, a Napoleonic dream of bravura on the field, complete with those visions of hard-charging, furious, saber-wielding gallops in clouds of dust.

Reform was needed in the context of a modernizing art of war. The officer had to consider himself as more than just a cog in a powerful institutional machinery. The officer, in the author's view, had a prominent social role, which required considering this role as a true profession, necessitating skills, psychology, and talent: "To consider instead the role of the officer under this new aspect of social agent, entrusted by the country less to prepare the arm of its children to fight than to master their minds, fashion their souls, and temper their hearts."[4] The officer had a deep moral duty.

Paris recognized in those pages the pen of Captain Lyautey. The army hierarchy squirmed, but in the end abstained from punishing the breach of the code of conduct, which required certification for any publication by an active member of the military. The intellectuals celebrated the author, and quickly Lyautey found himself lecturing on this bold new vision for an army that had, in twenty years, failed to truly reform itself and erase the infamy of its rout by Germany. Lyautey, as he spoke in public about his ideas, felt the thrill of public life and leadership. After giving a lecture to a rapt audience of young men, he wrote:

> I had that enjoyment, the fullest that I can conceive, of sensing an audience that is stirred by you and with you, that quivers and feels the thrill, that cuts you off at the end of each sentence. It's the sensation, at every moment, to have a hold on that young crowd and be united with it. It can only be compared to that of having a squadron that follows your every gesture and move; a squadron, right behind you, at full gallop, capable of overcoming any obstacle.[5]

This was a harbinger of what would make Lyautey such a charismatic chief, in tune with his troops in terms of both skills and sensibility. But what, in this demanding view, of the colonial officer? Who were the candidates to be such officers?

With all the noise about Indochina, French officers had begun to take a true interest in their own colonies beyond Algeria, and looked more to service abroad. These officers might have lamented British dominance, or heard of the plight of Catholics overseas. Throughout the ranks, a consciousness that the colonial enterprise could stimulate the nation, infuse it with a renewed optimism and energy, percolated. Not to be dismissed was also the significant pay increase for those risking their lives abroad.

Some officers of the French army simply saw the colonies as a space where one could escape that bland life of the barracks, contemplate an existence more adventurous, and be a leader of men. Gallieni, after a stay in France, could not remain idle for too long. No doubt this inclination was a question of temperament. "Go away!" would say his wife, when, later in life, he would take a few months of leave to end up utterly bored. First Gallieni went to Martinique, then he returned to West Africa from 1886 to 1888, where he commanded an area that stretched eastward of Senegal, named the Sudan—along the upper Niger River, corresponding to a part of Mali. Still with the famed Senegalese Skirmishers, allied local chiefs, and some officers who would eventually follow him to the Tonkin in Indochina, Gallieni chased and executed holyman and resistant Mahmadu Lamine, and then fought the Muslim cleric and ruler Samori Ture. War lasted many more years after Gallieni's departure before France could have a firm hold on what it claimed were her West African possessions.

In Indochina, leadership was still wanting. Human failure, in the assessment of many, had led to the debacle at Lang Son. Speaking of Herbinger, the ill-fated commander who had ordered the retreat after de Négrier was wounded, one observer commented: "He completely lacked that good judgment, that insight, that composure, that experience of men, that understanding of the terrain pertaining to matters of war that constitute the real leader."[6] These shortcomings were felt much more acutely in the particular case of the Legion. Hence Pfirmann's lucid diagnostic concerning the qualities most desirable in a colonial officer:

> In wild country, the lowest-ranking officer has a heavy burden: He must not only be a guide to his men, a wise counselor, but also, in difficult circumstances, he must be their protector. Hence the need to know your men in depth, to appreciate to its true nature their moral value, their physical endurance, in order to make the most of it. Hence the duty for the humblest officer to observe, to evaluate, to act with wisdom and prudence, to

draw lessons, to acquire experience, so that his men may benefit from it in return.[7]

The Legion surely had had its share of competent leaders. But the time of Lyautey and other famed leaders was still to come. The aftermath of the Lang Son episode, notwithstanding Tuyen Quang, demonstrated it.

Two months after the fall of Jules Ferry's government in 1885, while France faced increasing challenges from Russia and Japan, China signed the Treaty of Tientsin with France, recognizing the French protectorate over the Tonkin for good. In Paris, despite the serious doubts that de Négrier's misfortunes had raised, the new government voted the subsidies to pursue the colonization of Indochina.

One of the most consistent errors of the French military establishment during their colonial adventure in Southeast Asia, however, was to underestimate the strength of Vietnamese patriotic sentiment. They viewed the poverty and illiteracy of a population spread out over a sinuous, diverse country as antithetical to nationalism. Hence General Henri Roussel de Courcy's difficulties when he took over the military command of Indochina. De Courcy was a man who favored strong methods over diplomatic niceties: Facing a national resistance against French colonial ambitions, he took the imperial capital of Hue by force in the summer of 1885 and replaced Emperor Ham Nghi on the throne with a puppet ruler. Annam and Tonkin were eventually united under French authority.

Ham Nghi, who had fled Hue to seek refuge in the mountainous regions of Annam, issued a call for resistance that gave its name to the patriotic wave of resistance to the French: the Can Vuong edict, "Loyalty to the King." The French faced a new surge of opposition, complicated by the Black Flags and the Chinese deserters who had chosen to remain after the signature of the Treaty of Tientsin, all men who seemed very much alike from the colonialist perspective, and whose shifting, contingent alliances among themselves made them a very difficult enemy to identify properly. The villager that sold his chicken to the French soldier during the day, or labored in infrastructure projects, turned at night into a stealth enemy.

In bands that numbered from a few dozen men up to a few hundred, so-called "bandits" and "pirates" roamed the country, especially in the mountainous regions of the Tonkin, trafficking in weapons, opium, and women. They lived off villages, terrorizing those populations. They attacked

French military convoys. They were like "fish in water," almost impossible to grasp in their own milieu. The misnomer "pirates" allowed the French to justify their military occupation as a fight on behalf of the emperor they had put in place. Officials of the Vietnamese mandarin elite, meanwhile, often played a double game, assuring their new masters of their loyalty on the one hand, and supporting resistance on the other. For China's own bandits the notion of the border was meaningless; they fought in their own cohorts, or in conjunction with the Vietnamese. France's official protests elicited at best bemused assurances from China.

This lack of insight was a grave mistake, both for the French and for all subsequent invaders of the country. How could the Vietnamese not have forged a sentiment of belonging together after centuries of Chinese invasions? This mistake made French control highly unstable, at least until men such as Gallieni and Lyautey arrived in Indochina. Poor coordination between military commanders and civil leadership, thousands of miles away in Paris, made the task even harder.

The military occupation of the Tonkin, consequently, was still a logistical nightmare, and the Foreign Legion was at the center of it. Neither plain nor mountain was a better alternative than the other. Legionnaires policed the Red River Delta in columns, stumbling perchance on walled strongholds protected by added layers of palisades and trenches garnished with bamboo stakes, all of it sunk into the thickest high brushes. Mortal skirmishes, sometimes harsh combat, ensued. Tents were useless, and so serving in a column meant sleeping in muddy, vermin-infested huts that could be found along the way. Sleeping outdoors, had it not been for the humidity or the cold that came in the winter, would have been an enviable lot. Lucky were those who could find shelter in a pagoda. Life in the outposts of the Tonkin mountains was hardly better. By the time the legionnaires had built some decent accommodations on top of a mountain, they were usually displaced by other corps like the Marsouins, and were sent to renovate another post left in a sorry state by the Chinese. Food arrived rotten most of the time, leaving the troops to rely on local supplies.

The rules of the game were merciless. The lighter columns that allowed swifter action had a notable disadvantage, the legionnaire Flutsch would learn later from Tonkin old-timers:

> There were no wagons, so if there was a sick or wounded man, it was awful. It was often in the worst spots where, if we left a chap, we would find him butchered by the pirates who came to enjoy

cutting him or to stick a pug up his ass until it came out of his
shoulder.[8]

Each head taken from the Legion had a price depending on rank. A simple
legionnaire's head was worth fifty taels, the local currency, to those who
brought it back to the armed bands's chiefs. The French troops replied in
kind: Villages were often pillaged and burned, the women raped, the population massacred. It is difficult to assess the exact role of the Legion in the
murky but persistent evidence of misdeeds. A French soldier wrote:

> We were allowed to kill and plunder everything when the villagers
> did not show up to submit. We left at night around ten or eleven,
> we went to the villages and surprised the people in bed. We killed
> everything, men, women, children, at gun butt and with the
> bayonet, it was a real massacre.[9]

Likewise, the resident-general in Indochina evoked the "rumors circulating
on the actions of the column that operated in the delta, under the orders of
de Négrier," in a letter to the chief of staff of de Courcy.[10] When Pfirmann
saw a legionnaire trying to rape a woman, he intervened to free her, incur-
ring the ire of the soldier.[11]

Since in guerilla warfare tactics resisters to colonial invaders were peasants by day and fighters by night, the ambiguity led to tragic mistakes, or to
a cynical strategy where some officers killed innocents rather than let enemies
escape. "Every time we wonder how many innocents and how many pirates
lay among the dead bodies, I firmly think that the balance tilts heavily
toward the side of the innocents," declared the physician Gaston Dreyfus.[12]

What Dreyfus also saw was a darker motive to the atrocities, directly
related to what it meant to be a good colonial officer, if not a good officer of
the French army in general. Who could tell, back in Paris, whether the scene
of that glorious battle, as it was described by the military leadership, was not
in fact a smoldering Vietnamese village with civilian bodies pilled high?
Medals, some earned for true courage, others rewarding base ambitions,
cascaded on chests proudly puffed. The colonies were a *terre à galons*, a land
were military stripes were easily earned.

Pfirmann, who arrived in the Tonkin after the debacle at Lang Son,
observed what was left of the first battalions who had come earlier, those that
Sergeant Bolis had witnessed on the docks at Oran: "The men did not have
the martial air common to legionnaires. Without their uniform, one could

have taken them for brigands."[13] A few years later the situation had hardly improved. Lyautey voiced his dismay when he discovered further evidence of neglect, namely in the quarters of the Legion in Haiphong: "The lodging of the First Foreign is so bad except in Phu Lang Thuong that it's impossible to find a worse one in the Tonkin. That does not even deserve the name of barracks. Almost all men lack shelter against sun or rain."[14]

The unsanitary conditions in the camps made them breeding grounds for disease. Bodies weakened by tropical humidity were hardly resistant to heat stroke or skin irritations. After days spent crossing rice paddies, or moving incessantly between colder mountain and hot plain climates, drinking dirty water, the men fell ill. Dysentery, cholera, and malaria were endemic. Concerning malaria, medicine still struggled to identify what timing and dosage of quinine could ward off the malady. The military had issued a guide in 1886, the *Instruction élémentaire sur les précautions hygiéniques à employer au Tonkin*. It hardly made a difference.

A Soldier in the Legion, by George Mannington, and *Life in the Legion*, by Frederic Martyn, both of whom were Englishmen, described vividly this period of the early 1890s when the French struggled to control the Tonkin. Mannington served in the Tonkin from 1891 to 1895, fighting against the infamous rebel De Tham (Hoang Hoa Tham) in the Yen The region before obtaining a desk job in Hanoi. Martyn came from Britain with experience as an officer in an unspecified Hussards regiment. Martyn hinted at past misconduct: "I had been a fool and had altogether lost conceit in myself."[15] Thus he joined the Legion after bumping into a dashing gentleman coming out of the army's recruitment office on the Rue Saint-Dominique, where he heard the usual warning from the *commandant de recrutement*. The man he had met on the street, a Russian named Petrovski, eventually became an inseparable companion. Thanks to this Russian's seemingly endless resources, they took a rapid train to Marseilles, got a few hours to spare and booked themselves a room at the Grand Hotel Noailles just to take a warm bath and rest before hitting the town, "big cigar in mouth and feeling very well satisfied with ourselves."[16] This first chapter of Martyn's flavorsome adventure ended in an epic brawl with other soldiers at a luxury restaurant, and later on the hardwood bed of Marseilles's *salle de police* rather than the comforts of the Noailles.

A mere three weeks after discovering Sidi Bel Abbès, all the novelties of the colonial town in the Algerian backcountry exhausted, Petrovski casually dropped: "'Let's go to the Tonkin.' 'Righto,' answered his co-legionnaire Martyn. 'When shall we start—tomorrow?'"[17]

Beneath the humor and legionnaire swashbuckling of Martyn's narrative, sobering facts are evident, as illness took many more lives than the so-called pirates of the Tonkin. Likewise, Mannington describes in stark words the even-more-dreaded blackwater fever, a most often fatal complication of malaria, in his *A Soldier of the Legion*:

> Its commencement, like ordinary malaria, is generally announced by shivering fits, during which the sufferer experiences a sensation of extreme cold. The hands and feet are numbed and glacial; the teeth chatter continually, notwithstanding the fact that the thermometer in the veranda is often, in such cases, at 95 degrees. This is succeeded at the end of an hour or more by a feeling of burning heat; perspiration ceases, the sufferer's temperature rises to over a hundred; he is a victim of terrible pains in the head, and is often delirious . . . Hard drinkers were often longer in resisting the attacks of the fever fiend, but once the illness got a hold upon them, the results were generally fatal.[18]

In Martyn's memoir, Petrovski fell ill after suffering a bad wound. Then the author himself caught the terrible blackwater fever—he survived after a month in the care of the Sisters of Mercy of the field hospital, and he also saw his friend recovered. They both had been extremely lucky: Between 1886 and 1896, the four battalions of the Legion present in the Tonkin lost to disease an average of 153 soldiers every year.[19] Medical personnel, understandably, was powerless. Coffins, slathered with lime, were placed directly under the beds of the dying who had made it to the hospital. Evacuation to France or Algeria on the troop carriers was often the coup de grace for the sick.

So, when a legionnaire settled in the Tonkin, the *cafard* depression usually affected the legionnaire's morale, and if there is a key word that is essential to describe the legionnaire's type, there it is. It's an irresistible pull toward nothingness, explained Pfirmann, who suffered from it as he stood guard somewhere in the Tonkin, on Christmas Eve. "During the two hours of my watch, I relived of the film of my life. At no point could I hang on to the thought that the life of my comrades depended on me, and that my duty was sacred. Like a sleepwalker, the memories of the past dominated me, it was crazy. They told me it was that, the *cafard*."[20]

Were religious sentiments of any consolation to the legionnaire's peculiar depressive affliction? The authorities at the Legion of those years did not allow a chaplain, at Sidi Bel Abbès or during campaigns, because under the anticlerical rule of the republicans, religion was seen as divisive. Chartrand des Écorres, the Canadian who fought in the early 1880s in Algeria, went to military mass once, but he explains that soon after that, worship under official army sponsorship was prohibited. Although he observed that the soldier "is generally not devout," he still found mass to be a consolation, for reasons that had less to do with higher truths. "Military pomp enhanced the service. And it attracted such beautiful women, such elegant demoiselles, on which our troopers laid such chaste looks."[21]

In the Tonkin, the legionnaires found opportunities to interact with clergymen. Father Louis Girod described his ten-year-long mission in the Upper Tonkin, preaching to both Vietnamese and the French military. Among the legionnaires, his most amenable subjects were found in the hospitals, on their deathbeds, sick with tropical diseases. Otherwise, the healthy soldiers would likely have exhausted the patience of this most saintly and perseverant of all missionaries. Save for a few, Girod found them to be of the "prodigal son" species. It's not that they lacked human qualities: "What endurance in the midst of all kinds of deprivations! What courage under fire! What contempt for death!" Girod introduces the legionnaire Émile Kurtz, an Alsatian who, like so many of his countrymen, joined the Legion to avoid serving Germany against France. Kurtz was rowdy and drank too much, but he also liked to fight and dreamed of a promotion to corporal in the Tonkin; before leaving for a mission he always visited Girod to tidy up the affairs of his conscience. He died in January 1895, "gun and rosary in hand."

There is also a German named Dausch. This one staggered into the presbytery to ask Girod if he could celebrate a great mass for a comrade who had just passed away at Hanoi's hospital—"he is now eating the banana trees by the root," muttered the drunken fellow, nearing stupor. Girod tried to explain that he was short on the paraphernalia required by Catholic pomp. Dausch, mistakenly, thought that the money he had offered was insufficient, and so he piled up piastres on the table, growing animated, banging his fist with enough energy to show he meant business: "Enough, Monsieur Chaplain (he now roars with a guttural Teutonic burr), keep everything, I'm telling you. I swear I'm not thirsty anymore. But if you refuse my money, well, I'm off to the Chinese drinking hole round the corner and, I swear, I won't be held responsible for what happens next." He then gave Girod a bone-crushing embrace, and stepped off, "proud, head held high, with a conqueror's air." The next day, Girod found him at the infirmary, hung over and considerably less assured. Dausch gestured to hand him his money back, Girod heard: "No, no, chaplain, I know what I've said; for once I did something good after drinking, there is surely no reason to withdraw my offer."[22]

Legionnaire Dausch's reaction to Girod took the unlikely form of emotional blackmail: He would cause harm to himself if the priest did not satisfy his wish to honor a comrade. It's quite fitting in a situation involving a priest, whose duty it is to help. Therein lay the legionnaire's paradoxical ethos of defiance and feelings of worthlessness, perhaps the motive for which he fought in the ranks of the Legion, for which he defied death, and the reason why his figure would soon exert such a powerful attraction on the public.

Another manifestation of the *cafard* was revelry, excessive revelry no less dangerous. Local *choum-choum*, a rice spirit, hit you on the head like a sledgehammer. A system of comfort women also figured highly in the advantages of campaigning in the Tonkin. Most Europeans disliked how indigenous women in Vietnam varnished their teeth in black and chewed betel leaves that made their saliva blood red, but it's not that they cared so much about their smiles or conversation. Surely those who did not smile were the Vietnamese men, if we trust this song lamenting the occupation:

Thirsty with lust the French soldiers	*Avides de luxure les soldats français*
Day and night search for women	*Jours et nuits cherchent des femmes*
Alas! The Annamite whores	*Hélas! Les putains annamites*
Can eat without laboring	*Peuvent manger sans travailler*
Together with the Frenchmen	*En suivant les Français*
Now the sky is beneath	*Maintenant le ciel est en bas*
And the earth up in the sky.	*et la terre est en haut.*[23]

To enter into a civil contract with a so-called *congaï*, as the female companions of the troops were called, was an easy move for the legionnaire and contributed to the idea of the Tonkin as a tropical, seductive heaven. The French authorities turned a blind eye to these arrangements. At least it prevented rapes, they claimed, or excessive sexual promiscuity. A large number of daily consultations at military dispensaries related to venereal diseases.[24]

Between bouts of the *cafard* and the hangovers emerged the solidarity that bound a cohort, as Mannington saw it when he witnessed the ravages of the tropical fevers:

It was a quaint and touching sight to watch one of these bearded mercenaries, as he passed from cot to cot, and note his efforts to repress his own impatience and clumsiness, as he piled blanket after blanket on a shivering sufferer, changed the damp linen of another, who had broken into the beneficent sweat that denoted the termination of an attack, or calmed, with a voice which he tried to render gentle, the ravings of a delirious friend, standing the while to change every few minutes the wet bandages on the burning brow of the stricken ones.[25]

Pfirmann noted how that solidarity extended beyond death: "We encountered in the forest tombs of legionnaires. A stone, a plant, a inscription on a wood plank testified to the loyalty of memory that the living kept of these anonymous deaths."[26] What the legionnaires could rely on to survive was not a French colonial establishment in dire need of competence and leadership, nor the artificial paradises of a land that despised them, but themselves as corps. Again, Mannington paints a picture of camaraderie underpinned by a keen sense of fatality as he shows a quiet resting scene, at night:

> Their bivouac echoed with the rollicking choruses sung by the men as they sat around the fires. Between songs they would crack jokes at each other's expense, and enter into friendly discussions as to who would be the next to "eat bananas by the roots," which was their playful way of suggesting a hurried burial in soft soil.[27]

Legionnaire Bôn Mat, in an earlier memoir dating from the first expedition of 1883, depicting the same kind of scene of rest, emphasizes the lingering blues of the legionnaire.

> Despite the drizzle that starts again at nightfall, the clothes that one tries to dry in vain, the stomach that demands more food, the prospects of a bad night under the tent and on the damp ground, gaiety reclaims its rights. *Lieders* of the homeland succeed conversations. And in these chants slow and stern like church anthems, one hears a soft and sad lament, that of all those broken hearts that cruelty, injustice, sufferings of life have gathered here so far away from their country, under the same law of duty and sacrifice.[28]

As difficult as these beginnings of the French colonial rule in Indochina were, the nightmares would be quick to fade, so powerful was the spell of the Tonkin in the stories of those legionnaires who came back to speak of its riches: the scent of patchouli and burning aloeswood wafting in the streets of old Hanoi, mysterious women, visions of dragons curling in the haze of incense and opium smoke. There were cheaply paid boys to take care of the soldiers' everyday needs, and an abundance of wonderful food. One could even hunt tigers. Being sent to the Tonkin was considered a reward by the troops, reported Lyautey as he assessed the morale of the Legion, while on his tour of duty there. In 1900, Captain Abel Clément-Grandcourt wrote: "Indochina is the second motherland of my legionnaires. Its particular charm infiltrates their blood together with malaria and they cannot part with the vision of sunlight splashing the rice paddies."[29] Northern Vietnam became the Asian counterpart of Algeria, a name denoting emotional attachment and nostalgia.

Even the dreaded mountains exerted a strange spell, wrote Legionnaire Louis Carpeaux, as he moved about with his cohort:

> We passed through primeval bamboo forest thirty meters high, which immense lianas, hanging down to the ground, embraced. Often we had to cut these lianas with our machetes. Sometimes we saw gigantic trees, banyans or camphor trees, the dwellings of families of whistling monkeys. At other times we saw oaks, almost the oak trees of our regions. At some point we walked high enough to dominate the clouds, at a height of two thousand meters, to find rocks barren and covered in white frost at the summits; two hours later, back at the bottom, we were making our way through luxurious groves of banana trees in full bloom. And behind each banana tree trembling under the breeze, we expected a pirate to jump out, gun in hand, ready to sow death. The figure of the pirate is indispensable to the poetry of this splendid nature . . . He keeps the heart in a perpetual state of emotion that makes you experience the beauty of things more fully![30]

Martyn, so overwhelmed did he become with the perfume of these forests ("imagine, multiplied a thousand times, the scent of an old-fashioned garden"), fell asleep one day, the narcotic effect of the flowers emphasized by "the gentle swaying of the treetops."[31] He woke up with a black eye: Was it a bat, a bird, or a spent bullet?

The worst scandal ever to engulf the French Army, and arguably France as a whole, began in October of the year 1894, when a Jewish army captain, Alfred Dreyfus, was arrested and accused of spying on behalf of Germany. Dreyfus was publicly degraded, and sent to a penal colony in Guyana. Quickly, it would become obvious that the captain was innocent, but the army authorities refused to recognize the truth. The consequences went beyond a story of corruption. It also went beyond the virulent anti-Semitism that was taking deeper roots in France, after the publication of Drumont's bigoted pamphlet *La France juive*, in 1886. Soon the scandal stunned the entire nation, and carved deep rifts in its political terrain, giving rise to forms of political extremism. The "affaire Dreyfus" did raise deep suspicions about the integrity of the army, which still had barely recovered from another scandal. In 1889, a military strongman named Georges Ernest Boulanger had won enough votes in a parliamentary election in Paris and sufficient popular support to raise fear of a coup d'état—he later fled France and shot himself on the grave of his mistress.

As far as Lyautey was concerned, causes for chagrin extended beyond the army's woes. Pope Leo XIII, as expected, published in 1892 a landmark encyclical that enjoined the French clergy and Catholic citizenry to accept the reality of the republican regime. Royalists such as Albert de Mun could not have suffered a more severe blow, but their faith demanded they accept the pope's pronouncement. A year later, the right suffered a devastating loss in the legislative elections.

After a long eastward trip that took him to Budapest, Constantinople, and Athens, back in France, Lyautey faced the reality that once again he was going to live the bland military life of a small provincial. In October of 1893, he was named chief of staff of the French army cavalry's Seventh Division, based in Meaux. His newly found celebrity, it seems, had not led him to envision the realities of military life in France as a challenge he could take on. Then, he lost his father, Just, in March of the following year. "I am sick of this isolation, sick with sadness, and, above all, sick with the horror of my duties and military men in general."[32]

Another source of worry contributed to the awkwardness of these two years. Having befriended a young painter named Paul Baignères, Lyautey spent much time with Baignères's family. In the Baignères salon, Lyautey, who still made quite an impression even though he now had reached the age of thirty-nine, caught the attention of the painter's sister Louise. The two struck up a friendship as well, writing to each other at length, and soon it became obvious that the young woman had fallen in love. Her parents communicated that they would gladly acquiesce to the marriage, but that was quite far from Lyautey's preoccupation. With much tact, but quite firmly, he told her that their friendship would remain just that.

A man with an extraverted sensitivity, in whom his closest collaborators observed a feminine side, Lyautey did not shy away from voicing open admiration for men's physiques and beauty. He admired men as noble warriors and surrounded himself with cohorts of young officers. He judged men as others judge fine steeds and he waxed enthusiastically about the beauty of exclusive, passionate friendship between men. Georges Clemenceau is said to have crudely quipped, speaking of the Lyautey's ambiguous attractions: "There is an admirable man, with courage, and quite a set of balls down there . . . even when they are not his own."[33] But the fact is that the only reliable testimony concerning Lyautey's sex life represents him in the company of a woman. It comes from a legionnaire who served at Aïn Sefra, a military town where Lyautey would later be based. To contradict the rumor that Lyautey had taken a friend of his as a mistress, this legionnaire, named Richard Kohn, wrote: "Very often, in the evening, my pals and I would meet our chief [Lyautey], walking back to the fort in the company of those ladies of the café-concert for an evening of louche entertainment [*partie-fine*]."[34]

Following the fallout with Louise Baignères, or perhaps out of boredom, but in any case out of a pronounced existential malaise, Lyautey asked his superiors for an assignment in Indochina. The request for a transfer was approved. He boarded a liner in Marseilles on October 12, 1894, and saw the shores of the motherland fade to the horizon. "I must confess that I felt, as I leaned on the poop deck, the classic pang of the heart that takes you over physically when the shores drown behind the horizon," Lyautey wrote upon his own departure.[35] Corsica, Stromboli, Sicily succeeded each other, followed by the shores of Algeria, where more troops of the Legion eagerly waited to join in the journey. Officers, changed into their white colonial uniforms, fought *ennui* as they could. Meals succeeded card games. Under the white cloth stretched above the decks to ward off the relentless sun, the dedicated read about the strange countries they would soon get to know, and the books slipped from their fingers as they fell asleep.

Travelers had ample time to forget about the homeland, and forge powerful expectation, for distances create myths. Martyn, by the time Lyautey left France, had lived yet another chapter of their adventures. Returned to Sidi Bel Abbès and fully recovered from the diseases he had contracted in the Tonkin, he had found military life in the barracks and the Algerian countryside again all too predictable. The calling of faraway adventures was still strong. When the Legion sent a force to the African kingdom of the Dahomey, to subdue King Behanzin, he and his Russian companion jumped to attention. Arriving in July of 1892, the two fought together next to rising men such as Paul Brundsaux, who commanded the second of four Legion companies, and Polydore Minnaërt, the Belgian giant of the early Tonkin campaign, who at last earned a promotion to sergeant.

Martyn and Petrovski saw the shores of Algeria again in the early days 1894. They were bringing back with them yet more stories—stories of incredible hardship and suffering in the tropical war theater, but also the kind of extraordinary stories that defied the imagination of the wildest novelist: infamous fighting scenes against King Behanzin's two thousand beautiful Amazons, the female warriors that could put to shame the most aggressive of their male comrades; the entry into Behanzin's sacred and immense temple of sacrifices, centered around a courtyard paved with human sculls, and a path leading to a stone pool caked in human blood. All proof of the colonies' awe-inspiring and mysterious cruelties, and above all of the legionnaire's capacity to find solace in his fertile imagination.

CHAPTER 5

Oil Slick

The Can Vuong resistance movement, which began when Emperor Ham Nghi fled to the mountains in 1885, almost caused the collapse of the French war machine. By 1892, however, the threat had waned, the resistance having fizzled because the spontaneous movement uniting both peasants and learned elites never formed a common project around the institution of the emperor, a tired one. The French were still far from dominating the Tonkin, though. The circle of mountains that dominated the Red River Delta, especially to the east and northeast, harbored some armed bands that, under the leadership of warlords, reached at times the size of small armies. Burgeoning French infrastructure projects were good targets for these bands, including the new railway that snaked through narrow mountain corridors from Hanoi up to Lang Son. There were kidnappings of civilians as well.

Three men came to overturn this situation. Jean Marie de Lanessan was named governor-general of Indochina in 1891. A professor of medicine who found a calling in politics, he applied the characteristic firm belief in progress and the powers of human reason of the Third Republic to bringing order to Indochina. Lanessan carved up the upper regions of the Tonkin into four military territories and placed them under unitary military command. The leader of those military territories was Joseph Gallieni, newly arrived after digesting his observations in Africa and ready to apply new principles in what the French referred to as "pacification." Under Lanessan and Gallieni's leadership, a general strategy to fight the so-called "pirates" of the mountains and secure the territory by both military and political means emerged. They called it the "oil slick," an image conjuring the slow, steady, and permanent progression of French colonial power.

Lyautey arrived in Hanoi in November 1894. In the chief of staff's office, he supervised the logistics of military operations in the Tonkin, as well as the administration, both civil and political, of all four territories. Eventually he was elevated to interim chief of staff. Gallieni he met a few weeks after his arrival. His superior charmed him right away: "He is forty-four; he just spent eight days here and won me over as a lucid sire, precise and with wide views; then he made quite a lot of noise about my article, which did not leave me unmoved."[1] The relationship strengthened when a first tour in the Upper Tonkin took them first to Lang Son, along the railway line besieged by the rebels, and then along the Chinese border to Cao Bang, and finally in a wide circle back to Hanoi.

The Foreign Legion represented a vital resource in these expeditions. Four battalions, their members drawn equally from the First and Second Regiments of Sidi Bel Abbès and Saïda in Algeria, were in the military territories of the Tonkin in 1895, a year after Lyautey's arrival. Troops had been provided with uniforms adapted to the climate, notably a jacket in a brownish *cachou* color, with a distinctive collar adorned with scarlet insignia showing the seven-flame grenade emblem in blue (a distinctive sign of elite infantry troops throughout the French army, this emblem had officially become part of the legionnaire's dress in 1875). Although lighter-weight trousers had also been thought of with protection in mind, Mannington observed that the legionnaires supplemented them with leggings to protect themselves from cutting leaves and parasites. Last but not least, weapons had improved. The Lebel model 1886 (8mm; modified), considered to be one of the first modern rifles of its kind, offered the advantage of repeating, smokeless fire, compared to the earlier standard Gras. It was no small advantage for the soldier who needed to remain under the cover of thick vegetation during a fight.

Since the heavy columns that de Négrier organized to roam the delta had been cumbersome and ineffective, formations with fewer soldiers carrying their own supplies were put into place. They marched more quickly. If three of those light columns, leaving from different points, could trap an armed band and cut off its escape routes, then the coordinated attack had much higher chances of success. For that kind of mission, the Legion fit the bill perfectly.

At the very end of the year 1895, the French command set its sights on pockets of resistance in the Upper Tonkin, between the Upper Lô and Cam rivers, right below the Chinese border, where the warlord A Coc Thuong operated. Lieutenant-Colonel Jean Vallière, himself a veteran of Senegal under Gallieni, oversaw the operation and took Lyautey, naming him his second in command. Gallieni had left after only a few months in Vietnam, called by the French government to Madagascar, the new war theater in the Scramble for Africa. (Longstanding tensions between the Madagascar government of Queen Ranavalona III and the French, on the subject of what the protectorate treaty signed in 1885 actually represented, had reached a tipping point, and the French were mounting a new punitive expedition.) Vallière and the first two battalions departed for the second military territory, land that included the cities of Lang Son and Cao Bang, where much of the action to assert final French dominance took place.

Lyautey, who had until then been burdened by his desk duties and missed opportunities, looked for a good *fait d'arme*, a feat of arms. What kind of soldier is one who has never been shot at in a real engagement? On February 10, 1896, he fulfilled his wish, perhaps not with the kind of brio that his character demanded. On that fateful day, Lyautey was to be found in the most difficult of positions, in a vertiginous scene of steep sugarloaves of limestone, covered with jungle cascading into deep, dark gorges. Squeezed with the Legion on a narrow rocky ledge, he hung in the middle of those mountain cliffs, dodging bullets shot by the bandits. Night was falling, and rain, too.

The adventure had begun when Vallière's light columns converged from the southwest, but some of A Coc Thuong's bands, numbering at least a thousand men, headed for the delta instead of retreating toward China, and threatened to control some key communication points along the rivers. All French defensive posts, having contributed to the principal operation, could hardly spare any more soldiers to stop this unexpected movement. Communications with Vallière, who marched northward, were impossible, because foul weather rendered the optical signals useless, and the carrier pigeons had not been sufficiently trained yet. On January 13, the armed bands ambushed a detachment of legionnaires above Bac Muc, causing many casualties. Lyautey, who was sailing upriver to reach Vallière, retreated to Tuyen Quang and organized the resistance with assurance, still fearing an attack on the storied citadel: "I see myself starting Dominé's epic all over again, but in the most unfortunate circumstances."

On January 20 he reached Bac Muc, where the legionnaires's column attacked a week earlier was reconstituted. The following day, with a detachment of sixty legionnaires and sixty Skirmishers under the orders of Captain Girardot, he joined another reinforcement of legionnaires from the Third Battalion and Skirmishers: Both pushed the bands back north where Vallière operated. Meanwhile, Lyautey reorganized communication lines and ordered the installation of new telegraph lines. When Lyautey met Vallière at Ha Giang, he learned that he had missed the largest battle of the French conquest of Indochina, at Khau Coc (January 21–23), where more than three thousand soldiers fought to take a position at an altitude of fifteen hundred meters (close to five thousand feet). Thanks to the legionnaires' fighting spirit, and support from the artillery, it was a triumph. Still, with his swift initiatives, albeit less glamorous ones, Lyautey had contributed to a reversal of fortune on the front closer to where most civilians lived.

Some very last pockets of active resistance nagged the French, however, and taking them out gave Lyautey an opportunity to show valor in combat and create lasting bonds with Legion troops. The lair of the bandit Le Chi Tuan and his two hundred and fifty rifles, deep in the Nui Ken Mountains, south of Ha Giang, had to be cleared. Three hundred and fifty men of the French forces, split into three groups, two of them covering possible retreats of the enemy, converged on Nui Ken.

On February 9, Lyautey and his group closed in on the mouth of a narrow gorge that twisted into the mountain, but they were met with a barrage of bullets. Their adversaries had all the approaches covered from a vantage point. The French soldiers found a better position under cover of artillery fire, and dislodged them. On the morning of the tenth, Lyautey found this first enemy camp empty. The bandits had disappeared down the gorge and into the mountains, under the cover of the thickest forest imaginable.

Two teams went on reconnaissance. Hearing shots, Lyautey decided to supply backup, through "an inextricable chaos of rocky crests, needles, torn shapes, all that rock textured like a sponge, something you climb for a hundred meters, your hands bloody, dangling in the void, to go down again into vertiginous abysses, and up again." Fire intensified from down the gorge, the Chinese horns blared louder with their lugubrious war calls, calls and shots that echoed in the deep valley. They encountered one of the groups sent earlier. All was fine, so they proceeded through a curtain of fire, to which they responded with equal vigor.

This is when Lyautey and his men got stuck: "Finally, here we are at half past five, at night, the hundred of us hoisted on a needle of rock like those on the Normandy Coast, drowned in a sea of trees and less than two hundred meters from the action, but separated from it by a chasm where one cannot venture anymore due to the darkness." Still unaware of the second team's where-abouts, Lyautey asked the bugler to sound the refrain of the Legion's company he was with. On the other side of the ravine, in the same precarious position, was that second team, with four dead men and six gravely wounded. That, at least, was the little information they could exchange.

Both in darkness and in daylight, retreat was impossible; they'd end up broken down the mountain, or shot like fowl on that wall. The only way pointed forward. This is how Lyautey and his men spent the night hanging from the branches, without water or food, in dropping temperatures and thickening rain. Shots pierced through the night, just often enough to keep them awake.

Morning brought brighter prospects. They learned that combat had raged the day before, but their arrival, unbeknownst to them, had precipitated the outcome. The lair of the enemy was deserted:

> Darn! Sensing our movement, they've jumped ship, but what a mess! Fourteen dead bodies: It's been awhile since they've left their dead; traces of blood in the trampled vegetation show that they took some with them. Under the blown-up shelters, forsaken rice, hats, utensils, rags, and cartridges too, most of them Winchester. Much ado about nothing! Anyway, they've repaid us for the night.[2]

In the mountains of Nui Ken, at last, Lyautey had experienced what he described as "a really good fire, seasoned with a spicy sauce of emotions and incidents." His true "baptism by fire," and thrill of fighting with legionnaires had actually taken place the year before, in April 1895, on a mission to dislodge the bandit Ba Ky from a retreat at Ke Thuong. By his own admission, the experience had not lived up to the kind of heroics he envisioned. Much more prosaically, this first fight had given him a chance to hone his skills in organizing military logistics: "I dream bags of rice, cases of flour," he had quipped in the middle of the action.[3] And so the action in the mountains of Nui Ken, less concerned with bags of flour, was elevated to a primordial experience.

Lieutenant-Colonel Vallière found that Lyautey had demonstrated courage under fire. The report he wrote later to the chief of armies in Indochina, on March 22, 1896, certified that Lyautey had been a "valiant soldier" at Nui Ken, and that "it would be equitable if the career of this high officer benefitted from the exceptional services he performed on behalf of the army and the colony." The citation that Vallière recommended specified that at Nui Ken, Lyautey "had very aptly served his commander when he went by the enemy flank with two infantry groups, a movement that powerfully pushed the Chinese into a retreat."[4]

Sergeant Ernest Bolis of the Legion was a little more forthcoming about how he lived his first engagement, in the Tonkin, in the year 1891: "My head was heavy and I could not hear anything. Hair risen, big beads of sweat dripped from my temples."[5] He did not think of food for an entire day, he explains, left as he was with an overwhelming sadness. That, it's worth noting, did not make him less of a brave warrior.

Following these high-altitude heroics, Lyautey set his sights on taking full control of the area north of Ha Giang, which meant mapping the territory and locating optimal sites for posts along ways of communication and the border. A Coc Thuong had fled to China. Now, building those outposts near the border presented challenges of another order, since the line between the two countries was far from established; it involved diplomacy with the Chinese officials, a task for which Lyautey had many talents. With an escort of about thirty legionnaires of the Second Company of the Second Regiment, he set out from Ha Giang to Bao Lac, and then to the outpost of Coc Pan on March 6, through lands laid waste by the bands' ravages. Lifestyle improved noticeably: A copy of the *Revue des Deux Mondes* arrived by post in Coc Pan. The camp was treated to readings of poetry. An officer of the Legion present there, Charles de Menditte, turned out to be an acquaintance of the family. After graduating from Saint-Cyr, he had spent a year in Sidi Bel Abbès.

On March 9, the envoy of Marshal Sou, the mandarin Hoang Van Cao, honored the French camp with his presence and that of a numerous retinue. The French hoped to impress the Chinese with their hospitality because their first encounter, on the other side of the border, had been a feast worthy of any high-end Parisian restaurant. But a kitchen fire caused by the cook burned the whole canteen down. How to host a high-level diplomatic conference with some charred food remains? It seemed impossible. But that was to discount the ingenuity of the troops, Menditte's memoirs explain:

> On that occasion, our legionnaires proved to be incomparable; a sumptuous shelter was improvised in just a few minutes, a new menu devised. The camp's pig had escaped the flames of the fire only to fall under the knife of a legionnaire: Cutlets, sausages garnished the table only three hours after he was prancing around the camp full of life and carefree.[6]

Lyautey even thought, in retrospect, that the fire might have helped the French save face. "Our [earlier] good dinner paled next to theirs, and thanks to the fire and our apologies, they could imagine that we had prepared an

extravagant feast."[7] When the mandarin Hoang Van Cao left hours later—
"his fur-trimmed gown spread on his horse; the red of his umbrella, the violet
of his own mandarins in violet, the scarlet and blue of his guard unfolded on
the twisting road, shimmering under the sunset"—both parties had reached
a suitable treaty on how to cooperate as good neighboring powers.[8] France
and China looked toward more effectively peaceful relations.

By 1897, thirteen years after the launch of the Tonkin campaign, the French
commanders breathed a sigh of relief. New strategic methods showed their
effectiveness. Moreover, after getting rid of the heavy columns of the past,
the military leaders had learned to combine occupation of the terrain with
political action. First, the posts formed a systematic network. To show the
enemy and civilian population that the French had settled permanently,
structures built in masonry replaced old ones built out of bamboo in vulnerable sites. This in turn did well for the morale of the troops. Commanders
tried to relieve soldiers every forty-five days. Hygiene conditions improved,
as well as medical help, and although dysentery and blackwater fever still
took lives, they were much less a death sentence than a decade earlier. Roads
ensured better communications, while transmissions relied on optical telegraph. Gallieni put it this way:

> Any forward movement of the troop must be sanctioned with an
> effective occupation of the terrain, this principle is absolute.
> Every time war circumstances require one of our officers to act
> against a village, that officer must never lose sight that his first
> duty, once the inhabitants have submitted, is to rebuild the
> village, to immediately create a market, to establish a school.[9]

Near the French army forts, villages enjoyed relative security and a chance to
benefit from the occupiers. Outside the post, officers established contact
with local elites, supervised the creation and arming of local militia, launched
public works projects, and dispensed agricultural and economic advice.
Purchasing fresh food from the market was both a comfort to the troops and
a source of revenue for the farmers. At night, when the optical towers of the
French blinked their mysterious messages, it did appear that the all-seeing
Argus of colonization was effectively spreading all over Southeast Asia.

Charles de Menditte, whom Lyautey had met at Coc Pan, left in October
of 1896 to set up one of these forts in the mountains, at Tien Phong. Building

the fort necessitated leveling the top of a mountain with dynamite, which the legionnaires did effectively and fast, but with a disregard for safety that left Menditte horrified. Once the peril of explosives had passed, it was time for good fun: "With huge wood levers, everybody, officer first, we moved formidable pieces of rock, and when those rolled down on the side of the Chinese border, we had such a good laugh."[10] Since the troops included men with skills in wood and iron working, brick making, and other trades, the quality and appearance of the fort surprised visitors. There was a wood oven to bake bread, and a vegetable garden. At some point, Menditte and his men had the scare of their life: It turned out that Tien Phong had been built in Chinese territory by mistake, and that all their hard work risked benefitting the former enemy. Thankfully, since the border delineation was still a work in progress, all parties agreed that renaming the fort Chang Poung would suffice to make the topographers satisfied, and so Menditte and his legionnaires stayed.

There were few discipline problems, save for a Belgian legionnaire who terrorized everyone—a real Hercules worthy of a county fair show, according to Menditte. By most accounts, the Legion ranks featured some very healthy, tall, and physically fit men. Flutsch, in his memoirs, evokes "one of those colossi whose specimens were not rare in the Legion: height nearing two meters, the powerful build of a man of one hundred and twenty kilograms with almost no body fat."[11] Now, Flutsch did see this fellow reduce an officer to a pulp with the sheer strength of his fist. At Chang Poung, under the command of Menditte, the Belgian beast was a permanent guest at the prison, or rather the wooden cage that they used to contain him. Strong as he was, it seems he could easily have blown up his tight quarters, but that never happened. Rather, says Menditte, when he was outside he satisfied everyone and even "gave many proofs of absolute devotion" to the corps.

Entertainment was wanting, at least at the newly named Chang Poung. In other forts, the legionnaires proved as resourceful in entertainment as in other domains. Mannington describes twice-weekly shows of shadow theater, "adaptations of some of the most popular dramas and comedies of the day," although he concedes that legionnaires in the audience grunted when the female voices were not convincing enough. "We would fall on the floor of the little mat-shed hut, where we would lie convulsed with laughter, until the noisy public threatened to pull down the house unless we continued the play."[12] This sort of drag show was not as rare as one might think. Flutsch speaks of a theater show where "the young Foussnecker played the role of a lady of a manor. He was endowed with magnificent blond hair and appetizing breasts, baits that were all the more abundant that only the artist's judgment set their size."[13] Magnus, another legionnaire, heard of "some splendid female impersonators" that roused the crowd in the barracks.[14] Lyautey witnessed a play given by a company of the Legion during his first tour of the Upper Tonkin, "one of the most comical, incongruous, and risqué" shows he had ever seen. He did not specify the type of risk.

So, short of the resources of those carousing legionnaires bent on gender trouble, there was much time left for a man to ponder life's great questions and truths, in those solitary forts by the Chinese border. Menditte made the most of it; his temperament, and thoughts of his family in France, immunized him against the dreaded *cafard*:

> I got used to my absolute solitude on my stark rocky plateau; I knew every path on it and its rather hard climate fitted my mood. I enjoyed that long-distance view over the peaks of the Dong Quan, a view that the backdrop of the Lung Cam mount closed, I liked the great voice of the wind that, at night, came in to howl around the walls of my post.[15]

Sometimes, as he lay absorbed in his thoughts, at dusk, "The bugler of the Legion sounded his instrument." He adds, "The man who has not heard this retreat call at an outpost by the Tonkin's border, does not know how long a good clarion of the Legion can make it last."

Lyautey returned to Hanoi on March 25, after Nui Ken and the encounter with the mandarin, facing the prospect of pages and pages of reports to write for Paris's armchair generals. "Nothing written, nothing done," he lamented. For now, gone were those days when men forged true bonds of friendship in action, in an awe-inspiring land, through all sorts of hardships. He missed the company of those free spirits who, like him, had left the constraints of civilized life just as one sheds a well-tailored but hopelessly stiff uniform, with relief. His letters waxed lyrical about simple gatherings under the stars, when conversation rolled at will on war tales, lewd jokes, and literature. He slept rolled in the burnous he kept from his days in North Africa.

It's not that Hanoi was still the rough town of Garnier and Rivière's days. Life in the Tonkin's capital offered a pleasant counterpart to daily labors, and a suitable place to spend a leave for the soldiers confined in isolated posts. Along wide avenues rose impressive buildings in a European style. Elegant crowds animated the cafés at the end of the day; they drank absinthe or vermouth before the theater. After lengthy stays in the mountains, it felt like stepping back into Europe, assures Mannington. Those in need of local color could easily venture into the old town, by the other side of the Sword Lake, to enjoy all sorts of pleasures. This is where the true legend of Vietnam as a heaven for the legionnaire was forged.

More than one hundred thousand Vietnamese lived in Hanoi. Lyautey's correspondence abounds in information on the rich spectacle he saw. He missed the noble air of the Arab warrior, however, and compared the Vietnamese population with those he had met in North Africa in racist terms.[16] At the same time, he appreciated the deep historical culture of Vietnam, marveling at the great source of wisdom that had flowed from Tibet throughout Southeast Asia, along the Mekong. He set himself up a cozy home, which he filled with Buddha statues and outfitted with a mock opium den. There, he could read the latest literary news from Paris, write to his ever-closer friend, Gallieni, or entertain parties of younger officers who were invariably described as "charming" or "nice."

The governor-general who succeeded Lanessan, Armand Rousseau, named Lyautey chief of his military cabinet and took him on a two-month-long tour of Indochina—since 1893, Indochina had also included the Kingdom of Laos. Sailing down the coast on a warship, Lyautey visited the magnificent imperial capital of Hue, the bay of Da Nang where the invasion of Vietnam had begun in earnest in 1858 with the bombing of the town's forts. Before reaching Saigon, he stopped at Nha Trang, where he encountered Alexandre Yersin, a thirty-year-old doctor trained at the Institut Pasteur in Paris. Settled in Vietnam after exploring the country on geographical missions for the navy, Yersin was working on isolating the bubonic plague bacillus and producing a vaccine against it—epidemics of the terrible disease were still very much feared in Asia. He also introduced the cultivation of the rubber tree and found the firm Michelin as his first client.

What Lyautey witnessed in the work of Yersin evokes the best and worst of French colonial rule in Indochina: generosity at the service of human welfare, and ruthless exploitation. The new rulers built hospitals and schools. They founded the famed École Française d'Extrême-Orient, which helped describe and preserve the region's artistic treasures. But in the end, the goal remained the enrichment of France, and investments never benefitted the Vietnamese people. The cultivation of rubber in plantations eventually became a huge source of profits for French investors, at the cost of a brutal mistreatment of local labor. Meanwhile, it was expected that taxes laid on these workers would fund infrastructure developed with foreign exports in mind, since banks preferred extracting profit from financial operations, and Indochina never became a colony of French settlement.[17]

Lyautey, by then, had perfected his philosophical vision of colonialism. He envisioned development as mankind's duty on the earth. In his view, colonial warfare represented a new kind of war, "a life-creating" war, as opposed to the destructive conflicts that consumed Europe.[18] He had found meaning in his life in those three years spent in the Tonkin. The revelation, it seems, had come sometime between the missions in Ke Tuong and the Upper Lô River. To a correspondent who wondered then if this colonial enterprise so costly in lives and money was worth the effort, he admitted that surely it had to be more than a matter of "healing his heart and mitigat[ing] his moodiness."[19] But it was worth it, he insisted. Indochina could be the jewel of the French colonial crown.

The exotic wonders of the lands the French conquered made it all the more worthwhile to him. Continuing to Cambodia after Saigon, he discovered the archeological site of Angkor, an immense city of colossal temples and palaces asleep in the tropical jungle, ruins that held the Khmer civilization's secrets. He spent a moonlit night wandering alone in Angkor Wat, the main temple, to the accompaniment of Buddhist monks' chants and bullfrog calls. The rules of divine harmony, he thought, are one. By the sacred mount of the Khmer, the Phnom, in the monastery, he found himself irresistibly drawn back to his days at the Grande Chartreuse in the French Alps: "I can see him, the old priest, so fervent, striking up the refrain of each psalm, arms wide open before the high altar, almost Catholic, all lit up."[20] Some treated their *cafard* with a bottle of brandy; his temperament was prone to aesthetic inebriations.

On November 16, 1896, having returned to Hanoi, Lyautey received a telegram: His service was required on the island of Madagascar, where Gallieni, who had not forgotten his protégé, tried with the Legion to subdue rebels opposed to French colonial hegemony. This time, Lyautey would test French-style "pacification" on a much wider scale. It was to be the scene of French colonial history's worst military disaster.

CHAPTER 6

Grim March

Off the southeast coast of Africa is the island of Madagascar, at 226,000 square miles the fifth-largest island in the world. People originating from Southeast Asia, from the island of Borneo, settled there in times immemorial. Their boats came pushed by yearly monsoon winds. African populations from the southeast coasts of the continent joined them, to form a mosaic of different ethnicities, a patchwork of kingdoms. On a fertile central plateau, where broad valleys benefit from a mild climate and rainfall, the most powerful of these kingdoms emerged, the Imerina kingdom. Centered on their capital, Antananarivo, during the nineteenth century the Imerina extended their dominion over a larger part of the island, taking as vassals other people, such as the Sakalava of the eastern seaboard, or the Boina in the northwest. Europeans who visited Imerina in the nineteenth century found a developed country, social institutions, and evidence of technological advance. They found people who dressed just like them.

Abutting the steepest side of that central plateau, a narrow and long strip of forest covers much of the eastern seacoast of Madagascar. To the south of the island lies a parched region of wild cactuses and dry plants. The western side of Madagascar, on the much less severe slope of the plateau, provides the easiest access to the Imerina. Along this coast, mighty rivers such as the Betsiboka wash the soils of the highlands, discharging red alluvial waters in wide, low-lying estuary plains that caimans infest. The vegetation there alternates between low grassy expanses and marshland and, in the approaches to Imerina from the west, changes into richer and denser forests.

Jean Darricarrère, a physician of the French colonial army, describes a jungle forest in his memoirs of the French colonial expedition of 1895, writing somewhere halfway between the mouth of the Betsiboka and the capital, Antananarivo. Under a canopy of emerald leaves, plants in shapes and foliage never seen before form an "inextricable, admirable jumble that envelops the traveler with shadows and mystery." Hummingbirds and butterflies fly around twists of climbing lianas. Then comes a simple sentence in that description by the French physician. There, in this enchanted forest, says Darricarrère: "The legionnaire hanged himself."[1] There is no indication of who this soldier was, no name, no company, no battalion, no regiment.

The French Legion lived an ordeal in its first year on the "Grande Île," before Gallieni and Lyautey showed up in Madagascar, as European powers experimented and adjusted their methods of colonial conquest. There had been mass casualties from disease in the Tonkin, but that reality filtered through all the advantages associated with the soldiers' life in Southeast Asia. Madagascar never benefitted from this positive, exotic aura.

Ranavalona III, queen of the Imerina kingdom, was too independent for the French. The protectorate treaty that she had signed after the French attack in 1885 was ambiguous enough to let both parties interpret it the way they wanted. Meanwhile, the queen's authority suffered from weak leadership, corruption of the oligarchic class that effectively ruled Madagascar, and even armed opposition from her vassals. Predatory loans from French banks had pushed the state into bankruptcy. The French saw this as an opportunity to claim dominion over the island once and for all. Arguing for this move were the French settlers in the volcanic island Réunion, west of Madagascar, a colony since the 1600s. Great Britain had cultivated diplomatic relations with the Imerina monarchs since the early decades of the 1800s, a useful policy, at least until the opening of the Suez Canal. Then, the island lost its strategic importance to the British, and in 1890 Britain traded the right to occupy Madagascar with the French in return for Zanzibar.

When Queen Ranavalona refused to revise the protectorate treaty in 1894, the French decided on an expedition. A fleet arrived in view at Mahajanga, the town that guards the mouth of the Betsiboka. Fifteen thousand men constituted this expeditionary corps, to which one must add thousands of civilian aides recruited from as far as Algeria. General Jacques Duchesne oversaw the enterprise.

The soldiers who first landed in December of 1894 quickly noted how much the campaign plans laid out by officers and bureaucrats at the Ministry of War fell short. The planners were thoroughly ill informed of the terrain and novices in the art of organizing large-scale overseas operations. Mahajanga consisted of some houses dispersed in between mango trees, in front of a hill with an abandoned citadel. On lower sandy terrain, the French army slowly erected the buildings necessary to run the colossal operation and a wharf, but the wharf never extended beyond the violent surf and sea currents that made navigation on the bay's waters treacherous. With few boats available to unload the supplies, the preparatory phase of the invasion was lengthened needlessly. Horses and mules had to be thrown overboard and left to swim to the shore, which, thankfully, they reached safely. While the boats waited idle offshore, the cases of medication and material needed to construct and operate field hospitals remained on board. Duchesne, meanwhile, rushed the onset of land operations, his eyes set on capturing Antananarivo, two hundred miles away. An air of disorganization reigned. A putrid haze hovered over the marshy area that surrounded the camps.

The River Betsiboka yielded more trials. Because the French thought the river would provide easy waterway access to the inland region, cutting distance by at least half, Paris's brass had chosen to land on the west coast of Madagascar, even though the distance to the capital was much greater from that point. But the Betsiboka foiled their designs, because it was so difficult to navigate: In the dry season, the waters were too shallow for most of the boats, and sand banks emerged or disappeared with frustrating unpredictability. Riverboats arrived late, and assembling them took much time.

What to do, then, with the wheeled carts supplied by the Maison Lefebvre, hundreds of them, that the leaders relied on to transport material and supplies for the second half of the trip? These carts, pulled either by animals or even hired collies, were supposed to make this campaign the stuff of military legend. Building both a road and the bridges needed along the river up to where boats were supposed to arrive in the original plans became a priority for a commander seemingly obsessed with his Lefebvre carts. The path crossed grassy undulating flatlands, where once in a while a grove of mango trees offered some shade, but often yielding to swampy terrain near the river. Rocky ridges surged periodically, obstructing the way. Meanwhile, soldiers not constructing dirt roads under the scorching tropical sun went on reconnaissance missions. Their Imerina enemy, by many standards, held its own: It benefitted from good weaponry and English training. That enemy progressively turned elusive, however, retreating as the French advanced, leaving scorched fields and abandoned villages. The soldiers seldom saw more than glimpses of the enemy's white shawls, the *lamba*. One enemy leader, Ramazombazaba, was quickly nicknamed "Ramasse-ton-Bazar" ("Pick Up Your Stuff") by the troopers since he was nowhere to be seen, either. Hence, the French could hardly hire the civilian population they had counted on for their works.

A battalion of the Legion arrived at the end of April 1895 as part of the Regiment of Algeria, commanded by Colonel Oudri of the Legion. This regiment numbered eight hundred men and twenty-two officers drawn equally from Sidi Bel Abbès and Saïda. Under Colonel Metzinger, the legionnaires proceeded inland as the advance guard of the expeditionary corps.

The legionnaires bore the full brunt of the deteriorating situation. Their column proceeded through more hilly land, at times rocky and barren, or covered with lavish forest. Stopping in Marovoay, an important point on the river, on the ninth of May, they protected the site for a construction of a bridge. Then they marched again. Sometimes the track lost itself "in the sands of the Betsiboka, in the midst of the sun's blinding reflection in the waters and the golden, mica sands."[2] Conditions worsened: Red ants, mosquitoes, and the "*moukafouis*" flies tormented the legionnaires at night, rabid wild dogs roamed about. Caimans could easily cut your head off as you squatted by the water to seek relief from the heat with a splash of water. Cases of malarial fever in its virulent blackwater strain and dysentery appeared and multiplied, leaving bodies drained, teeth shattering in the heat. Medical help was inadequate. Heat stroke, no matter how dangerous, seemed almost like a preferable lot. The sick accumulated under tents where rising temperatures perfected the works of illness.

And so it became clear that the Imerina, from their windswept, temperate highlands, relied on two of their most lethal generals, "Tazo" and "Hazo," General Fever and General Forest in their language, to defeat the European invaders. In early June, the Legion lieutenant Paul Langlois noted a legionnaire's suicide:

> Sergeant Rohrman, shouts with an unforgettable voice: "Lieutenant, It's X . . . who just blew up his *caisson*." The wretched fellow had filled the barrel of his rifle with water, to make sure he would die on the spot: His entire head was blown to pieces, scattered around the rocky soil. They buried him with his waxen neck fringed in red, his waxen hands, on which blood stains created a glowing halo.[3]

With the legionnaires, drastic decisions tended to come in waves. "It comes over them suddenly and unaccountably, this feeling that they cannot go on, that it would be better to be dead than to go through hell," explains the legionnaire Adolphe Cooper, who claims to have witnessed dozens of such deaths at a stop near a burial ground in Algeria, when a desperate, morbid *coup de cafard* fell on the troops.[4]

The few engagements took on a character that in the other circumstances might have elicited less than heroic prose. The vanguard of the column with the legionnaires reached a strategic point of passage, the town of Maevatanana on the Ikopa, the branch of the Betsiboka that led to Antananarivo. The legionnaires crossed the river on June 6, neck-deep in the water with rifles held overhead, but there was more risk from the caimans than from the Imerina army: The artillery and the gunboat *Brave* had finally made it that far and had already mowed the local defense down. The transport mules, delighting in the refreshing bath, ditched the cases of supply and baggage in the water. Still, as told by some, the event rivaled the crossing of the Rhine by Louis XIV's army.

Three days later, the Legion climbed the steep cliff on which Maevatanana stood and took the town, but melenite shells of the French artillery had preceded them—these shells, stuffed with a newly produced explosive based on picric acid, packed an incredibly strong destructive force. The legionnaires, exhausted and angry after the civilians protested the confiscation of their pigs, went on a rampage, beating every man they encountered, which Langlois found to be quite comical:

> They are beaten in a magisterial fashion, and nothing is more
> comical than their desperate cries, their terrified shrieks. Nothing
> is as hilarious as their scouring back into their lairs under the
> clubs of our good legionnaires, who can hardly keep beating so
> hard they laugh.[5]

War turned uglier in conditions such as those lived by the French troops of the Madagascar conquest of 1895. The legionnaire Adolphe Cooper, while serving in Algeria, reported hearing from older legionnaires "gruesome tales of things perpetrated on that island." Those stories related to the art of curing human skin, especially that a woman's breast, to make tobacco pouches.[6]

The next stop for the advancing column was eight kilometers away, in Suberbieville, which had been founded by European gold prospectors. There was no resistance there at all. The most significant battle of the campaign took place in Tsarasaotra, on June 29, but Skirmishers from Algeria fought it, not the legionnaires.

General Duchesne ordered the construction of the road farther toward the capital, under the supervision of the Fifth Regiment of Military Engineers. This required crossing some high mountains, a fact that the Paris planners had ignored. The physician Hocquard, who followed the troops, appreciated the legionnaires' skills in laying out a camp: "Two or three hours after setting up camp, these huts rise out of the ground seemingly by magic. Well aligned, they form in the Legion's camp streets that intersect at a right angle; these streets lead to a central square, where food is distributed and where a sentinel guards the flag."[7] Hocquard also noted, however, the poor condition of the companies. Down the river, at the hospital of Ankaboka, between twenty and thirty soldiers died every day. Darricarrère, the other doctor based in Mahajanga, worked in the midst of "teeth chattering of the coming chill, noisy deliriums born out of terrifying illusions, precipitating flights before a terrorizing hallucination, coughing fits that tear at the bronchial tubes, abundant spurts of vomit against the floor or the walls.[8]" Next to the camps that lined the road at regular intervals, white crosses and crescents spread at a steady pace.

The legionnaires, whipped by hot winds, their faces caked with red dust, labored all day on Duchesne's road, pausing between ten and three. Wine and quality rations were a distant memory. Their task was to carve portions of the road climbing on mountain cliffs. At the milepost 750 on the military map drawn at the time, a depression of one hundred and fifty meters appears, and cutting a road through this wall of rock required moving thousands of cubic meters of stone. From his tent, Langlois contemplated the scene:

> From my own construction site, on the very top of the slope, I can enjoy the strangest spectacle imaginable: Below me, lines of men, indicating the hairpin turns of the future road, are stacked up at smaller intervals the farther I look down into the valley. The incessant clamor of shouts, curses, pickaxe blows rises.[9]

The two brigades visible to Langlois included legionnaires, Algerian troops, and soldiers from other corps such as the Marsouins, and totaled one thousand men. It took them four days to build that segment of the road. The route progressed, crossing more mountains, and the deaths accumulated. Some were found dead sitting on the side of the road where they had paused, cigarette hanging from the corner of the mouth. The Lefebvre carts now evacuated the moribund:

> What misery, these evacuation convoys of the sick. They consisted of the food supplies carts that went back empty. Three or four men were packed in there, and the Kabyle driver departed. There

were seven more or legs to the trip under the sun, with the bumps of a vehicle without suspension, on a pothole-riddled and almost unusable road. What suffering did these moribund endure, lying next to cadavers or bodies sick with dysentery, shaken in their own dejections![10]

Weeks later, by the end of August, the road reached the town of Andriba, without encountering any significant resistance. Another legionnaire was found dead from suicide.

Duchesne, at last, decided to form a light column that would march and take Antananarivo, still two hundred kilometers away. He organized a review of the forces that were gathered. Langlois recalled:

> We were silent, not a shout, not a whisper, not a breath, and yet, fifteen hundred men were lined up. They were, in truth, so gaunt, so depressed, that you would have thought they were dead men rather than alive. Clothes reduced to rags, shoes to pieces, their helmets, too wide for their thinned out faces, fell on their shoulders, covering almost all of those yellow faces, where only eyes animated by fever expressed some life.[11]

Legion reinforcements of about one hundred and fifty soldiers arrived, including a tall adjutant-major, "with a sapper's beard, Paul Brundsaux, wearing on his chest the Legion of Honor and medals from the Dahomey and the Tonkin."[12] Brundsaux had also commanded the Fifth Battalion of the First Regiment of Algeria. The light column, the soldiers' legs shaking under the heavy backpacks, departed on September 15.

The salient fact of this column's mission was not that, against all odds, it took Antananarivo in the very last days of September 1995. The terrifying melenite bombs quickly convinced Queen Ranavalona and her minister that raising the white flag over her palace was her most prudent option at that point; she signed a stronger protectorate treaty a few weeks later. Rather, it is how they got there at all. The legionnaires, always facetious in the most awful circumstances, nicknamed the carts "*voitures la fièvre*" instead of Lefebvre and their pickaxes "rifles model 1895" instead of Lebel model 1886. Meanwhile, the column earned its nickname "Marche ou Crève"—"March or Die." This hyperbolic expression, a defining one for the Legion, was born in a literal sense.

Before entering the fertile lands of the Imerina, the column faced its most challenging geography yet, a geological roller coaster that took the soldiers from windswept crests to suffocating flats, all in the midst of a rocky valley. Right at the beginning of their march, in the narrow pass of Tsinainondry, Metzinger's men met a strong enemy sustained by nine cannons. "But! They're shooting at us, those *bougres*!" dropped one captain. The French found that Malagasy artillery was quite capable. The poor quality of their shells marred their effort at stopping the invaders, however, because they often failed to explode. Brundsaux showed a magnificent attitude under fire. On September 26, at Sabotsy, yet another defense barrier was toppled. Legionnaires Tornafoni and Woehrel, even though they were seriously wounded, returned to the battle line and earned the praise of their officers and fellow soldiers. Metzinger cited the courage of all at Sabotsy, but he also gently chastised his legionnaires for exposing themselves to enemy fire with reckless courage.

The Imerina retreated again, now leaving the villages standing instead of burning them. Herds of cattle wandered, bellowing. The grandiose landscape of the mountains slowly yielded to the populated land of the Imerina, with tidy rice paddies and villages of pretty houses, with flowerpots on the balconies—almost like a small Switzerland, noted an observer. On the roadside, crowds of well-to-do Malagasy bourgeois looked at the ghostlike invaders. Still, Langlois recorded another suicide:

> Around two o'clock, a shot is heard. It's a legionnaire of the Fourth Company that just blew his brains out . . . I don't know anything that's more unsettling than these suicides. Some kind of madness takes over your mind . . . You worry that this destructive fever might possess you at any moment.[13]

Another legionnaire, clinging to life but unable to continue, blew up one of his legs with his rifle. The ghostly army, limbs swollen, faces carved by harrowing work, finally made it to Antananarivo and took the town.

A month later, after the capitulation of the Imerina monarchy, what was left of the Legion in the ill-fated Regiment of Algeria marched back to Mahajanga, on that same road that had cost so much effort. Langlois found many corpses rotting in the open air. Some were exposed from their hastily dug graves. "There is a Kabyle driver who sat to die next to his mule; by some prodigy his body stripped of its flesh stood straight, the grimacing head still wearing the red chechia, and in his eyes, those eyes that saw, laughed, and cried, big white maggots were having an orgy."[14] They sailed back to Oran on December 3, and that killed many of the survivors. Out of a contingent of eight hundred and forty-five legionnaires who left Algeria as soldiers in the First Battalion of the Regiment of Algeria, three hundred and fifty-eight boarded the ship returning to Algeria. The official log of the regiment registered eleven deaths by suicide.[15] An officer from another corps found that suicides were more prevalent in the Legion than in the other corps of the expeditionary force. The actual number of these self-inflicted deaths remains impossible to know, given how officers, in all likelihood, counted many of them as death by disease.

When the legionnaires arrived, the citizens of Oran adorned their houses with flowers and flags, the streets with garlands, and built an arch of triumph on the Place de la République. It rained oranges and cigars on the cortege, champagne flowed, and some pretty girls even shouted, *"Vive la Légion!"*

Lyautey arrived in Madagascar sixteen months after the end of Duchesne's sordid march and five months after General Gallieni's own landing. A new battalion of the Legion had showed up in the meantime, but two years went by before Lyautey had an opportunity to command them. Lore has it that Gallieni had requested the battalion when he received the governorship of Madagascar, claiming: "I solicit the authorization to take with me a battalion of the Legion, so that I may, if need be, die properly."[16] The Legion was the troop of the last stance with panache.

The island had erupted in general rebellion—the Revolt of the Menalamba, the Red Shawls—against French subjugation and formal annexation, hence the presence of General Gallieni as governor. Pacification methods might have favored a careful political approach, but emergency circumstances called for drastic measures. The general put two of Queen Ranavalona III's trusted men before the firing squad after a dubious trial, and eventually abolished the Malagasy monarchy by sending the queen into exile.[17]

Lyautey, who was quickly promoted to lieutenant-colonel, was ordered to take control of a vast region northwest of Antananarivo, around the upper Ikopa and Betsiboka rivers, and then, farther to the west and down the coast, part of the Sakalava kingdom. He captured the dissident Rabezavana and quickly secured the territory under his control. To counter Imerina influence, he then practiced what Gallieni had done in the upper regions of the Tonkin, the *politique des races*, which the latter had explained this way:

Any grouping of individuals—race, people, tribe, or family—
represents a sum of common or opposed interests. There are also
hatreds and rivalries that one must trace and use for our own
profit, against each other, and relying on the ones to better
convince the second . . . To sum up, any form of political action
consists in discerning and using the political elements that are
available, and to neutralize and destroy those that are useless.[18]

This "politics of the races," in other words, practiced the old adage "divide
and rule" on a grand colonial scale, and with a wide variety of interlocutors.
In Sakalava country, Lyautey explained how he held long discussions with
indigenous chiefs wearing a loincloth and holding a spear, and paid homage
to queens who had a fetishistic power over their people. "We're far from the
[Imerina] in tailcoats and knickerbockers," he commented.[19]

Madagascar's occupation also consisted in building infrastructure and
promoting culture. Hospitals and schools rose from the ground. A medical
campaign sought to eradicate rabies. In Ankazobe, whence he commanded
his territory, Lyautey drew the plans for a new city and was delighted when,
upon returning from his tours, he saw new streets and elegant buildings
taking shape. The infamous road between Mahajanga and Antananarivo
needed consolidation for intensive use: He took the route and still saw
cadavers from the ill-fated 1895 expedition blackening under the sun.

"Et vive la méthode Gallieni!" Lyautey exclaimed. That method, however,
necessitated capital that Madagascar's exploitation could hardly provide, yet.
On May 24, 1899, both Gallieni and Lyautey boarded a ship bound for
France with a mission to secure funding for their projects. The two found a
challenging political situation in their homeland, but also some ears more
receptive to colonization.

On June 22, 1899, Pierre Waldeck-Rousseau had formed a moderate
government in the midst of the Dreyfus Affair's most tense period, when a
tribunal set aside the original military verdict against Dreyfus because new
revelations showed that forged documents had been used to incriminate
him. Then, in January 1898, the novelist Émile Zola had written his famous
open letter titled "J'accuse!" in which he excoriated the bigotry of the Jewish
officer's opponents. France was split into opposing camps of Dreyfusards and
Anti-Dreyfusards, the latter openly blaring their anti-Semitic views through
the voice of newspapers such as the Catholic *La Croix*. They denounced what
they saw as campaign to shame the army. If France's political spectrum had
until recently organized around the poles of republicans and monarchists,

the Dreyfus Affair reconfigured the political field with the new dynamic of right-wing nationalism. The writers Maurice Barrès and Charles Maurras, the founder of the movement Action Française, represented this current and defended the idea of the nation as an organic whole, founded on "blood" and "soil."

Gallieni and Lyautey never played a role in this movement. Gallieni avoided politics; his duty consisted in serving his country. In that he once again appears to be the quintessential Third Republic army officer, faithful to the principle of political agnosticism. Lyautey referred many times to the Dreyfus Affair in his correspondence to denounce the fanatic nature of the Dreyfusards. Although Lyautey carried out overseas the nationalistic ideas of Barrès, he never showed the kind of virulent xenophobia and anti-Semitism that Barrès displayed in the context of the Dreyfus Affair. "I feel closer and closer to Action Française, Maurras, Bainville, setting aside those who insult and those who are violent, of which I will never be part."[20] In March 1898 he wrote to a friend: "I suffer more than anyone else all that is currently dishonoring France: I know that when I'll be back I shall be even more isolated among those who wear my uniform and among those who share my education and my milieu. I find them to be mad. I sense that many think like me and don't have the courage to voice their opinions."[21]

What shocked Lyautey was the mob mentality that reigned in France; he found it vulgar, which casts an interesting light on the royalism of his first years. His right-wing politics retrospectively appear to be an aristocratic and aesthetic position. For both Gallieni and Lyautey, the scandal was a disaster, shattering any illusion that the military institution could be the vanguard of a deep renewal of French society. A career in the colonies, away from this fetid miasma, appeared ever more desirable.

What Waldeck-Rousseau's government represented in terms of colonial politics was continuity. Théophile Delcassé was minister of foreign affairs. It would be hard to overstate the role played by Delcassé in turn-of-the-century French foreign policy, and especially the colonies. In 1893, this man had headed the modest Undersecretariat for the Colonies, and when this office became a full ministry, Delcassé remained. Meanwhile, Oran's deputy in the National Assembly, Eugène Etienne, channeled an ever more dynamic group of colonial interests. The perpetual rivalry with Britain had been exacerbated in 1898 when two military missions from each country claimed rights over the post of Fashoda, in the Upper Nile region of Africa. Delcassé, who by then had become minister of foreign affairs, ordered the French commander, Jean-Baptiste Marchand, to withdraw, given the army's lack of resources on the field, and instead dedicated himself to forge an alliance with Great Britain that would do much to free France's hand in her future colonial takeovers.

There were critics of colonialism who protested with strident voices France's actions overseas, at a time when the Dreyfus Affair laid open the corruption of the military establishment. Journalists denounced the brutality of Madagascar's colonization—Malagasy historians now estimate that tens of thousands died during France's conquest. The infamous Code de l'Indigénat denied the indigenous populations the rights enjoyed by the colonizers: They could not travel freely, they paid more taxes, and were forced to labor in France's projects, such as the construction of a railroad between Antananarivo and the east coast—an enterprise as deadly as Duchesne's ill-fated expedition. Critics argued that the concentration of power into the hands of military viceroys such as Gallieni not only betrayed France's republican and democratic ideals, but also most likely explained the terrible excesses of colonization.

Undaunted, Gallieni and Lyautey lobbied to activate networks of influence and promote public relations. In January of 1900, Lyautey published in the *Revue des Deux Mondes* an article conceived as a sequel to his first one on the social role of the officer. In "Du rôle colonial de l'armée," he maintained that the military officer, provided that he was properly shielded from tired, antiquated methods of the military establishment, was France's best hope of building an empire. He saw that officer not only as war chief but also as builder, topographer, physician, politician, and administrator.

The Universal Exhibition opened that year. Throughout Paris, grand buildings and public works such as the Grand and Petit Palais, the railway station on the Quai d'Orsay, and the new subway line along the Rue de Rivoli emerged to brand France as a modern power. Naturally, the colonial empire was highlighted at the exhibition. The wealth of resources that an officer such as Lyautey intended to create in the colonies was featured in the pavilion dedicated to Madagascar. On the hill of Chaillot, opposite the Eiffel Tower, a grand structure housed a recreation of the Malagasy people's geographical and agricultural environment, including huts, animals, and what were euphemistically called "samples of population." When not performing native dances or practicing their crafts for the entertainment and education of the visitors arriving from all over Europe, these Malagasies attended French school classes in public intended as an example of France's civilizing mission in action.

Upon his return to Madagascar with Gallieni, subsidies in hand, Lyautey received the command of the huge southern section of the island, comparable in size to a third of France. He commanded it from the town of Fianarantsoa. This time, he had both full civilian and military powers as a colonel. In the spring and summer of 1901, he took a long tour of the island. Expeditions were the opportunity for him to be the accomplished colonial leader he imagined himself to be: "I conceive of command only as direct and personal presence on the terrain, on a never-ending tour, as its realization through speech, intimate seduction, and visual and oral transmission of the faith, of enthusiasm."[22] The Legion, this time, was on hand:

> Slept and dined in Ranomafana, chief town of Lieutenant Prételat's district. I find again my beautiful camps of the Legion, reminding me of the Tonkin, with these legionnaires so precious when well guided, builders, industrious, good for everything. I found two that marched with me on the Lô River.[23]

> Ah! Our good old legionnaires! What a colonial troop, what founders of cities, what resources! This Behara [settlement], sprung from the ground under the touch of a magic wand, is one our best elements for pacification. In it, the neighboring indigenous people see our force, our resolution, and our designs for the future, and they bow.[24]

Together, Lyautey and the legionnaires marched through strange regions, proud and confident messengers of the benefits of French civilization, as they demanded the submission of populations that, to them, seemed to have barely emerged from the dawn of time.

How glorious was such a life lived outside, under the sun, far from "the deadly squirrel wheel" of military bureaucracy and pettiness.[25] "*La joie de l'âme est dans l'action*" (The Soul's Joy Lies in Doing), proclaimed Lyautey in a motto inspired by the poet Percy Bysshe Shelly. The mirror of the sea in the distance, they traversed fantastic forests populated with naked trees extending branches like tentacles, cactuses contorting in sinister forms, red flowers beautiful in appearance, only to reveal petals cutting like razor blades if touched. It all evoked those extraordinary ancient tales of Homer, except that the heroes here, far from thinking of themselves as the playthings of the gods, saw themselves as both heroes and gods, weaving the epic tale of France's imperial conquest.

Lyautey departed from the big island in the summer of 1902 after a stint at an outpost at the island's northern tip called Diego Suarez, where the military command envisioned a stronger base. Earlier, Lieutenant Paul-Frédéric Rollet had arrived on the island, three years after joining the Legion in Sidi Bel Abbès. The meeting of two officers who were rising fast in the ranks, and who were destined to be important figures in the history of the Legion, was not to happen yet.

Rollet was the son of an infantry captain, and he too had graduated from the prestigious Saint-Cyr military school. His superiors widely recognized him as very capable. Yet he was also a bit of an outcast, an independent, anticonformist type, with a high-strung edge: "An excellent officer, could also take the wrong path," had noted his teachers at Saint-Cyr.[26] On his way from Algeria to Madagascar, Rollet first visited Marseilles, taking time to tour the best restaurants, music halls, and *café-concerts*, then he embarked on the ship *Djemnah* for that three-week-long journey to Mahajanga. He set foot on the island on February 1, 1902. From Mahajanga he reached Morondava, to be greeted by the local Legion commander, who was none other than Paul Brundsaux of the 1895 expedition. Rollet's orders were to command the legionnaires at the isolated post of Belo.

Belo, a small farm in the midst of Madagascar's wilderness, was not much to cheer about at first view. The challenges Rollet faced there were nonetheless hard enough to require the true mettle of a legionnaire. He countered Sakalava resistance to French colonization and built new villages to win over the population, following the principles of the "oil stain" prescribed by Gallieni. Other tasks included surveying the terrain to draw maps, establish a land register for the areas destined for development, and conduct a census.

The legionnaires in that district could be both superb operators of and troublesome obstacles to French rule. Months after arriving in Belo, Rollet had to return to Morondova, where a new chief of the French army had allowed a severe breakdown of discipline. The soldiers had fathered many children in the indigenous communities, and when the command tried to restore order, they broke out in a riot one night. One French civilian was almost stabbed to death in the mayhem. Rollet wrote to his father that holding these wild legionnaires was hard, but that he still could do it. Along with the Sakalava warriors and the legionnaires, the local caimans represented another of Rollet's sources of worry.

Through harshly dry and then rainy seasons, the fevers that incapacitated his men miraculously spared Lieutenant Rollet, allowing him to enjoy the spare time he had. Suppressing violence against indigenous women did not mean that less violent forms of contact were forbidden. Rollet speaks openly of the "wife" he took there, a *ramatoa* described as a "small girl of about twelve or thirteen years." She drove Rollet's orderly mad by stubbornly refusing to wash her feet before entering Rollet's bed at night. Perhaps this motive of conjugal discord explains why Rollet cultivated other personal hobbies. His archive includes a precious collection of observation on the customs and legends of the Sakalava, including transcriptions of the tales "The Hawk and the Chicken," and "The Caimans and the Parrots." Rollet claimed that he liked this "good life of the outback." By 1904, Brundsaux could write the following appreciation: "Monsieur le Lieutenant Rollet, hardworking and very intelligent, proves to be an excellent officer, capable of fulfilling all the mission he would be given to his chief's entire satisfaction. A brilliant officer with a future, he'll need to be pushed up the ranks this year."[27]

Like Lyautey, Rollet ended his stay at Diego Suarez, to the north, where he contributed to setting up a new defense plan for the base. On March 23, 1905, after three years spent on the island, he returned to Algeria, followed soon thereafter by the entire contingent of legionnaires, who would not return to the infamous island of Madagascar for a long time.

Part Two

CHAPTER 7

In the Legion

Life swirled like at a ball dance in the Paris of the Belle Époque, tinged green by that mischievous fairy, absinthe. Darker undercurrents ran beneath France's glittering society, however. The army still lived in a funk in the wake of the Dreyfus Affair. Then, the Waldeck-Rousseau government inaugurated a staunch anticlerical stance, which led, under the next government, of Émile Combes, to two scandals. In 1904, the Affaire des Fiches revealed that the government kept index cards tracking the religious habits of military officers, noting, for example, how often they went to church. The information was then used to stall the career of unsuitably secularist subjects. In 1905, a law that can be considered the first act of French-style institutional secularism, *laïcité*, was enacted: "The Republic does not recognize, give salaries on behalf of, nor grant money to any religious cult," said article 2 of the law. Since the distinction between state and church remained blurry when real estate was concerned, enacting the law required taking inventories of the Church's possessions. Ugly scenes where government administrators entered churches and convents followed.

Théophile Delcassé remained as minister of foreign affairs until 1905. Turning the Fashoda fiasco to France's advantage, he crafted the 1904 Entente Cordiale with Great Britain. Having let go of their old rivalries with a mutual recognition of their respective claims to Egypt and Morocco, Britain and France completed their colonial expansion as they saw fit without fear of military or diplomatic confrontations between each other. The progressive takeover of Morocco would soon begin, and by 1912, France's empire spread over more than ten million square kilometers (about 3.8 million square miles), and counted fifty-five million inhabitants.[1] Delcassé kept an eye on Germany. From now on, antagonism with the hated enemy of 1870 would be waged by proxy, in the colonial theater, until the outbreak of World War I.

Meanwhile, under the trepidation of the Belle Époque, officers like Lyautey and those young men of the Foreign Legion searched for an alternative to what seemed to be an increasingly materialistic, disenchanted existence. Efficiency, industry, and capitalism thrived in this Belle Époque. Actually, the colonies provided a firm support to the system, as the purveyor of money, labor, and raw materials. The colonies, in many ways, were conquered, protected, and administered by men who rejected the very culture that promoted and benefitted from colonialism. Ernst Jünger understood well that *ennui* of Europe's young who left the continent: "those young persons who, in the foggy dark of night, left their parental home to pursue danger in America, on the sea, or in the French Foreign Legion. It is a sign of the domination of bourgeois values that danger slips into the distance."[2] This movement intensified after World War I, when the supremacy of technology and efficiency culminated in savage war.

Seen from this angle, a string of legionnaires' writings published in the first two decades of the twentieth century give not only a precise picture of military life in the Legion, especially in Sidi Bel Abbès, but also created a cultural mythology. Some of the stories published during that period, including Jünger's novel *African Games*, forged the image of the Legion that Percival C. Wren's novel *Beau Geste* would consolidate for good in 1924. Many of these memoirs did not exactly cast a flattering light on the Legion. They were part of a German effort to stop the flow of recruits to the Legion and Sidi Bel Abbès, which turned out to be a source of diplomatic and military tensions. In many cases, these memoirs of the century's first decades describe an administrative itinerary that, in the eyes of young recruits, took on the meaning of an initiation, an existential journey.

The adventure of the recruits still began at a recruitment bureau, in France, in Paris on the Rue Saint-Dominique, or in cities near the border with Germany, the country of so many legionnaires. Showing up there, they waited in the company of strange characters. After a brief medical visit, aiming at rejecting candidates the most obviously unfit for service—eyes had to be healthy, teeth strong enough to bite into the hard biscuit of field rations—they met again with an officer, to sign the contract that, for five years, would put their lives in the hands of the Legion. With a small allowance in their pockets, still in civilian clothes, the would-be legionnaires took that train to Marseilles, where they stayed until enough recruits were gathered and a ship could take them to Algeria.

Adventure truly began as they stepped out of Marseilles's Saint-Charles Station, a burst of "impressions as incomplete as the memories of dreams."[3] The walk down the Canebière, the boulevard leading to the seaport, offered the first impressions of new worlds, since Marseilles was a crossroads of Mediterranean cultures. Jünger, still beaming with excitement after joining, got a foretaste on those faraway lands he wanted to visit:

> Shrieking excited crowds pushed past each other on the stone
> quays between the stalls of the fishmongers, between baskets full
> of mussels and sea-urchins and the rows of chairs at little harbor
> bars, set out under the open sky. The air was full of the smell of
> strange races, of great warehouses and the refuse of the sea.[4]

The sight of the Fort Saint-Jean, the lodging in Marseilles, dampened enthusiasm. Imposing and gloomy, on the right side of the port and over-looking the narrower passage leading from the docks to the open sea, the old fort, around which "swam a floating girdle of green seaweed and brown wrack," was a maze of damp, narrow courtyards and endless obscure corri-dors.[5] For the legionnaires in waiting, lying on rows of beds, it was the stench of humanity that made adventure concrete at this point.

At the turn of the century, they were men between the age of eighteen and forty, most of them in their twenties. The First Regiment, in 1897, listed 1,612 Frenchmen, 1,551 men from Alsace-Lorraine and 1,441 Germans in its force of 7,066 soldiers. In 1909, Germans made up 22% of that regiment's contingents, the French 25%, while the proportion of men from Alsace-Lorraine was reduced to 11%. The Belgians, the Swiss, and the Austrians constituted another smaller part of the troops.[6] Russians came later, after the Bolsheviks took over their country. The rest was a mix of Spaniards, Italians, Danes, Britons, and some Americans. There could be the odd Turk, and even a New Zealander.

The faces conjured a wide variety of stories. Fresh young faces of romantic types like Jünger, who dreamed of adventure, wanting a military life but not a placid existence in a provincial garrison. Other faces were rugged, looking more like those of the soldiers one encountered at the Bataillons d'Afrique (Bat' d'Af), the penal regiments. The Legion did harbor types who sought to escape the keen eye of justice. They were rarely hardened criminals, but rather individuals, such as Antoine Sylvère, with enough of a background to prize the anonymity afforded by the Legion: soldiers who had deserted another army, or been pursued for bad behavior; gamblers who had failed to realize that Lady Luck had abandoned them a while ago; boys who had fathered an illegitimate child. The prodigal son variety caused problems of their own. One aristocrat, for example, after exhausting his fortune, making a dent in his wife's own, and cheating on her, joined the Legion. She still paid him a generous allowance, which he spent on drinking parties for his company.[7] You never knew next to whom you were eating, fighting, and sleeping in the ranks of the Legion, asserts Legionnaire Maurice Magnus:

> The times are countless when a detective from some part of Europe entered the Legion's barracks, and, when the company was at dinner, looked for his man, tapped him on the shoulder, motioned for him to follow, and disappeared with him—none never knowing who he was, what he had done, or what became of him.[8]

Other recruits bore the etched wrinkles and frowns of tragic stories. Adolphe R. Cooper, who joined the Legion for the first time in 1914 at the age of fifteen and under the false name of Cornelis de Bruin, eventually rose to the rank of corporal, although his record of service was marred by incidents of insubordination. His memoirs tell the story of a Swedish legionnaire named Kosh, six feet tall; "typical of his race, he was fresh complexioned and looked very fit and healthy." One night, Cooper heard this Kosh open a packet he kept with him: "I heard in the darkness a rustling of paper, which I guessed was the parcel, and a few minutes later what I took to be a muffled sob, although with the other recruits snoring it was hard to be precise."[9] Unbeknownst to Kosh, Cooper found out that the parcel contained a doll, in a tatty shape. The day Kosh was caught cuddling the doll, he became the laughingstock of the entire regiment. His story spread through the entire Legion. When he took two bullets in the chest, it was finally time to tell his story to Cooper. He was the only survivor of a car accident that claimed the life of his wife and three children. The youngest, his favorite, had died with that doll in her hands.

There were tanned faces that showed the marks of lives spent working exposed to the elements, with callous hands thickened by manual labor; other had the delicate complexion of sheltered lives, with hands made more for holding a pen, or moving over piano keys. The meager salary paid by the Legion, about five cents a day, much less than a British private's pay at the same time, hardly enticed anyone to abandon a civilian job for the Legion. Nor did the modest retirement paid by France after fifteen years of service explain why such a variety of characters had ended up in Marseilles.

Orders to march out of the Fort Saint-Jean eventually came. As recruits boarded one of those vessels of the Messageries Maritimes, fresh, salty air signaled that a new life was beginning. Some saw themselves as successors to the Roman legions, traveling to make the Mediterranean the *mare nostrum* of Rome, a lake for France. Epics of the Roman conquest sustained the Legion's mythology since Bugeaud's days, and so dreams regained a promising backdrop to all this blue of the sea. But with the first pangs of seasickness, reality manifested itself. Pity the would-be legionnaire who had to face the forty-eight hours that the crossing to Oran required, if the Mediterranean, instead of showing its blue colors, tested their fortitude with a storm.

Algeria appeared, but there was little time to contemplate the principal coastal town of Oran, which, like Constantine and Algiers, commanded one of the *départements* into which Algeria was divided under French occupation. The crew of recruits, usually between thirty and forty of them, boarded a narrow gauge train. The scenery of the Tell, the rich, temperate region of Algeria that borders the sea, looked underwhelming to some. Legionnaire Étienne Boulic, perhaps already homesick, compared the landscape unfavorably to France's: "These fields, these immense vineyards with their vigorous stems, they are not as gracious as our smaller properties in France, and this countryside gives more an impression of agricultural power rather than of beauty."[10] They were heading straight toward the city of Sidi Bel Abbès, which, as the *maison-mère*, the home base of the Legion, its main garrison and hub, had grown to sizable proportions.

There was still not much to write home about Sidi Bel Abbès for those who fancied exotic wonders. Bel Abbès resembled a banal French provincial town, with its pompous buildings typical of the Third Republic, albeit a town where palm trees replaced plane trees. Legionnaire Erwin Rosen provided this impressionistic look:

> The atmosphere was yellow. Yellow were the old-fashioned ramparts of Sidi Bel Abbès, built by soldiers of the Legion many years ago; yellow was the fine sand dust on the streets; glaring yellow everywhere. The green gardens on the town's outskirts seemed but animated little spots in a great compact mass of yellow. Far away in the background the colossal ridges of the Thessala towered in gigantic shadows of pale yellow. Even the town's buildings flared up in pale yellow.[11]

Behind the high ramparts and their moats, military life had shaped the town and permeated its everyday aspects since its founding in the mid-1800s. By 1913 the population had grown to more than twenty thousand, needing the market, the schools, and the theater. The sound of a military band, whether playing for a crowd of civilians on Carnot Square, bidding farewell to a departing company, or saluting the arrival of a new contingent of would-be legionnaires, inevitably reminded the traveler of the town's military essence.

The walk from the train station to the Quartier Viénot, the barracks named after the legionnaire hero of the Crimean War, was short. Legionnaire Flutsch, the central character in Antoine Sylvère's 1905 novel, says that a band playing "Le Boudin," the march of the Legion, accompanied the troop.[12]

We are crafty ones	*Nous sommes des dégourdis*
We are rogue ones	*Nous sommes des lascars*
Unusual types	*Des types pas ordinaires*
We often have our bouts of the cafard	*Nous avons souvent notre cafard*
We are legionnaires	*Nous sommes des légionnaires*

They entered a large courtyard covering about two acres, framed on three sides by tall buildings, to be greeted with a cry: "*Les bleus! Les bleus!*" *Bleu* is French military jargon for rookie, after the blue uniform that new recruits once wore. Hundreds of faces showed up at the windows of the barracks to the rumble of steps down staircases. Crowds of inquisitive, bantering, bearded legionnaires surrounded the new recruits.

After this first inspection, the recruits received a service number, noted on a *livret individuel*, a personal record book that also detailed disciplinary measures for the rest of a man's career in the Legion. They took their uniforms and fatigues, a kit in a knapsack. Rifles and bayonets would come later. The time for a vigorous scrubbing under the shower and a shave had come. Shedding dirt and parasites marked the Legion's new recruits' entry into their new corps, a new life. The Legion prided itself on neatness. The communal bedrooms, in contrast to those at the Fort Saint-Jean, appeared immaculate and well ordered, with rows of beds with linens neatly folded. Rosen marveled that for each legionnaire, "even the most trivial of his belongings has its proper place."[13]

At the end of a very long day, the recruits sat back in their rooms, fed at last—meals in the Legion were served at the kitchen and eaten back in the room. Their first *soupe* consisted of a hearty stew of meat, potatoes, and vegetables, to be finished with a portion of French bread and washed down with thick Algerian wine.

One advantage of joining a French army corps, especially when basic training began at five-thirty in the morning, was the morning supply of strong coffee. *"Au jus! Au jus!"* Recruits had too few minutes to tidy up their rooms before assembling on the central ground of the Quartier Viénot. They walked to the *plateau*, an area right outside the town's walls where exercises were held and met the noncommissioned foreign officers who had risen through the ranks, as opposed to higher-rank officers coming from France's military schools.

Training, led by those corporals, featured the repetitive moves that built endurance and a quasi-instinctual obedience to orders, essential to performing under live fire. Physical exercise included physical jerks and boxing. Basic moves of the infantrymen consisted of foot drills, forming lines and columns to attack, positioning to protect artillery and ambulance. The new legionnaires then observed how, not only in the daily life in the barracks but also on the field first and foremost, precision and perfection of execution were hallmarks of their corps. Sometimes the soldiers performed in wider regimental drills, and, much less often, in a divisional demonstration before a general.

By the time the soldiers performed in such larger exercises, it mattered little if they could make any sense of barked orders in an unconvincing French—you had the moves drilled into your reflex system. Regulations demanded that these officers know a list of five hundred basic French words, and yet many strained under French grammar rules. As far as linguistic abilities were concerned, the Foreign Legion still passed as a remarkable assembly of polyglots. Legionnaire Flutsch mentions a foreigner named Pachoud, capable of delivering verses from Corneille and Racine perfectly.[14]

After all drills were performed and maneuvers executed, the legionnaires learned their most valuable lesson: that they would often have to fight with a stubborn, no-holds-barred determination to win. Legionnaire Flutsch recalled the criticism that one of his instructors directed at an otherwise perfectly well-executed simulation of an attack:

> "You could have been a great model for a painter wanting to represent the scene 'Taking the Green Hill.' In the Legion, this is worth nothing, because in reality, you would all be dead. But nothing is as innocuous as a dead man, and personally, I'd rather deal with five thousand dead men than ten resolute ones. You're going to come back to your starting point and start this maneuver all over again, not to provide me with a parade, but as a real troop of legionnaires, each of whom has decided to live to fight, and

thus takes advantage of any stone, of any patch of grass, of any mound of dirt, of any path that will allow him to strike unexpected blows. Let's go!"[15]

A legionnaire, in other words, used any possible advantage to win, even if it required him to ignore panache, and fight dirty.

What followed these exercises was also a vivid reminder that one did not join the Legion for some antiquated notion of bravura. Once the training of the day was over, it was time for hard labor, the chores of sweeping the courtyard and floors of the barracks, cleaning latrines, or peeling potatoes. This was not just a job for *les bleus*. Legionnaires in Sidi Bel Abbès were often lent to the city, and their talents were put to good use in public works. Men with former professions constituted a remarkably resourceful corps. There was not much time to think, and that is why most of them found the ranks of the Foreign Legion suitable.

After their last meal of the day, at five o'clock, and until bedtime at nine thirty, they were free to use their time as they wished. Some washed and repaired their uniforms, shined buckles. Others went out for a stroll in Sidi Bel Abbès when the doors of the Quartier Viénot opened at six.

Since most of the civilian women of the town would have rather died on the spot than acknowledge an appreciative glance from a legionnaire, the soldiers ended up chain-smoking at a *café maure*, moorish café, or visiting the town's brothels. Officers fared much better in the ruthless competition for female attention. They generally lived in rented apartments in town, and gathered at the *cercle militaire*, the officer's club.

Paul-Frédéric Rollet, before he left for Madagascar, formed an opinion on smart living in Bel Abbès. The newly arrived officer, with temper and energy in inverse proportion to his height, fancied himself a connoisseur. His superior noted on his record: "Vigorous officer, tireless, full of energy, still young in temperament, lets himself drift toward pleasure too easily, and even exceeds the limits of authorized gaiety; he has the necessary stuffing to become an excellent officer if he rectifies this defect."[16] His biographer mentions the "*maisons de tolérance* that he honored with his visits" and spoke of in his diaries.[17] In Bel Abbès, according to Rollet, the local women were not prudish: "Hair color is rather dark, the eyes generally pretty, nice teeth, waist slim and lithe, hips rather heavy, the clothes fresh-looking and nicely cut, flowers in their hair, maybe a little too many bracelets and necklaces."

Of course, there was always wine to help one forget. Served by the liter at the military canteen, or the drinking establishments of the town, wine's artificial paradise was the bottomless cask into which the legionnaires' meager salary was thrown. The Legion had a reputation of harboring alcoholism. Magnus explains that rules forbade drinking establishments in Bel Abbès to serve anything besides wine to legionnaires, "but liquors could be obtained on the quiet for double price." Rollet, at first, seemed unimpressed: "If there are some men under the influence of alcohol in the streets of Sidi Bel Abbès, those are rather calm, they don't look for a fight with the passers-by, and they generally content themselves with braying songs in all kinds of dialects."

Eventually, Rollet realized that on payday, drinking parties crowded the smoke-filled bars and ended, past the chanting of nostalgic German songs, in solid brawls, especially between men of different army corps. His own batman, as some point, remained intoxicated for three days in a row. The Legion made halfhearted efforts to lessen the problem, with not much effect, because drinking was an integral part of the culture. The story has it that if you somehow found your way back at the barracks gate in time for the eleven o'clock curfew of leave days, past the inspecting gaze of the officer, you were safe: That inspector never turned back to see what happened once you staggered into the courtyard.

The detention cells at the Legion were a busy scene. Rollet says that on pay day, they put in the "cellar . . . all the drunkards as they came back home," until it burst with "one hundred and fifty guys who crawled about, and fought."[18] Some of the Legion's recruits were indeed outcasts, types not shying away from drinking on duty or selling some of their equipment for a few quick francs.

What about the image of an ironclad discipline enforced by cruel lower officers with a sadistic fiber that the Legion evoked, especially after the novel *Beau Geste* appeared? Cooper describes a Corsican named Suzini as a man "who took pleasure in seeing me dejected and in pain."[19] These, presumably, were the kind of officers who administered the *crapaudine,* a punishment in which a man was restrained, flat on his stomach, feet and arms crossed and tied in the back, for long, excruciating hours under the Algerian sun. They were the men who would put soldiers into one of those underground silos the peasants used to store their grain, silos where "you could not stand or lie." There is fact and fiction concerning this legendary topic of punishment. Much of that negative reputation came from German anti-Legion propaganda that flourished before and after World War I, or derived from the confusion between the Legion and the Bat' d'Af. Those infamous silos might indeed have been used to immobilize a recalcitrant legionnaire, but they were in all likelihood expedients of missions spent outside of regular military

camps. Hair-raising stories of dungeons where depraved officers put prisoners into sexual slavery must be treated with even more suspicion.

The types of crimes that certainly warranted serious action were violence
toward an officer and, much more frequently, desertion. The 1890s saw a rash of
desertions in the Algerian frontier lands. Thick dossiers in the French diplomatic archives show intense conversations held between diplomats and the
Ministry of War. Why were the soldiers deserting? Were living conditions in
the Legion truly that awful? Dispatches explained how newspapers such as
Strasbourg's *Post* or Geneva's *Tribune* denounced the forced enrollments of
unsuspecting youth who spoke no French and were thrown into trains to
Marseilles after signing off five years of their lives, the meager pay over there,
the harsh punishments. After investigating, the Ministry of War denied such
accusations. Diplomats sometimes transmitted requests from German families
who claimed that their sons had acted on a whim, and wanted them freed.
While most requests had to be turned down, the Ministry of War occasionally
granted releases from service. One Xavier Meyer of the First Regiment, for
example, was released from his service in 1894, when his family, doctor's
certificate in hand, proved that the father, in ill health, required his son. It did
help in this particular case that this father had fought for France in the war
against Prussia.[20]

A soldier could not venture farther than seven kilometers outside of Bel
Abbès. Beyond that limit he was considered a deserter, which might lead
him to the disciplinary battalions in the area called Colomb-Béchar, and
even the firing squad. Mostly, those disciplinary battalions were confined to
labor camps and construction sites, spending months breaking stone. But
if the straying soldier came back within a few days to his barracks, he was
spared the disciplinary council, and faced ordinary punishment instead.
Legion discipline was intended to sanction misbehavior, but also to ensure
the cohesion of the group, not only in how it prevented insubordination but
in the way the officers administered discipline as well. Officers knew when to
wink at their men's misdemeanors, and they were well aware that they meted
out judgment before an entire corps. According to Flutsch:

> The strict discipline of the Legion had nothing to do with military
> rules; infractions were tolerated that would have been deemed
> unacceptable anywhere else. That was common knowledge, and
> only those judgments sanctioned by the community carried any
> weight. Even officers could not escape that collective pressure on
> their judgment, under penalty of being declared "non-legionnaire."[21]

So, most legionnaires accepted punishment like men who were part of a cohort: additional chores, drills in full equipment, and, yes, confinement to quarters while one's comrades strolled in town, trying to get a glance back from a pretty Bel Abbésienne.

Sometimes the bugle sounded in the middle of the night. Cohorts of bleary-eyed legionnaires assembled in the courtyard, ready for a dreaded exercise that was at the core of their mission. In turn-of-the-century Algeria, there were no motorcars and no railways to the remote regions where French rule was less established. One of the prized skills in the Legion, then, was still to march fast and under any circumstance.

Equipment, perfectly organized and loaded around the body, was heavy, and could weigh up to sixty pounds, sometimes even more. The standard gun at the turn of the century, the repeating Lebel model 1886 weighing 4.2 kilograms (more than nine pounds), would already strain a man in average physical condition if carried for hours. The rest of the equipment included a haversack filled with rations and food, a two-liter water bottle, and ammunition and bayonet on the side. The knapsack, a wooden structure wrapped in tarred canvas, contained the soldier's own kit (items of clothing, more food, and ammunition), but also parts of the tent and cooking utensils. Rolled or hanging on the side of the pack were blankets and boots. "I found it so heavy that I tottered like a drunken man," writes Adolphe Cooper.[22] Leaving Bel Abbès with this load, the legionnaires disappeared in the night, singing marching songs.

While they wore a plain cotton vest for everyday action, out on a march or a mission in Northern African terrain, the legionnaires wore the iconic blue greatcoat, the *capote*, "which is made so that the skirts can be buttoned back to leave the ties free," over khakis and boots. A blue woolen sash wound around the waist added warmth and acted as back support. This silhouette would not be complete without the kepi hat, and, specifically, the type of kepi that sported a cloth cover and back flap (*couvre-képi*) to protect the cap and legionnaire's neck from the from the merciless sun. In truth, this cap and cover item dating from the 1850s had been used by all French army troops, in France in the summer months or overseas in hot climates. The standard issue of this kepi cover was cut from a khaki cloth, but the harsh sunlight of North Africa and frequent washings lightened it to white. The legionnaires took a fancy for this cap covered in bleached cotton. It was a bit showy, officers protested that the *couvre-képis* made for some rather visible targets when under fire—this might have made the white kepi even more valuable to some daredevil legionnaires.

Distances for marches varied according to the urgency of the mission. A company covered more than forty kilometers (twenty-five miles) in one day, and much more at the accelerated *pas* (step) *gymnastique*. The fertile plain yielded to the arid terrain of pre-Saharan Algeria, vast expanses of stony ground where vegetation was reduced to bunches of alfa grass and thyme. The nights turned colder, the days hotter. Excessive heat and blinding sun soon tested the endurance of the hardiest legionnaire, barely rested after a bad night under a thin blanket. Acid sweat burned your skin. Each breath of burning air stung. Temperatures easily reached fifty degrees Celsius (about 120 degrees Fahrenheit) in the summer months in Algeria. Water supplies had to be supplemented by that found at wells on the road, and mineral elements gave that water an unpleasant taste. Then there were the flies, innumerable, relentless. Staggering, their feet bloodied in their new boots, the straps of their equipment cutting through their skin, this is when the new recruits might have wondered what cruel twist of destiny had led them into a burning, blinding hell of nothingness.

Legionnaires learned quickly that they could hardly give up, demand medical help, or, even worse, end up being carried by their peers. Deep solidarity already cemented the troop, just a few weeks after they had been walking down the Canebière in Marseilles:

> When everything goes badly, you faint and someone takes care of you. A guy who tries to dodge because he's in pain, it's like a guy who won't fight, you despise him. If you fall, unless you won't wake up even if they throw a bucket of water at you, you stand up again as soon as you can and you take your place again. You march with your shoes full of blood, and when you arrive, you do the chores just like the others, and then you lie down just like the others. And you're not going to get any compliments for that. You're just going to be a legionnaire like the other ones.[23]

This is how a recruit turned out to be a true legionnaire, by finding the limits of human endurance, to push those limits back, right there, in the middle of the infinite and arid plains of the Algerian outback.

CHAPTER 8

Beyond the Desert

At the edge of the Great Western Erg of the Sahara, under the blinding sun, before yellow and tormented waves of sand stretching to infinity, Lieutenant Achille-Jean Guillaume exclaimed, "Indeed, there was that real desert we had been waiting for, the one we had dreamed of, the mysterious virgin territory where nothing lives, where one will only find solitude and the great silence!"[1]

In the reality of Algerian and Morocco's borderlands where the Legion operated, epic images abound, although the vast expanses of southern land that stretch between Algeria and Morocco are for the most part of another aspect than the great sea of sand. In their most barren form, that is, on the plateau of the Guir Hamada, the landscapes take a desolate aspect: a monotonous, stony flatland covered with rocks, a furnace of flat rock with no end in sight, nothing to distract the eye. Hence Guillaume:

> The dunes give the Erg unevenness with their varied and bizarre contours, and the traveler keeps hope that he might find other horizons all of a sudden. In the Hamada, no illusion of this kind is allowed: One has the certainty that, till the end of the trip's leg, and the day after, the eye will only see an inhospitable plain of barren and scorched rocks.[2]

This Hamada is the actual desert of legionnaire lore. Confronting this desert proved too intense for many legionnaires, and generated a serious bout of the *cafard*. Legionnaire Cooper explained:

Many legionnaires become known as "*les solitaires*" because after a long periods in the desert they shun their fellow men and become immersed in their thoughts; they become peculiar in their behavior, but all this by a slow process, until the time comes when their commanding officer finds it necessary to have them transferred to some garrison town in central Algeria or Morocco. This often becomes apparent to the officer or NCO after a suicide attempt.[3]

Jean Martin, while he traveled in those desolate regions years later, experienced the same malaise:

> During a pause, a cold chill shook me. I was learning the fearsome effect of the Hamada. Its immense solitude does not fit well with the unhinged nerves of Europeans who suffer from chronic agitation. To be able to stand it, you need the indifferent stoicism of Arabs, or many years of roaming in the countryside, which make you accustomed to the desert and its silence. The hallucinating emptiness added to fatigue had given me that fever.[4]

Landscape abstraction induced contemplation. Sergeant Lefebvre remarked how in the desert's stillness, one forgets time, one does not know what day of the month it is. Man feels suddenly reduced to an imperceptible atom in the burning and empty vastness. "In the desert's solitude, man can listen to his heart," wrote Legionnaire Ehrhart.[5]

How intriguing that these men could experience such pangs of the heart in the very countries where they wreaked havoc. But the violence of the desert is an integral part of the mystique: living in incredibly harsh conditions, enduring heat and thirst, weathering the sirocco wind that halts the caravan and blows all night, infiltrating tents. You wake up in the morning, drenched in sweat, face caked with dust, dreading the stale bread and the can of sardines that will crack under the teeth. An old saying proclaims, "The sirocco's dust will even penetrate the eggshell." And yet, through such trials, from the country of light that Edith Piaf sang of in "Mon Légionnaire," European soldiers reemerged reinvigorated and purified. After the storm, the air is crystal clear, the senses are sharpened, the minutest objects appear in vivid detail. One feels like a superior human being. And it was not only the military that fell for such powerful images: For a cast-out of the ordinary joined them in those nether regions.

* * *

From the town of Figuig to Béni Abbès, southward along the River Zousfana, a line of small oases and water holes separates the Great Erg sand desert from the Hamada and its mineral, calcinated desolation. Nomadic peoples such as the Ouled Djerir and the Doui Menia moved their herds around it. At the western, Moroccan, edge of the Hamada, before the Atlas range, lay the Tafilalet, a rich oasis dotted with *ksour*, fortified castles. For centuries, caravans coming from Timbuktu carried the material and human riches of sub-Saharan Africa to this region, and then to Marrakech or Fes. The Tafilalet is also known for its plump dates and, last but not least, for its warriors who rose when leaders of holy inspiration called for *jihad* against invaders.

This region between Morocco and Algeria was a place of surging colonial tensions in the early years of the twentieth century. The project of a train line extending toward West Africa had come up again. In 1900, the army launched a daring expedition, annexing the strategic southern oasis of the Tuat. That same year, a column marched toward Igli, along the Zousfana River. Legion troops, including Rollet, in the ranks of the Second Mounted Company of the Second Regiment, and Lieutenant Guillaume rode on that occasion. As France took bolder steps to assert its authority over the southern and western confines of Algeria, resistance from desert-dwelling Algerians and Moroccans grew. Bands stole horses, camels, and weapons. They attacked sentinels at night, convoys during the day.

Because previous accords between Morocco and France (the 1845 Treaty of Lalla Maghnia) had established a precise border only from a point on the coast down to a region that the French authorities considered useless at the time, more diplomatic agreements created a buffer zone between Algeria and Morocco to provide more security, in 1901, and again in 1902. Those arrangements failed to stop the Ouled Djerir and the Doui Menia from harassing the French. Complicating the situation was the uncertain nature of political authority over the part of Morocco that abutted Algeria, and indeed the lack of a precise border between the two countries. What did the decrees coming from the Sultan Abdelaziz's court in Fes and a line drawn on a map mean to the independent, nomadic peoples who considered the Hamada their own? The sultan's lordship fluctuated in the outer reaches of his kingdom. In many ways, he ruled over people much more than over a territory, and that power rested on allegiances in constant need of validation. That was the case in the Tafilalet, even though the ruling dynasty of Morocco, the Alawites, originated from that vast oasis.

On May 31, 1903, shots narrowly missed the governor general of Algeria, Charles Jonnart, while he visited the outer oasis of Figuig. The French replied by sending two heavily armed columns and thoroughly bombing the oasis with their melenite shells, on June 8. From the Tafilalet, the leader Ba Sidi seconded by his father, Moulay Mustafa, formed a pan-tribal army of thousands of warriors that headed for the Zousfana, circling around the Hamada via the north. Starting on August 17 for three days they attacked the legionnaires that guarded the fort of Taghit. Artillery power saved the day. Then, on September 2, a catastrophe etched the name of El Moungar in the annals of the Legion.

One hundred and twenty legionnaires of the Twenty-Second Mounted Company of the Second Regiment, under the command of Captain Marie Louis Vauchez, and elements from the Spahi corps had halted near Fort El Moungar at nine thirty in the morning. They guarded a civilian convoy of camels. Many factors exacerbated an already dangerous situation. The line of camels had elongated, creating gaps in the escort. The site of the halt, between a line of sand dunes to the east and a rocky crest to the west, was ill chosen and dangerously exposed.

Just a few minutes after the legionnaires settled, fire erupted from the top of the dune to decimate the legionnaires. The attackers were warriors who had participated in the earlier assault on Taghit; they wanted revenge. Legionnaires frantically moved to form a line of defense. One of the first officers to fall was Lieutenant Christian Selchauhansen, a Dane and a veteran of the Tonkin and Madagascar. He had resigned from the army of his country after a scandalous affair and had found in the Legion the place to redeem himself. When Selchauhansen's men moved to take him to safety, he chased them away. Hagiography wants it that he sighed these last words: "I don't fear death, because death is my destiny. I only fear oblivion in the memories of these brave friends and comrades of the Legion."[6] Perhaps a little too contrived a statement for a man agonizing in the midst of a merciless firefight, Selchauhansen more realistically would have given orders until he lost consciousness.

Under a hail of bullets, the legionnaires' position was hopeless. The enemy gained terrain. A section of legionnaires tried to charge, bayonets forward. They failed. Captain Vauchez fell wounded, though perhaps the desperate attempt of the company charging with bayonets allowed their comrades to reach the rocky crest. There, Vauchez continued to direct the defense. The attackers hid behind brush, or used the mass of the camels to approach the crest, and so the bodies of the dead and the wounded legionnaires piled up in the small gulley between the hillocks as the hours went by. Some extracted bullets from their wounds with pocketknives. Mercifully, a smaller group had a better position and offered some cover. Help was uncertain. Other convoys, also with their military escorts, were on the road, but they were too far apart to intervene fast in case of an attack, tens of kilometers away. Ammunitions reserves dwindled.

At around five thirty in the afternoon, a cloud of dust announced reinforcements, enough to convince the fighters that it made more sense to retreat with their loot of camels. Had the reinforcements arrived an hour later, they would have found a company annihilated. The dead were buried the following morning, most of them on the spot. Both Vauchez and Selchauhansen eventually died from their wounds, the latter after he was found in a pile of corpses. There were thirty-four legionnaires dead and forty-eight wounded.

A few days after El Moungar, by the bedside of the wounded legionnaires at the hospital of Taghit stood Father Charles de Foucauld. De Foucauld came from an old aristocratic family. While a student at Saint-Cyr, and then an officer in a regiment of the Hussards, he had lived a rake's life. When his regiment moved to Algeria in 1880 to join the fight against Bouamama, his existence took on a new meaning. He gave up on late-night dinners with ladies of dubious reputation to learn about North Africa and take Arabic lessons. Then emerged an incredible project: to travel through Morocco, which was off limits to Christians at the time, to provide a topographic and geographic survey of the land. Undaunted, de Foucauld dressed up as a rabbi—indigenous Jewish communities were accepted in old Morocco—and, from June 1883 to May 1884 he crisscrossed the kingdom of the Alawites, pretending to be a Russian Jew named Joseph Aleman.

The sight of the desert struck de Foucauld as a revelation. The piety of Muslims also impressed him. Upon his return, while preparing his 1888 *Reconnaissance au Maroc*, he realized he had found his calling. Three years later he was ordained a priest. He wanted to bring his own faith to the desert, and so he founded a Saharan monastery in Béni Abbès, down the Zousfana River in Algeria. With his white *gandoura* (gown worn by Arabs), leather sandals, and deep-set black eyes, de Foucauld left a profound impression on those he met. Some found him to be a new breed of soldier-monk. Apparently he did not disdain wearing the military kepi to protect himself from the sun.

The legionnaires accepted his company when he rushed to their side upon hearing of the disaster at El Moungar, riding for hours in the desert. Captain Adolphe de Susbielle, who commanded at Taghit, recalled asking, "So, Father, were you well received by our wounded?" To which de Foucauld responded with a twinkle in his eyes, "We need time to know each other, but it will come, and I'm happy to be by their side."[7] While it is difficult to discern between truth and legend in de Foucauld's life stories, at the very least he ended up winning the legionnaires' trust.

Lyautey, who knew de Foucauld from his early days in Algeria, in 1881, met the priest later, during an inspection tour in Béni Abbès. He still found him a striking character. Lyautey recounts a mass that de Foucauld celebrated during their encounter in the desert:

> Before that altar, a mere white wooden table, before those sacerdotal garments of rough fabric, those pewter crucifix and candleholders, before all that misery, but also before that ecstatic priest, who offered the Eucharist with a fervor that filled the place with light and faith, we all felt such a strong religious emotion, such a sentiment of grandeur, one that we have not experienced even in the most grandiose of cathedrals. Beyond those humble walls of dirt, beyond those few Muslims who had spontaneously come to associate themselves with the prayer, it was this vision of Saharan immensity, of this Sahara and its waves that crashed on the door steps of this church, and on which de Foucauld truly reigned by the force of his prayer, of his virtue, of his sacrifice, and there he gave France the benefits of the love and respect that he inspired.[8]

De Foucauld represented for the spiritually dispossessed Frenchman that idealized ego, that man who had had the courage to follow his highest inclination to the fullest.

Eventually de Foucauld moved to Algeria's southernmost regions, in 1905, to the Hoggar desert, where absolute truths might been even more evident. He also nurtured temporal aims. De Foucauld affirmed that his goal was to convert the "infidels."[9] His best hopes, then, rested on the success of the French colonization.

> It seems that with Muslims, the way is to civilize them first, to instruct them first, to make them into people like us: That accomplished, their conversion will be a task almost accomplished too, because Islam does not hold up before instruction. History and Philosophy do it justice without any discussion. Islam falls like night before day.[10]

Dwelling in a *borj*, a fortified compound, in Tamanrasset, de Foucauld lived a life of prayer and charitable acts, while also acting as a relay of information for the French military. Fascinated by the Tuaregs, this "white marabout" wrote a dictionary of their language. Some of his time he spent at a retreat he built in the mountains, at an altitude of 2,780 meters (9,120 feet).

On December 1, 1916, in the tumult of the Great War, an armed band of thieves broke into de Foucauld's fortified monastery. Their goal, it seems, was to kidnap him for a ransom. They ended up killing him.

Lyautey showed up in Algeria a month after the massacre at El Moungar. Facing a continuing crisis in the aftermath of the attack, the new governor, Charles Jonnart, needed a man with resources; the veteran of the Tonkin and Madagascar, back in France and already facing the dreaded *ennui*, would not miss such a grand return on the North African colonial scene. Jonnart gave him full military authority as a *général de brigade* over the South Oranais. He also insisted that Lyautey report to him instead of to the Ministry of Foreign Affairs. Lyautey settled in Aïn Sefra, the hub of the so-called *confins algéro-marocains*, the vast, arid regions that stretch between Algeria and Morocco.

In one of his first gestures, Lyautey visited the wounded of El Moungar. He shook their hands one by one, expressing sympathy. He asked those who could stand, "Well boys! Who has ever walked with me?" The rest he narrates in a letter to a close correspondent:

> Five or six step out of the rank: "I did, *mon colonel*, I was with you at Mirken . . . I was with you at Ke Tuong . . . I was with you at Fort-Dauphin . . . I'm the one who escorted you that day . . . I'm the one who brought you that information." And it's the same at every post that I visit and where I find my old legionnaires. And you can barely imagine how good that feels—each time I tear up—to see in those braves that they've given me trust a long time ago. They also seem to tell me: "Let's go to the brawl once again together, it'll work out!"[11]

Still fervently representing the Gallieni method of colonization, Lyautey relied on the Legion. For the moment, though, the time had not come for the niceties of resuscitating village markets and creating schools and dispensaries. The legionnaires' task was to secure an endless region. What these people of the desert and its oasis needed, philosophized Lyautey, was the craft and display of force first and foremost.

The French faced nomadic men who rode fast. They had the uncanny ability to vanish into thin air, and reappear in a flash at stunning distances. With an enemy like that, surely the heavy European columns were headed for failure. Nor did Lyautey believe in erecting what he called a "Wall of China"— a hermetic border to protect Algeria. He crafted a strategy of building forts in strongholds and strategic locations, and adapting his forces to ensure "permanent policing" of the desert. The legionnaires often guarded those forts, and so the two-hundred-kilometer stretch along the River Zousfana became known as the Boulevard of the Legion. These are the forts that literature and Hollywood would incorporate into the classic images of the Legion, providing a narrow, but no less essential, perspective on the rich history of the corps.

The accords that France signed with the Sultan of Morocco allowed pursuit and reprisal into his sovereign land, under a clause called *droit de suite*, right of pursuit. The first elements of this police were indigenous fighters whose tasks consisted of exploring the region to detect, deter, and fight the formation of armed bands. Stationed at the forts, infantry and artillery, including the Legion, provided resistance in case of an attack. The task of some of the Legion troops, however, was also to intervene as support in both attack and withdrawal.

For that, Lyautey relied on special mounted units within the companies of the Legion. These formations had operated for a long time, at least since de Négrier's campaign against Bouamama, but Lyautey created new ones and made the best use of the resource. Mules offered some crucial advantages over horses: They are more robust and frugal. Considering that the companies operated in the desert environment, moving with animals required bringing forage on expeditions and finding adequate sources of water. Also, under attack, tending to a large herd was inconvenient, as the 1882 attack at Chott Tigri had revealed. Hence, the companies used one mount for two men. Every hour, at the call of *"Montez! Chargez!"* the legionnaire would give up his place to his acolyte who had been walking near him. The mule, with its step approximating a man's walk, then stood out as an even more sensible choice. Such companies could easily travel twice the distance that a regular cavalry unit would have covered.

Each animal carried a tent, food, and cooking supplies, two liters of water per day for each soldier, and forage—camels carrying barrels filled with forty-five liters of water followed for those longer columns in the driest country. Often there was even wood for the fire, for a total load of up to one hundred kilograms. Contemporary pictures show that the legionnaire's outfit consisted of canvas vest and slacks, and the typical colonial helmet, rather than the iconic kepi. The blue topcoat offered cover at night, or in the colder months. The Lebel 1886 rifle still reigned supreme, and it did until 1916, when the *mousqueton*, less cumbersome for riding and with a five-bullet cartridge, replaced it. Each officer had his own horses. An additional mule carried the wine supply for the company, in two fifty-liter barrels.

The legionnaires considered serving in the mounted companies a privilege; it brought the kind of action that chased the *cafard* away, and yet it was extremely harsh service. Lefebvre describes his ragged lot, returning to his home base from a mission in the Tafilalet:

> We form a group of legionnaires, Skirmishers, Spahis, Saharans, and artillerymen. All are dressed in the most fanciful way one could imagine. Some are in their underwear, others sport a shirt, and many Skirmishers wear what looks like a bathing suit. The whims and fancies of the troopers inform the most bizarre head-dress. Some sport Arab hats, other helmets or chechias, or are wrapped in desert shawls. Add to this mules, horses, and camels; on the faces and clothes that water has not touched for the last ten days, a coating of dust and sweat, hirsute beards; savage cries and the monotonous songs of the indigenous fighters, and you'll get a picture, still imperfect, of our column.[12]

Days under the inexorable sun of North Africa extended excruciatingly. Before resting for the night, soldiers had to build a low, square wall of protection. The enemy lurked. Only after this last chore did they find themselves in the stillness of the desert, in its silence at once beautiful and oppressive.

The legionnaires of the mounted companies progressively secured the South Oranais, relentlessly chasing the bands that roamed through the territories France aspired to fully control. Lyautey, meanwhile, was living again those early years he had described with vivid colors. Out on a mission, he rode preceded by the young son of a local chief who had cast his lot with the French:

> He had taken his most beautiful horse, his most prized harness of fine leather embroidered in silver, and, all day, he seconded me in the manner of a medieval equerry, following my step, holding his rifle high in the most difficult passages, the first one in my tent asking me how my night went, preparing coffee, arranging

my burnous: a youthful Saracen warrior straight out of the
Gerusalemme Liberata, beaming youth and elegance. What pretty
chivalrous mores![13]

Lyautey relished life in a tent, where he held long discussions with local
chiefs to highlight the benefits of French authority, with promises of security
and economic benefits. He impressed them with his deft use of ritual Arab
greetings and a showing of the sword his grandfather had fought with in
Napoléon's army.

Orientalist fantasies aside, straight out of Renaissance epic tales of the
Crusades in Lyautey's description of the young "Saracen," it took little time
before frictions appeared not only with the sultan of Morocco, but also with
the French government itself. Heard louder in Paris were voices arguing that
France's manifest destiny was to complete its dominion over the Maghreb, to
rule from Tunisia to the Atlantic. The Moroccan question held the last imperial chance at this point in the sharing of the earth, remarked Eugène Etienne,
the leader of the colonialist circles in Paris. For the moment, Lyautey displayed
restraint, as the good apostle of the "oil stain" colonial philosophy: "We will
need to 'digest' Morocco and not conquer it. For the moment, as far as I am
concerned, I've prepared, I think, some good outposts—and I'm firmly set on
extracting from the mixed police and the accords all they can give."[14]

In 1903, less than two months after his arrival, the French army of the
South Oranais, including the mounted companies of the First and Second
Regiments, took the ksar of Bechar (or Colomb-Béchar, as it became known)
in what the accords had defined as Moroccan territory—to the north of the
Hamada, where tribal warriors congregated. Bechar, which otherwise
numbered about three hundred inhabitants, had abundant water. Théophile
Delcassé, the minister of foreign affairs, thought that French ambitions
should for the moment rely on diplomacy with the Moroccan government,
the Makhzen. Nevertheless, Bechar remained a central piece of the French
upper Sahara military chess game. Soon the railway line reached it from Aïn
Sefra. In June of 1904 the French took another, farther oasis, Berguent, to
the considerable irritation of Sultan Abdelaziz. The year 1905 saw more
steady progress. Topographical expeditions scouted for watering points, wells
were dug out, more outposts were established. An extensive communication
network emerged. Rollet, together with the mounted legionnaires of the
First Regiment, created a 185-kilometer-long (150 miles) track from Mecheria
to Berguent in just two months. The mounted legionnaires patrolled the
desert to pursue marauding bands.

The year 1906 witnessed how precarious the situation remained, in spite of the many tribes offering allegiance to the French. In the Tafilalet, on the other side of the Hamada, religious and political leaders called for war against the invaders. Rumor had it that an army of unprecedented size had formed. Had the time come to make a decisive move toward eastern Morocco, even up to the capital, Fes, and present the politicians in Paris with a fait accompli? Lyautey did confess an "irresistible itch to do stupid things."[15] Still, he exercised restraint. Taking over the Tafilalet, far away from his Algerian bases and with a large, partisan population represented too risky a challenge. In the meantime he advanced his chess piece further, in yet another strategic place nearer Morocco: Boudenib.

Aïn Sefra, the nodal point of this French military expansion in the desert, grew. Military quarters, administrative buildings, barracks, and a hospital were built on an elevation between two mountain ranges and a huge sand dune. The buildings faced the civilian town across the river. The barracks of the Legion—the Twenty-Second and Twenty-Fourth Companies of the Second Regiment—consisted of three rectangular buildings featuring elegant arcades on each of the three levels.

Aïn Sefra showcased all that one would expect from a frontier town through which troops passed constantly, on their way to the outposts, or back from leave. The Café du Progrès reminded this transient population of the Third Republic values that sustained their mission, while the cabaret La Môme Qui Pue ("The Gal That Stinks") provided an alternative to those who found progress wanting as a source of inspiration in the hardship of war. Drinking was the cult that rallied everyone, and on the Legion's payday, woe to the citizen who ventured outside. Even the highest-ranking officer had to watch out on those days. Lyautey learned his lesson when, upon returning from the military circle, he found his legionnaire orderly sleeping off his absinthe in his very own bed.[16]

There appeared another of these characters who found in North Africa the appropriate landscape to satisfy their wanderlust and comfort their loathing of European conformism. Isabelle Eberhardt, born in 1877 of Russian parents in Switzerland, had first visited Algeria with her mother. The desert cast its spell on her, and it would never let go: "I love my Sahara with an obscure love, mysterious, profound, inexplicable, but real and indestructible . . . My life is forever linked to this land, which I can never leave."[17] Eberhardt flouted society's conventions to the extreme. In Algeria she converted to Islam, learned Arabic, and set out to discover the country dressed as a man, calling herself Si Mahmoud. Eventually she married an Algerian who worked for the French administration. With a deep interest in the mystical religious current of Sufism, she found work as a journalist for a newspaper, *El Akhbar*, enough to allow pursuit of her wanderings.

In Aïn Sefra, where she arrived one week before Lyautey in 1903, Isabelle did not fail to cause a sensation among the legionnaires, with her white *gandoura*, leather boots, and shaved head. Chain-smoking, with a habit of drinking and smoking hashish, she struck a cord in what she described as "the blond men from the North, tanned, burnt under distant suns, in the colonies."[18] The existential connection ran deep. Her own half-brother Augustin had joined the Legion in 1895, after leading a dissolute life—he took his life much later, in 1914. Orschanow, the central character of her novel *Trimardeur*, is a Russian who is haunted by visions of the desert and eventually chooses to become a legionnaire. Eberhardt visited the wounded of El Moungar, about whom she wrote an article: "Very *sympathiques*, these poor devils that suffered and risked dying for business alien to them, and for which they don't care."[19] Legionnaire Kohn recalled how she would walk up at the end of the day to the military quarters to spend time with the troopers. Conversation in German flowed on sharing adventures in the *bled*, the North African countryside. "Not one of my comrades, nor me, would have used foul language in front of her. Moreover she had nothing to provoke and was far from pretty."[20] The legionnaires minded their manners when not patronizing La Môme Qui Pue.

Very much smitten with Isabelle was Lyautey. "No one understands Africa like her," he averred.[21] "We understood each other, that poor Mahmoud and I, and I shall forever keep the exquisite memories of our evening conversations. She represented what attracts me the most, a *réfractaire* [an objector]. To find someone who is true to herself, who lives free of any prejudice, of all subjection, of all clichés, and who passes through life as free as the bird in space, what a treat!"[22]

On October 21, 1904, the legionnaires of the garrison at Aïn Sefra heard a tremor. Rushing to the edge of the terrace of the fort up the village, they witnessed, powerless, a flash flood destroy and carry away entire houses from the village down below. Isabelle Eberhardt had returned from one of her pilgrimages sick with typhoid, and was resting in her house when disaster struck. A legionnaire named Schandelmeyer found her body under mounds of bricks, beams, and mud, one of twenty-six victims. Lyautey insisted that in this chaos the legionnaires also find a manuscript she was preparing. They did. That manuscript, published in 1906 under the title *Dans l'ombre chaude de l'Islam* (*In the Warm Shadow of Islam*), featured haunting pages describing long trips to tombs of holy men, deep in the desert, as far as Morocco, in places so cut off from the world that one feels at the edge of existence.

CHAPTER 9

Morocco That Was

On the morning of March 29, 1907, a column of troops led by Colonel Henri Felineau stood in view of Oujda, the largest Moroccan town near the Algerian border. Lyautey arrived shortly after by car and seized the town. Oujda was a convenient outpost to keep an eye on Morocco and, possibly, enter it from the east.

Thus began in earnest the long-foreseen French takeover of Morocco, the last great prize in the Scramble for Africa. Old Morocco fascinated the French. The kingdom had been off-limits to Christians, but on many occasions, travelers on diplomatic missions had brought descriptions, some produced by great artists. In the 1830s, the painter Eugène Delacroix spent five months frantically covering his sketchbooks with delightful drawings and watercolors of what he saw. While Charles de Foucauld's *Reconnaissance au Maroc* served more pragmatic aims, in 1885, the novelist Pierre Loti wrote a travel narrative that set standard orientalist images of the kingdom.

There, tucked in the northwest corner of Africa, shielded by the Atlas Mountains, yet with a history bearing the imprint of many a civilization, lay a mysterious kingdom of fascinating traditions. Starting in the seventh century, Arab conquerors had brought their culture and Islamic religion to the native Amazigh population. To this day, the country still bears distinctive traits of these two groups. There is also evidence of Roman presence at the archaeological site of Volubilis. In the medinas, those typical dense, labyrinth-like towns of Morocco, there are the mellah quarters, where Judaism's diaspora found refuge, especially after the Jews' eviction from Spain in the late 1400s. Sub-Saharan Africans, brought by the Arab slave trade through the desert, appeared everywhere. Moroccans in pre-colonial

Morocco lived under a monarchy, represented since the 1600s by the Alawite dynasty. The Alawite sultan of Morocco, originating out of the Tafilalet, that region of staunch resistance to colonialism in North Africa, claimed to descend from the prophet Muhammad.

Central authority was weak in what an English journalist and author of an essential contemporary memoir, Walter Harris, called the "Morocco That Was." In the words of Lyautey in 1916, commenting a few years after the French invaded the country:

> We found ourselves before a historical and independent empire, jealous of its independence, rebel to any servitude, an empire which, until these last years, still looked like a constituted state, with its hierarchy of government officials, of foreign envoys, its social organisms which still exist to this day, in spite of the failures of Morocco's central authority.[1]

The French made the most of this unstable situation. Sultan Abdelaziz, like his immediate predecessors, faced chronic deficits and dangerous challenges from rebel chiefs such as Bouhmara, a pretender who had proclaimed himself sultan in 1902. At the end of that year, and again in 1904, Abdelaziz took loans from the French secured by 60 percent of his kingdom's customs revenue and a contract that gave French military officers the right to modernize his royal army. The fiscal reforms Abdelaziz initiated turned out to be widely unpopular. His people viewed him as subservient to European interests. The sultan's lifestyle left his subjects aghast as well. A man with a passion for everything modern, he spent fortunes on cars and photographic equipment, or played bicycle polo tournaments in the white, sun-splashed courtyards of his palaces.

The Germans, who had financial and industrial views of their own concerning Morocco, signaled that they would not afford the French a free hand in taking over the country as the British had done after the Entente Cordiale. In late March 1905, Emperor Wilhelm II landed in Tangiers and, on March 31 gave a speech that championed the independence of Morocco and freedom of commerce. French public opinion howled.

Ten months later, at the Conference of Algeciras, European powers sought to diffuse the tension over Morocco. The French had the support of Great Britain, and they were also free to negotiate with the Spanish, who claimed for themselves the northern part of the kingdom—for centuries Spain had held on to a few ports on the Mediterranean coast, Ceuta and

Melilla. They obtained a diplomatic victory. The conference's official declaration emphasized the independence of Morocco, but these words meant
little considering how the French tightened their grip on the customs revenue, infrastructure contracts for the ports, and forces that policed those
ports. Jules Ferry's fierce opponent in the 1885 colonial debates that followed
the Lang Son debacle, the radical socialist stalwart Georges Clemenceau,
became minister of the interior, and then president of the Council of
Ministers in 1906. Much water had run under the bridges as far as
Clemenceau's stance on the colonies was concerned. He now pursued the
policies of his predecessors and presided over France's progressive takeover
over Morocco.

Meanwhile, famine and internal disorder wreaked havoc on Abdelaziz's
people, and the sultan's reputation sank even further. Not only did his
subjects see increased European presence in their cities, but they also heard
of how Lyautey, from Algeria, progressively tightened his control over the
eastern side of the country, beyond the Atlas Mountains. It would be a
stretch to speak of a Moroccan nationalism in this early context. That said,
the subjects of Abdelaziz considered that their monarch had a political and
religious responsibility to ensure the integrity of the *umma*, the community
of believers in his land.

On March 19, 1907, a French doctor named Émile Mauchamp left his
medical dispensary in Marrakech to walk back to his house a few hundred
meters away. Mauchamp practiced under the auspices of the French
government, in an effort to convince the Moroccans that French involve-
ment in their country was beneficial. Mauchamp had a distinguished record
of serving abroad and bringing health care to the people of countries as
diverse as Brazil, Russia, and Turkey. Many in Marrakech had grown increasingly suspicious of these motivations, however. Was Mauchamp a spy?
Wasn't he installing a wireless telegraph in his house that would facilitate a
military invasion?

Mauchamp went home early that day to take down a flagpole in his
courtyard that created further suspicion of spying. Walking in the narrow,
meandering street of the medina in the company of assistants, he encountered a group of men. A commotion ensued. Men shouted, women ululated.
Moments later the body of Mauchamp, bludgeoned and stabbed to death,
naked, was dragged through the streets. The mob looted his house. Eventually
Marrakech's governor had the corpse retrieved from the yard where it had
been dumped. The French authorities brought him back to France as a
martyr of civilization and buried him in his birthplace, Chalon-sur-Saône.

Outraged political leaders and army chiefs demanded swift action, and this is how Lyautey ended up before Oujda in March of 1907.

Tensions between France and Morocco culminated a year later at the port of Casablanca. Under French control and management, workers hastened to build a wharf, using carriages on rails to transport stones from a quarry north of the town, along the edge of a cemetery. On July 30 a group of men enraged by what they perceived as lack of respect for the dead in the cemetery killed the workers, nine of them. Local leaders—who had political motivations of their own—demanded the expulsion of Europeans from the kingdom. Quickly it became obvious that Casablanca faced the threat of a riot. The European population, which numbered about six thousand out of an estimated thirty thousand citizens, took refuge on boats in the harbor or in the consulates of Great Britain, Sweden, Austria, and France.

Clemenceau estimated that the threat in Casablanca required resolute action, and agreed to send in a force. The battleship *Galilée* left Oran and arrived in view of Casablanca two days after the massacre of the workers; by then, anarchy had taken over in the port city. On the morning of the fifth, a contingent of seventy French marines forced the gate overlooking the harbor and charged forward toward the consulates, spearing anyone who opposed them with their bayonets. The rioting intensified and became an all-out massacre. The tribesmen targeted the Jews, plundered and destroyed their stores and houses, raping and killing.

The Legion arrived shortly after, on board the *Jeanne d'Arc* and the *Gueydon*, carrying half a battalion of the First Regiment each. A thorough bombing of Casablanca started, setting the Arab neighborhoods on fire. From the consulates, through the whizzing of bullets, one saw dark clouds of smoke rising, glowing red underneath. General Antoine Drude led the entire French force that took over Casablanca on the seventh. Braving Casablanca's infamous ocean swell on shallow rowboats that the French called *barcasses*, the legionnaires landed to find the scene of an eviscerated town. The stench announced streets filled with burnt rubble, abandoned plunder, and cadavers swelling with putrefaction in the August heat. What was left of the civilian population wandered around, haggard and terrified.

The French faced ongoing riots, a public health catastrophe, and looming danger from the tribesmen whose ranks were growing outside the town. Order in Casablanca needed first to be established. Drude ordered his men to secure the strategic points and a safe perimeter, allowing them to shoot on the spot any armed Moroccan they found; taking position on minarets was expressly forbidden, however. Between August 16 and 23, twelve Moroccans caught armed, spying, or stealing were executed. Meanwhile, the civilian population cleaned up, while those parts of town that were deemed impossible to rebuild were burned. Three hundred Muslims and thirty Jews were buried. Curling toward the northeast of Casablanca southward, a vast military camp grew to accommodate the troops in the next few weeks. Two more battalions of legionnaires arrived from Algeria as reinforcement, forming with other troops of Algerian Skirmishers the Marching Regiment in Morocco. True to form, the sections of the camps set up by the Legion stood out with their order and neatness under the scorching weather.

The orderly rows of the Legion camp stood in marked contrast with the behavior of some of the soldiers during the battle, as it turns out. In the fog of battle and general chaos, the legionnaires' discipline had broken down in the ranks. Those left to guard the town on the seventh of August were drunk. General Drude requested permission from the minister of defense to bring "cases of indiscipline in the Legion" to a court-martial, including two men who had stolen merchandise and two others who had shot and killed two Moroccan women.[2] Drude hastened to say that these were isolated cases. Due to the murky circumstances, the idea of the tribunal was abandoned, and the legionnaires were sent to the disciplinary corps of their regiments in Algeria.

Nevertheless, a serious problem threatened the Legion's reputation for excellence. Lieutenant Kuntz, a good observer of military affairs and an eye witness to the landing at Casablanca, explained that forming marching battalions with elements taken here and there from the Legion's ranks was a mistake: Group coherence and solidarity were the backbone of the Legion, more than in any other corps. Leadership was also at fault. Going to the Tonkin was an eagerly awaited reward for service, but instead of sending entire companies, the Legion sent officers and soldiers on a schedule, depending on the length of time they had served. That was a factor of disintegration in the corps, too. Finally, Kuntz noted how the increasing numbers of French recruits contributed to the worries: "These Frenchmen are not from the top of the basket and are mostly from the colonial infantry regiments where their reenlistment was denied. These are factors of diminishing morale value that we must remedy."[3] Such an influx of Frenchmen compensated for a noticeable decline in the recruitment of soldiers from Alsace-Lorraine, and these were widely considered as the best, since the leadership estimated that they showed both attachment to France and Teutonic hardiness and discipline.

*   *   *

Clemenceau's determination to protect Morocco on behalf of France's economic interests stopped at the idea of waging a full-scale war. Hence, Drude's orders were to not venture beyond the immediate surroundings of Casablanca. The Moroccans interpreted this constraint as timidity, and on the eighth of August they besieged the camp vigorously and claimed the Legion's first victim since the landing, Legionnaire Motz. The attackers were also fired up by a newly emerged leader, the brother of Sultan Abdelaziz, Abdelhafid, whom the ulemas, the members of the high clergy in Marrakech, had proclaimed as the one legitimate leader in view of the sultan's weakness before the Europeans. The French strongly suspected that the Germans supported this Hafidiya movement, but it remained, in essence, motivated by popular religious sentiment. On the twenty-first there was yet another attack, which the French warded off with the backup of cannon fire from their warships. Powerful searchlights from the cruisers swept along Casablanca's white walls and the beaches while the staccato of machine guns tore through the night.

On September 3 Legion troops set out to find their enemies, which they encountered at the village of Sidi Moumen, about ten kilometers from Casablanca. Hindered by a rigid square formation, facing volatile tribesmen of the Chaouia Plain who made the most of the terrain, the French learned what a foe these Moroccans from the plain could be, even when they suffered many more losses. The French could not engage successfully with tribes of the Chaouia on the battlefield, limited as they were in their range of actions. Their hopes consisted in attacking directly the enemy camps, which lay a short distance away. But the only thing they found on their September 11 and 21 raids were empty tents. By October, the troops of Sultan Abdelhafid in Marrakech were showing up in increasing numbers.

The French government grew impatient with the continuing unrest and opted for new leadership. General Albert d'Amade, a veteran of the Tonkin campaign in 1885, took the command of the French occupation forces on January 6, 1908. His new mandate recognized that holding Casablanca without the Chaouia Plain was unrealistic. D'Amade first took Settat, on January 15, then changed his strategy.[4] The troops were divided into two mobile columns, with some left in the outposts as defense and reserve.

The legionnaires became part of the Column of Tirs, led by Colonel Boutegourd, comprising nine companies, two squadrons, a battery of 75mm field guns, and some machine guns. Weeks of arduous marches followed, still with uncertain outcomes for quite a while.[5] At a place named Sidi el

Rhnimiyne, on March 15, Boutegourd surprised a camp counting more than a thousand tents. This gathering followed a holy man named Bou Nouala. After weeks of fruitless march, the French soldiers were champing at the bit to engage and they walked fast. Sowing death by machine-gun fire, Boutegourd's legionnaires then finished off any survivor they found with their bayonets. One witness numbered the deaths at fifteen hundred.[6] Fire raged on the camp until cold rain brought an end to the hellish scene and announced a miserable return through the soaked, muddy plain of the Chaouia. The men had covered a distance of seventy kilometers in twenty hours, including four hours of fighting.

First envisioned by its leaders as a good, clean, modern example of colonial warfare, and eventually drawn by necessity into the grim reality of scorched-earth tactics, the Legion's campaign in the Chaouia went on till mid-May.[7] The violence, cynics thought, had the merits of finally bringing stability to the region. Although their mobility gave them considerable advantage, the Chaouia tribesmen were mostly horsemen who never set foot on the ground, and they made ineffective shooters, poor fighters in close combat, and even less effective defenders of their camps. "From the point of view of general tactics, it's the frank and rapid offensive that succeeds the best before the Moroccan cavalry," noted a journalist who followed the campaign.[8]

Lyautey and the French representative in Algiers, Eugène Regnault, arrived in Casablanca at the end of March on a fact-finding mission requested by an increasingly anxious Clemenceau—Lyautey, since the end of 1906, was general of the military division of Oran. Both men reported progress, so much so that the Sixth Battalion of the First Regiment and the Fourth Battalion of the Second Regiment made their way back to Algeria. The legionnaires who stayed built roads and bridges or installed communications infrastructure, future manifestations of the "oil stain" perhaps, but essential elements of a long-term occupation for the moment. A newspaper in French appeared, aiming at the growing population of French speakers. Lieutenant-Colonel Charles Mangin attempted again to reform the sultan's army. On July 14, a review of the troops to the tune of the "Marseillaise" marked the celebrations of the French national holiday.

The last episode of General Drude and General d'Amade's campaign in the Chaouia featured the Legion prominently, but far from featuring prowess in combat, it once again fueled concern about the cohesion of the corps and the loyalty of its best elements in this first decade of the new century, and added further tension to worsening Franco-German relations. On the night of September 25, 1908, a small group of men climbing aboard a *barcasse* on the beach, while a military ship idled at a short distance away, was spotted by a patrol of legionnaires. They recognized some of their own. After some fighting, all ended in the water, and then before French military authorities. As it turns out, the men on the beach were a group of German legionnaires attempting to escape. Desertion was a rather common occurrence in the Legion, but the French had not realized how much of an unofficial but well-funded German sleight of hand caused it.

The presence of German recruits in the Legion, as it turns out, was still very much a thorn in the side of Emperor Wilhelm and his chiefs of staff, all the more so in the context of strained relations with France. They lamented that some of their best recruits would serve in the *französische Fremdenlegion*. Committees formed in Germany to help the deserters, while a propaganda campaign sought to dry up this precious resource for the French. Through graphic posters, newspaper articles, novels even, young Germans were told to what extent the heroic image of the Legion concealed brutality, disease, even sexual abuse. The Legion represented a form of modern slavery for pennies a day.

Direct testimony seemed like the best way to strike fear in the impressionable minds of German youths who might be tempted by a stint in the desert. Raimund Anton Premschitz, a former lieutenant in the First Regiment, published his *Meine Erlebnisse als Fremdenlegionär in Algerien* (*My Adventures as a Foreign Legionnaire in Algeria*), in 1904. The subtitle did not seek to hide its main objective: *Warning Cry to Everyone Who Is Bound by Military Service*. Premschitz's *Adventures* featured a gallery of legionnaire rogues types, quite varied in their life experiences (a missionary, a count, an artist) and living in squalid conditions. Legionnaires, apparently, were the object of unfair and bestial punishments inflicted under the relentless African sun, and other turpitudes. "No one esteems the legionnaire. He is feared, but not respected"; "The Arab sees in him a man of lowly extraction."

Interestingly, Premschitz openly explains that half of the legionnaires were Germans from Alsace-Lorraine, Baden-Württemberg, or the Rhine Palatinate who had deserted from their own regiments because of ill treatment. However, "after spending a few days only at the Legion," he adds, "they can't find enough good words for their former regiments."[9] Books and pamphlets in Premschitz's style appeared frequently until World War I broke out.

For the French officers who read them, these documents represented gross exaggerations, but here and there one can pick up asides that suggest, indeed, that discipline was not what it used to be in the African corps of the Legion, and that the presence of those French low-grade rejects from other French units was a greater factor in the breakdown of morale and discipline.

The number of German recruits, which had been declining since the late 1880s, possibly after reports of the devastating loss suffered in the Tonkin and in Madagascar, had dropped.

The French representative in Tangiers, Eugène Regnault, reported in a telegram that "desertion of German legionnaires happens continually and there is not a week that groups of two or three [German] soldiers arrive in Rabat." On September 26, 1907, the same Regnault reported to the French minister of foreign affairs:

> The [German] deserters [from the Legion] are smuggled back to Europe on the many German ships that arrive quite frequently in the harbor [of Rabat]. Yesterday's departure occasioned an incident particularly painful to us. Five or six old legionnaires went on board chanting the *"Wacht am Rhein"* and shouting in German: Down with France. The vice-consul of Germany, Mr. Neudorfer, took them on board and saluted them many times by waving his hat.[10]

Since the landing in Casablanca a year earlier, 217 legionnaires had bid adieu to the elusive glories and comforts of the Foreign Legion, including 114 Germans, and the French commanders could little to stem this flow, constrained as they were by the laws of Morocco and the international agreements signed in Algeciras, in 1906.

As far as morale in those troops who remained faithful to their mission was concerned, Legionnaire Flutsch, who in Antoine Sylvère's autobiographical novel served from 1905, recalled unmistakable strain:

> Noises concerning Germany's opposition to France's designs in Morocco reached the Legion. That stirred up the latent rivalries between the two nations and a very serious brawl took place in the room of the Seventh Company. Bayonets intervened, and, in sensibly equal proportions, the fighters were taken to the hospital, the infirmary, or the prison. There were deep wounds but no deaths. The ensuing report announced that any challenge susceptible to open a conflict of nationalities would be taken as crime against esprit de corps and unworthy of a legionnaire; it would warrant its author sixty days . . . In Kabylia [Algeria], in Mexico, in the Tonkin, German and French had united under the same flag to create one country that they all recognized: the Legion.[11]

In the deserters's incident of September 1908, in Casablanca, it was clear that the three legionnaires—named Meyer, Heinemann, and Bens—were Germans who had conceived of their escape with the help of their consul. The incident caused a scandal of international dimensions. The Germans cared little for the contract their clients had signed with France, let alone for the symbolic ideal of the "Patria Nostra." They argued that under the current agreements with the Sultan the men were under their jurisdiction and that, indeed, their liberation was the only possible solution. The diplomatic corps in Tangiers thought that the trigger of war had finally been pulled. *"C'est la guerre!"* But time for war had not come, yet. France and Germany, after much vituperation from both sides, reached an agreement in November, ending the dispute.[12]

In eastern Morocco, south of the Oujda region that Lyautey now controlled and around the Hamada, legionnaires made further and more decisive advances against those many Moroccans who resisted French invasion on the other side of the Atlas Mountains. The Hafidiya movement, following the king's brother, aroused passions in the east, too. Emerging out of the Upper Guir, even tumbling down the Atlas Mountains, Moroccans answered the call of a leader whom the religious leaders of the capital, Fes, had declared legitimate. Leading the movement around the Hamada was a holy man named Moulay Lahsin. French papers in Oran were filled with frightening news of *harka*—an army—of as many as twenty thousand fighters.

Four military columns, each one with a backbone of mounted Legion troops, left Aïn Sefra, Berguent, Beni Ounif, and Colomb-Béchar to converge on a designated staging area, Aïn Chair, and report to General Léon Vigy. The Legionnaires Lefebvre and Boulic wrote accounts of these missions in detail. They first recorded the actions of the Twenty-Fourth Mounted Company of the First Regiment; the latter's text, titled *Souvenirs d'Afrique*, is a manuscript in the private papers of Lyautey, to whom it is dedicated. One of the first chapters concerns chiefly Boulic's activities in the Twentieth Marching Company, which, as we learn, was still reeling from a tragedy. In the night of February 1, as it moved near the post of Forthassa Gharbia, a winter storm had caught its men unawares. Thirty-four legionnaires had perished frozen, and many more suffered from injuries.

The columns at Aïn Chair formed an impressive army of five thousand men. In the camps, the exploits of the Twenty-Fourth Mounted Company of the First Regiment, which had arrived from Colomb-Béchar, dominated the conversations. On April 16, after Commandant Pierron ignored a message from a Moroccan chief who ordered them to leave the country or else convert to Islam, the legionnaires had pugnaciously withstood an attack at the oasis of Menabha. The fight ended in man-to-man combat. According to Pierron's internal report, one Lieutenant Huot of the Twenty-Fourth had carried the fight. "All the Moroccans that entered the camp were killed." "Calm, collected and brave," lauded their commander. Lefebvre—registered under service number 6853—was one of those whom Pierron singled out for recognition: "Showed much sangfroid while he led his section during the fight."[13]

From Aïn Chair, the columns marched toward the *harka*. The weather was beautiful and warm, Boulic recounted, and enough water could be found without too much trouble. The food, however, left all wanting: "Hunger often torments our guts, bread or biscuit is out of the question, we receive each day our two quarters of flour and with that we bake our *kesra* [Algerian flat bread] as best as we can, because combustible is rare too." Later, halting at ten at the end of a long day, "I was so hungry that I ate part of my rice from the special reserve, and it was almost raw because all I had to cook it with was some dry camel dung."

As columns of such magnitude made their way, supply problems became more acute, but the itinerary then went through more generous regions, and the troops could live off the land, that is, they robbed the populations, requisitioning crops and livestock, and let the mules, horses, and camels graze in the barley fields made green by springtime. No one made it a matter of conscience, since they suspected that the same populations gave fighters to the *harka*. Sometimes the columns set up camp in the field, looking forward to taking water or feed to their mules from the irrigation canals that lined those fields, but the inhabitants would then divert the flow of water upstream, inflicting long trips to a more distant watering point.

The legionnaires itched to fight, but the battle did not come until early May, when news came of the *harka*'s presence near Boudenib, which had long been a gathering point for the tribes. No doubt the Moroccans were hearing of d'Amade's progress in the Chaouia and the news prodded them. On May 13, the Twenty-Fourth Company took Beni Ouzien just a little distance short of Boudenib. The fight cost the life of a much-admired officer, Lieutenant Jaeglé, a survivor of El Moungar and a talented topographer. The day after, following another engagement in Boudenib proper, "The French flag floated over the Boudenib minaret, gaping from a shell shot, and we were amply paid back for all our miseries." Boulic then muses, philosophically, about what all this signified: "To serve, to accomplish one's duty and exhaust oneself to fulfill the duty, because that order came, because orders come from the superiors and they set a proper example."[14]

The legionnaires set out to build a post fit for a force of fifteen hundred men and five hundred mounts; they did it in two months. Boudenib is a rich palm grove that follows the River Guir for about three kilometers, encased between two rocky plateaus. The fort stood on the northern bank, while on an elevation to the south, the French also established a blockhouse to watch over the entire area. On May 23, Lyautey arrived to review and congratulate the troops. There remained the Twenty-Fourth and the Sixth Mounted Companies as garrison, waiting for the *harka*, watching over the Tafilalet, a mere hundred kilometers away. Torrid temperatures, a persistent sirocco, meager food, and the rising toll taken by typhoid fever made most of the news in the summer months spent at the edge of the Hamada. The legionnaires slept all dressed up, ready for combat given the state of emergency.

The *harka* at last manifested itself with a challenge, brought to the French commander of Boudenib on May 29 by a venerable-looking old man:

> May beneficence be on those who follow the upright life, those who humble themselves before merciful God and seek Justice. Know that, since your arrival in the Sahara, you have badly treated the weak. You have gone from conquest to conquest. Your dark soul made a mockery of us while you race to your destruction. You have made our country suffer immense harm, which tastes as galling to us as the flower of the bitter gourd. The courageous and noble warriors approach you, armed for destruction. If you are in force, come out from behind your walls for combat; you will judge which is nobler, the owl or the hawk. Do set the hour of this encounter of the braves, because this is the custom of our valiant ancestors in dealing with your ignoble ancestors.[15]

The challenge of an honorable fight elicited a derisive snicker. Still, having heard that this gathering outnumbered the earlier one by far, maybe up to twenty-five thousand soldiers this time, the French sent some reinforcements from Béchar.

The final showdown with the *harka* of 1908 truly began at Boudenib in the last days of August, when masses of Moroccan fighters began to appear forward. From the French positions in Boudenib, a day later, one could see myriads of white tents and innumerable fighters in their burnouses, either mounted on their horses or on foot. The core of the *harka* stayed at Djorf, about ten kilometers away. As usual, women followed the harka with their children, to support and profit from what had to be, in their mind, the blow that would dispatch the *roumis* back to their shores. At last, at two o'clock on September 1, a detachment of Spahis galloped back to sound the alert. The great attack had begun.

The battle lasted approximately sixteen hours, pitting the garrison at Boudenib with its legionnaires against thousands of Moroccans. Artillery struck first. As Lefebvre put it, this artillery "only had to punch in the pile, the rifles remained idle." The superiority of the French weaponry caused terrible losses in the attackers' swarms, who, as soon as they came within one hundred meters would then meet the firepower of the machine guns. The sounds deafened any conversation. Lefebvre saw mounds of dead fighters grow, as those who came to retrieve the dead were shot too. There were a few wounded in the fort as well.

By five o'clock the Moroccans determined that taking the blockhouse, which towered over Boudenib on the mountain tabletop (*gara*), represented their only chance. Barbed wire protected the one accessible side of the block-house, whereas on the nearly vertical slopes of the other aspects, shards of glass were copiously sprinkled all over. Thirty-five legionnaires and forty Skirmishers held this small fort. Thousands of Moroccans rose, till night plunged the scene into darkness. Their attack continued.

Optical communications allowed the legionnaires in the blockhouse to indicate to the artillery in Boudenib where to shoot. The log of their exchanges shows terse, slightly bemused exchanges: "Little short"; "Are the petards having any effect?"[16] The keepers of the fort also threw grenades when groups tore themselves out of the wire. Through the night, wrote Lefebvre, the shots of the machine guns evoked "some magical fireworks." "Finally, at one o'clock in the morning, the clamor subsided, and one could hear in the newly found calm the wailing of the dying."[17]

When the sun rose over Boudenib, the sight of the palm grove strewn with corpses offered a grandiose, horrible spectacle. The French waved at each other from the fort and the blockhouse. They counted their losses, minimal ones. A bullet had hit Lefebvre's mule. He reflected that if he had been the one to take it, it would have earned him the coveted Médaille Militaire. The Béchar column, led by Alix, arrived on the fifth and went after what remained of the *harka* right away, gunning down more.

The much-vaunted ideal of the *tache d'huile*, which Lyautey had spelled out upon his arrival in the South Oranais, clearly had met its limits. Lyautey put it in perspective: "Any indigenous politics must rest on a force, the only way to earn respect, especially in Muslim country."[18] The miserable remnants of the great *harka* of Moulay Lahsin, inspired by Abdelhafid, the brother of the sultan, went back to the Atlas and the Tafilalet. Many were peasants armed with stones and sticks.

Lyautey's career in the colonial service paused at the end of 1909, when his superiors transferred him back to France, to Rennes, as general and commander of the Tenth Army Corps. This time he hardly let out any manifestations of depression after leaving the sunshine of North Africa. The post was highly prestigious. Moreover, he did not live alone anymore.

In 1907, a hospital ship coming from Morocco had made a stop in Oran and Lyautey was there to salute wounded soldiers from the Chaouia campaign. On board was a nurse named Inès de Bourgoing, daughter of Napoléon III's grand equerry and widow of an army colonel, Joseph Fortoul. Inès, forty-seven years old, was attractive, distinguished, and quite rich. She and Lyautey went out for dinner twice and struck up a friendship. As his career prospects appeared ever more promising, Lyautey missed the presence of a woman by his side on social occasions. It must have been a bit strange to see the general, at an official dinner, dispatching his guests according to the *plan de table* he had devised. He made a proposal which Madame de Bourgoing accepted readily. Writing to inform Louise Baignères of his matrimonial project with Inès, he explained: "She is independent and used to a very active life, which, hopefully, will not suffer too much from mine's perpetual jostling."[19]

Hubert Lyautey married Inès de Bourgoing, *la veuve* Fortoul, in October 1909, in Paris. For the rest of his twenty-five years, she brought him friendship, which he returned with affection and respect. Apparently she also had a good sense of humor. Later in this marriage, the joke was that one day, Madame Lyautey found her husband in his usual masculine circle and declared, victoriously, "Gentlemen, I have the pleasure of informing you that last night I cuckolded you all."[20] While she took her place by his side in the extraordinary events of his career, she never abandoned her leadership role in the Red Cross. She traveled through Morocco or to Paris as a devoted advocate of health care and hygiene, working at establishing dispensaries and maternity wards.

Edit. Siboni, Bel-Abbès.

4. — Légionnaires du 1er Étrangers.

Legionnaires of the First Regiment in Sidi Bel Abbès, 1915.

This page:
Pirates of the Upper Tonkin, 1890.

Joseph Gallieni (front and center) with his staff in Madagascar, 1899. Lyautey stands to the left.

Facing page:
Entrance gate of the Quartier Viénot in Sidi Bel Abbès, 1907.

Legionnaires of the Second Regiment in Saïda, 1921.

Marching in the Algerian backcountry, ca. 1905.

Le Petit Journal

5 CENTIMES SUPPLÉMENT ILLUSTRÉ 5 CENTIMES ABONNEMENTS

Le Petit Journal
CHAQUE JOUR — 6 PAGES — 5 CENTIMES
Administration : 61, rue Lafayette
Le Supplément illustré
CHAQUE SEMAINE 5 CENTIMES

Le Petit Journal Militaire, Maritime, Colonial.... 10 cent.
Le Petit Journal agricole, 5 cent. ⁓ La Mode du Petit Journal, 10 cent.
Le Petit Journal illustré de la Jeunesse, 10 cent.

On s'abonne sans frais dans tous les bureaux de poste

SIX MOIS UN AN
SEINE et SEINE-ET-OISE.. 2 fr. 3 fr. 50
DÉPARTEMENTS......... 2 fr. 4 fr. »
ÉTRANGER.............. 2 50 5 fr. »

Les manuscrits ne sont pas rendus

Dix-huitième Année   DIMANCHE 6 OCTOBRE 1907   Numéro 881

LES TROUPES D'ÉLITE DE L'ARMÉE FRANÇAISE
La légion étrangère au Maroc

Facing page: Lyautey enters Marrakech through Bab Agnaou, 1912, by Maurice Romberg.

Resident-General Lyautey with Sultan Moulay Yusef (left), 1925.

This page: Le Petit Journal celebrates the "troupes d'élite" of the French colonial army, 1907.

Father Charles de Foucauld, 1880.

Isabelle Eberhardt, ca. 1895.

Abdelkrim, ca. 1918.

Aage of Denmark and a detachment of legionnaires near Taza, July 1925.

Aage of Denmark, ca. 1933.

Maréchal Lyautey, by Marcel-André Baschet, 1934.

CHAPTER 10

Baraka

araka is the sign of leaders and winners in Morocco. When the holy
man rises as a chief of the people, to take them to war, to defend the
community of believers, there is the *baraka*, the blessing, the energy
that testifies to divine presence. The sultan of Morocco is, naturally, a prime
holder of the *baraka*. The sultans of Morocco used to leave for month-long
journeys through their kingdom, in immense convoys called *mehallas*. They
collected taxes, reaffirmed or created allegiances, fought battles—in other
words, they revivified their *baraka*, the mark of their legitimacy.

The *baraka* flowed scarcely from Sultan Abdelaziz during the French
onslaughts of 1907 in the Chaouia and of 1908 in eastern Morocco. Eventually,
the *chorfas* of Fes, a class of elite citizens regarded as descending from their
prophet, also found the sultan's brother Abdelhafid more suitable for the
throne. Abdelaziz abandoned the capital, Fes, for another imperial city, Rabat,
and went after his brother's bands in a last gambit to reclaim his power. The
outcome was disastrous. In August 1908, in a battle at the foot of the Atlas
Mountains, Abdelhafid vanquished Abdelaziz. Abdelhafid's reputation surged
even higher when he captured the longtime pretender Bouhmara and his
acolytes. The Rogui, as Bouhmara was called, was paraded in a small cage for
a few weeks, then thrown into the lions' den at Fes's imperial place. The lions,
well fed, would have none of it. The palace's guards finished the Rogui off.
Meanwhile, his followers, after hair-raising torture, were hacked to death in a
public execution. Since news in this modernizing world traveled much faster
than it had before, "The civilized world was upset," recorded the French
ambassador to the sultan's court.

In the end, the stark reality of the European financial and military stranglehold caught up with Abdelhafid too. He borrowed money from the French after conceding to the terms of the Treaty of Algeciras, and wound up short of all the goodwill that his ascent had elicited.

The tribes of Fes's region rose and besieged Fes in the spring of 1911. The French, with troops still concentrated by the Atlantic, would not allow it. Diplomats in Fes feared for their lives; they needed a sultan they knew how to control. Bitter memories of the campaign to stabilize the Chaouia still hovered. General Moinier was sent with a military column to protect the sultan and the Europeans.

The Second Company and the Third Mounted of the First Marching Regiment—troops borrowed from the Second Regiment in Saïda—formed the backbone of this expedition led by Mangin. In the midst of the legionnaires was Rollet, who had operated at the Algerian-Moroccan frontier after Madagascar. He had been promoted to captain for his outstanding service, and then sent to Casablanca, on March 17, as an officer in the Third Mounted. Troopers called him Père Espadrille, for Rollet had a reputation for idiosyncratic footwear that had spread through the entire corps. Actually, he no longer wore the espadrilles, which were against regulations, mindful that his prospects for future promotions would suffer from such flights of fancy.

From Kenitra, north of Rabat, Rollet's legionnaires protected the supply column of thirteen hundred camels that followed the military heading east toward the imperiled Europeans in Fes. After Lalla Ito, where they staunchly defended the camp they had set up for the night against two hundred Moroccans from nearby villages, they encountered more difficult mountain terrain, but little resistance, except for a few skirmishes with Beni M'tir fighters. The Saïss Plain, at the end of which Fes lies, appeared devoid of obstacles. On May 21, 1911, having marched two hundred kilometers, according to their log, the legionnaires arrived in sight of the capital, weapons over their shoulders, advancing between rows of stunned Fassis, the citizens of Fes.

Rejoicing did not last long after the taking of Fes. The day after the legionnaires entered the city, a press dispatch announced that disaster had struck the Sixth Battalion of the First Regiment while on a reconnaissance mission closer to the Algerian border, about three hundred kilometers to the east. The French, keen on establishing safe communications between western Morocco and Algeria, had been slowly securing the small mountain ranges that lie to the west of Oujda. On May 15, a gray foggy day, the Beni Driss cornered the legionnaires of Captain Labordette's company in a narrow valley at Alouana, killing twenty-nine out of a troop of seventy-two. The men fought hard till rescue came, so much so that some ventured to call Alouana the Legion's second Camarón.

Legionnaire Boulic, the veteran of the previous year's campaign in the Upper Guir River, took part in the rescue mission that fetched the survivors and the bodies of the fallen; these were found, predictably, with gory evidence of mistreatment. "After demolishing a few kasbahs with our mountain artillery pieces, which we had taken up the mountain crests with untold misery, we came back with our lugubrious remnants, thrown over the mules." The day after, Boulic's platoon went on another reconnaissance mission and was shot at. The commanders decided to retaliate against a nearby douar, a camel-hair tent camp. Boulic doubted that the mountaineers would have lingered nearby as the legionnaires sipped their morning coffee, in what promised to be a beautiful day, if they had anything to do with the attack. They were pledged to be neutral in the fight against the French invaders. War followed another logic. "In any case, we needed to set an example. We gave it right away and it was terrible!" The two 75mm artillery pieces gunned down these people, and the legionnaires burned down the camp. "The survivors, rage in their hearts, fought with the energy of despair and harassed our rear guard for the length of our return," admitted Boulic. He concluded, "Even if it was necessary, it was still a bit nauseating, this massacre in the pure clarity of sunrise."[1]

The slow penetration of Morocco from within the Fes region and the northern sectors near the Algerian border continued. The Germans watched it with growing irritation. On July 1 the German warship *Panther* dropped anchor in the Bay of Agadir, in southern Morocco, triggering yet another international crisis. The Germans asserted again that they would not let their own commercial and industrial interests in Morocco be threatened; many saw the provocation as yet another signal that France and Germany were heading for catastrophe, yet this time again, the two powers found a negotiated resolution to the crisis. In exchange for a sizable part of the French colonial possessions in the Congo, the Germans agreed to let France take over Morocco as it wished.

On March 30, 1912, the French embrace of Morocco tightened to its logical conclusion. Abdelhafid, whose kingdom crumbled even more under the weight of its debts, made the fateful decision to sign a protectorate treaty that gave France full initiative to "institute in Morocco a new regime, including the administrative, judicial, educational, financial and military resources that the French government will deem useful to introduce in the

Moroccan territory."[2] A few months later, France and Spain would reach an agreement that gave the Spanish control over northern Morocco, with a capital in Tetuan. Tangiers, however, acquired the status of an international zone. From the French point of view, Morocco was theirs.

Fes erupted for a second time, and Lyautey again was called on as the man of the hour. On April 17, 1912, just a few weeks after the French declared Morocco a protectorate of their own, three thousand of Sultan Abdelhafid's elite Askar guard revolted. They resented not only the new political regime and the imminent departure of the sultan to Rabat, the capital designated by the French. They also hated the changes that French military officers who trained them brought to their traditions—carrying a knapsack instead of leaving such a burden to an aide, and a direct allocation of food rather than monetary compensation, which represented a substantial part of their living wages.

The minarets called for *jihad*. The French plenipotentiary minister, Eugène Regnault, was caught unawares. Followed by a mob made up of the city's poorest population, the soldiers found the French who, forgetful of elementary security precautions, had scattered throughout the city to occupy the finest palaces they could find. The Askars killed sixty-three French officers and civilians during two days of riots. Some of the victims were smeared in tar and burned alive. The Jews became the target of killings, rape, and looting, so much so that the sultan opened the gates of his palace to shelter two thousand of them.

When three companies of the Second Regiment arrived from Meknes on the nineteenth, soon followed by General Moinier, who took charge, the fight to retake the city from the mob began in earnest. It took days of combat through the narrow, tortuous streets of Fes to regain control, in true urban guerilla warfare style. Morning offered the staggering spectacle of piles of cadavers by the walls, so determined had the assailants been. Reprisals were terrible too. Under martial law, war tribunals promptly sent the rioters to the firing squad; some were shot on the spot. Moinier called Fes "the criminal city" on the tombs of the dead. Legionnaires carried out the executions. Many blamed the escalation on divergent views between civilian power, represented by Regnault, and the military authority of General Moinier. The French government, at wit's end, made Lyautey resident-general on April 28, 1912, giving him both civilian and military authority.

By the last week of May, and following Moinier's harsh reprisals, not only was the unrest in Fes hardly subjugated, but the revolt now extended to the vast surrounding regions, the fiefdoms of Amazigh tribes. Fifteen thousand of these warriors stood ready to descend from the surrounding mountains to attack the city, take it back from the French who occupied it, and drive them out of the country. While only the poorest had rioted in April, now the entire Fassi population seethed. The noble *chorfas* were said to be negotiating with the Amazigh chiefs to facilitate their attack. Facing them were a mere five thousand soldiers of the garrison. This time, a true leader, the *chorfa* Mohammed El Hadjami, united what could arguably be called a patriotic upsurge.

Lyautey entered Fes at four o'clock on May 23, greeted by the grand vizir, the pasha, and other elements of the city's elites who met him a few kilometers outside the walls in a show of respect. After landing in Casablanca on May 13, Lyautey had sent a telegram to notify the government how critically vulnerable Fes was when armed tribes were camping by the River Sebou. The infantry he needed: "three battalions including two colonials and one of the Legion which I formally request. It's a core troop [*noyau*] here indispensable and there isn't enough; we should be able to take one out of Algeria and replace it with a colonial or alpine battalion."[3] On the way to Fes he had met convoys carrying the wounded and relatives of the deceased from the initial uprising.

The political situation was impossible. Sultan Abdelhafid, whom he met the day after his arrival in a grand audience, wanted to leave the city and ground his teeth in distrust. The French government in Paris, and even some of Lyautey's high officers, offered to quash this city that wanted to keep its "barbarian ways." The ulemas, Fes's highest clergy, were telling Lyautey that it was too late to avert a disaster. "I found myself before an absolute void. People turned away, doors closed, they spat when I walked by."[4]

The night of May 25 to 26, a beautiful warm night, marked the nadir of the siege as far as the French were concerned. Rifle shooting began at ten in the evening. How to defend the centuries-old walls of the city, which were crumbled in many places and could yield before even a modest effort? The French artillery thundered from the two forts that guarded the capital, north and south, but the assailants concentrated their efforts to the east and the north. One Frenchmen who observed the attack from the higher part of the town still found beauty in the spectacle:

> The lower town laid out in tiers at our feet, with its innumerable minarets and superimposed terraces, still and almost asleep, while the moon, in its first quarter, poured its most caressing

light. There is no theater set that is more seductive and enchanting. All around this blue plane, silent and pure, a circle profound and obscure—continually shot through, in the midst of gunfire, by the savage shrieks of the attackers, and the fulgurating streaks of the bombs—created a spectacle grandiose and overwhelming.[5]

Assailants poured into the city, and at the various checkpoints the struggle raged mercilessly, culminating at two o'clock. What if the Moroccans reached the prisons where many of the April mutineers were jailed, the armory of the Sultan's palace, or even the French headquarters and supply house at Dar Dbibagh? At the southeastern kasbah Tamdert (east of Bab Ftouh), which the Moroccans had penetrated, the Giralt legionnaire group coming from Dar Dbibagh encountered such a barrage of fire at five in the morning that it had to call for artillery reinforcement.

Near the Bab Guissa and mosque, guarding the northeast quadrant of the city, the French defenders suffered many casualties. They were fired upon from the Marinids mount, a rocky ledge ranging parallel to the walls, about a hundred yards away. Other attackers, infiltrated through breaches excavated in the fort, took the minaret of the mosque overlooking Bab Guissa and caught the French between two fires. Wary of poisoning even further the relationship with those Fassis who remained neutral, the French command had given orders not to fire on any religious building. Eventually, religious sensitivities were set aside. In the first hours of April 26, Lyautey radioed the news to Paris, and put another urgent request for Legion troops. He learned that the attackers had removed the saintly banners kept in the shrine of Moulay Idriss, a sure token of *baraka*.

On the twenty-eighth of May, the swell of the attack surged again. Sultan Abdelhafid told Lyautey how much he lamented this degradation of his authority; the resident-general then met with the qadi of the town and the ulemas, to hear their own complaints about the tragic consequences of the French protectorate. Frightening news came that the Oulad Djama and Cheraga, tribes who were still pledged to the sultan, had defected to the insurrection. In Paris, the news agency Havas reported that according to diplomatic channels in Madrid, Fes had been taken, and Lyautey, Regnault, and other members of the French mission had been assassinated.

This is when Lyautey, sitting on his rooftop terrace under a bright starry night of North Africa, heard poetry through a cloud of blue cigarette smoke, while the grandiose spectacle of Fes besieged by thousands of Amazigh soldiers unfolded at his feet. When Lyautey woke up the day after, French military forces, including the Legion he relied upon most, had warded off that second attack. The Europeans inside were saved, the French protectorate in Morocco had survived an early demise.

On June 1, Colonel Gouraud dealt the final blow to the insurrection. Leading five battalions of infantry, three artillery sections, and other units, he launched his troops out of Fes in very difficult terrain (the northeast regions of the capital are cut with deep ravines and crests, and the flat surfaces are barred with hedges of prickly pear cactuses). One of the battalions in the main corps included the legionnaires of Giralt, supported by the mounted company with Rollet. The bulk of the *harka*, after several engagements sustained from crest to crest, appeared once Gouraud's troops reached the valley of the Sebou River: "We understood that they had adopted some kind of a formation by tribes, fractions, and *douar*. Standards in bright colors and infantrymen preceded them."[6]

The Amazigh tribes had not encountered the latest in modern weaponry; neither could they fathom how Europeans fought their wars. When the 75mm cannons opened fire at six in the morning, the entire *harka* disbanded. Still, combat lasted two and a half hours. Beyond a last elevation of the terrain, Gouraud's troops found a camp of hundreds of tents, from which El Hadjami had made a precipitated escape, leaving behind papers that proved how much a coordinated assault the last attacks had been, in contrast to the April events. The soldiers appreciated more the couscous and roasted lamb that had been prepared for the return of the victorious fighters. Eventually the entire scene was ignited into a raging inferno.

On June 2, before the old walls of Fes and Bab Guissa, at the foot of the hill from which the tombs of the Maranids guard the city, the troops paraded for the new resident-general. The sultan watched it from his palace, almost a kilometer away to the west. Convinced that Gouraud now had the *baraka*, he insisted that he should be the one escorting him to Rabat.

Lyautey, envisioning years of rule by the side of a sultan amply discredited, contemplated other options. He deployed his talents and charms to win over the elite classes of Fes, and with considerable success—the powerful Fassis, in the end, found themselves wary of the insurgency and the havoc it could bring to their city. Abdelhafid abdicated in favor of his brother Yusef on August 12, 1912, and left Morocco from Casablanca with a one-million-franc check that Lyautey handed him while they both stood on one of those *barcasses*, the boats that braved Morocco's Atlantic swell.

The diplomat and memorialist Charles de Baupoil, Count of Saint-Aulaire, together on the boat with Lyautey and Abdelhafid, accompanied the sultan onto a French cruiser bound for Tangiers—the ship, the *Du Chayla*, had bombed Casablanca four years earlier—and handed the illustrious passenger to the captain. "The commander of the boat, an old seafarer, knew little about courtly manners, including those at the [Moroccan] court," recalled Saint-Aulaire of those last moments with the monarch. "He asked me, pointing at the sultan who lay like a rag on a mattress [he was sea-sick]: Do I need to throw him overboard or offer him some champagne?" To which Saint-Aulaire politely replied, "Offer him some champagne."[7]

The siege of Fes might have been over, the nearest dangers eliminated, but the task of regaining control of the entire region was far from accomplished. The summer months of 1912 saw Gouraud, still with the mounted legionnaires of Rollet, furiously engaged in a contest for the region between the mountains that buttress the Rif and Middle Atlas ranges. On July 7 they defeated El Hadjami, at Moulay Bouchta, in spite of their "extraordinarily fierce" resistance.

Returned near Fes, Rollet's men set out to build a permanent camp at a location named Dar Marhes; it would remain the home of the Foreign Legion until Morocco's independence from the French in 1956. This was hardly their only labor as far as infrastructure was concerned. They redesigned the strategic road between Fes and the Atlantic, which Moinier had hastily laid out in 1911, and dotted it with better forts. The works, which stretched over eighty kilometers, were often interrupted to join other troops engaged in fighting, and they lasted a year and half, necessitating laying twelve bridges and many other complex constructions. Rollet and his team thus laid the first element of the infrastructure that the French colonization bequeathed to Morocco.

Lyautey, considering these achievements both military and infrastructural, easily understood that even with ample military resources, including the small but no less vital contingents of legionnaires, his conquest was far from fully assured. In Paris, experts had warned from the beginning of the occupation that it would take a hundred thousand men and thirty years of efforts to subdue the region. "One must be aware of the sudden nature and the violence of the movements that blow up in Morocco. These are true groundswells. Let us recall April 17, 1912," Lyautey chillingly wrote a correspondent of that day, as he remembered the bloody days of Fes.[8] The French in Morocco and those in their own country were less traumatized by the cascade of events since the protectorate treaty had been extracted. What would have happened if the entire country had risen to the call of *jihad*?

The dreaded torrent of resistance first surged in southern Morocco. Since May of 1912, a new charismatic leader named Ahmed El Hiba preached holy war beyond the High Atlas, where he incarnated the religious and patriotic leadership that Moroccans desperately wanted to see: "We don't know in what name we should pray, there is no more sultan," went the complaint.[9] Powerful warlords such as Thami El Glaoui had ruled over southern Morocco, despoiling its population; there was little that the last sultans could have done against this state of affairs, given their own weakness. Thus, Ahmed El Hiba also represented hopes for justice and welfare. Immense crowds followed this Mahdi, a "redeemer," on a wave of popular exultation and religious fervor, many believing he could actually achieve miracles. The man showed all the signs of a privileged holder of the mystical blessing. He crossed the Atlas and, once proclaimed sultan by the ulemas of Marrakech, took the city on August 17, 1912. Eight Frenchmen in the city were taken hostage.

"Allez-y carrément," (Go for it squarely), ordered Lyautey in his telegram to Colonel Mangin.[10] A heavy column of five thousand men moved from Casablanca toward Marrakech in early September while legionnaires remained in the north. At the village of Sidi Bou Othman, as the sun rose on the sixth of September, the French army met the forces of El Hiba. When the Hibist troops and crowds advanced on a wide front, holding about a thousand rifles, they met the fire of twelve 75mm field guns, eight machine guns, and twelve hundred rifles. One projectile killed seven men at once. A melenite bomb disintegrated a horseman. Only his legs, booted in red leather, were found. The French cavalry's four hundred horsemen then slashed its way through the remaining multitude. By nine o'clock, at least two thousand Moroccans lay on the ground. Some of the wretched had hurled themselves before the guns, chanting the name of their god.

Mangin's men, exhausted, had Marrakech high on their mind. A smaller detachment reached the city on the seventh to consolidate the victory at Sidi Bou Othman. By the time they arrived, the qaids (chiefs) had regained control. El Hiba fled back across the Atlas, his pronouncements that God would turn French shells into watermelons before his army was ridiculed.[11] One French officer exulted, "Marrakech! The city that the blue men conquered and lost! The famous capital of their ancestors, the Berber Almoravids and Almohads of Yusef ben Tachefine and of the black sultan El Mansour! The Christians who, in those long-gone days, formed their militias, are today the masters. What a destiny for that Berber people that commanded an empire of which Spain and Algeria were the jewels!"[12]

Lyautey arrived in October to decorate Mangin, salute the troops, and own the city. His automobile was the first ever to reach Marrakech; it came equipped with a machine gun. Madame Lyautey, who landed in Morocco in October, abstained from traveling to regions where trouble could still break out.

The legendary capital of Morocco's South stunned Lyautey with its sandy pink crenellated walls, gleaming on the backdrop of its rich palm grove and the Atlas Mountains' high summits. Peeking behind those walls, the shiny lines of green-tiled-roofs and the square minarets of the mosques, with, first among these, the elegant Koutoubia minaret, the landmark and pride of the city. In contrast to Fes, Marrakech feels rather airy and generous, it rewards more readily with its central, wide-open public square named Jamaa el Fna. Emerging from the maze of Marrakech's souks, leaving the bounty of Morocco and Africa piled high in boutiques—for Marrakech is the gateway to the High Atlas and beyond, the destination since time immemorial of caravans coming from as far as Timbuktu, Senegal, and the Sudan—the French conquerors stumbled onto a wide-open scene of snake charmers, Gnaoua musicians, storytellers, fortune-tellers, and amusers, a spectacle best seen at sunset, when the sun fires up the metal globe of the Koutoubia.

After months of continuing crisis in Morocco, Lyautey still faced daunting prospects. The new resident-general exercised "protective" authority on behalf of Sultan Moulay Yusef, a proposition that elicited deep hostility in the Moroccans, regardless of the sultan's political credit. In a long letter to his friend Albert de Mun, written from a "small pleasure pavilion surrounded by orange, pomegranates, olive trees, and cypresses," Lyautey explained how he conceived of the protectorate, that is, the principles that informed his military and political philosophy in Morocco.

Lyautey had consistently argued since his arrival that colonial conquest had to rely on the "oil slick" method he had practiced with Gallieni in Indochina and Madagascar. Political action went hand in hand with measured military gestures. The events of 1912 at Fes showed that Moinier's march onto Fes with a heavy column, the year before, had been a waste of time and resources. "It is essential that Force manifest itself from the beginning under two inseparable forms: Force and Interest," maintained Lyautey.[13] But antagonizing populations with massacres was poor politics, he also argued. Indirect rule, in the vein of what the British had exercised in India and Egypt, held much more promise. With help from the French, the Moroccans would be able to police themselves, and emerge from times the occupiers invariably described as rife with lawlessness and fanaticism.

Sultan Moulay Yusef, by the terms of the protectorate, remained the sovereign in his kingdom, and Lyautey carefully staged the appearance of this power, based on the sultan's prerogatives as imam and caliph of the believers in Morocco. Prayer was said in the sultan's name at the mosque. The English journalist Walter Harris had noted that before abdicating, Abdelhafid had "destroyed the sacred emblems of the Sultanate of Morocco—for he realized that he was the last independent sovereign of that country. He burned the crimson parasol which on occasions of State had been borne over his head."[14] Under Lyautey the parasol, the palanquin, and other elaborate rituals of the Moroccan court returned to manifest sovereignty.[15] Barely six months after the protectorate was declared, Lyautey declared Sultan Moulay Yusef his "most successful realization":

> I gave him back his traditional allure and his apparent integrity. I carefully put away all the European promiscuities, the cars, and the champagne dinners. I surrounded him with old-fashioned Moroccans. His temperament, that of a good Muslim and a decent man, did the rest. He restored the great Friday prayer with the age-old ceremonies. He celebrated the holiday of Aïd Seghir with a pomp and a respect for tradition unknown since Moulay Hassan.[16]

Since there could be no staging of the sultan's power without strong religious institutions, and a lived reality of religion and tradition in Morocco, mosques remained closed to non-Muslims under Lyautey's order. Religious brotherhoods were reopened, while Christian missionaries were banned. All matters pertaining to Islamic law, at least between Moroccans, remained the prerogative of the sultan. Given how recent events had demonstrated the need for a capital less exposed to insurrection, Lyautey transferred the seat of government to Rabat, one of the four sacred imperial towns of the kingdom. Last but not least, Morocco's cultural heritage was placed under strict protective measures:

> Piercing of walls, transformation of city gates, enlargement of streets, alignment works, even those works that are deemed of immediate necessity, works to embellish squares, gardens, to provide public lighting, and in general anything that is susceptible to modify the character of indigenous towns, can only be undertaken after early submission to the Beaux-Arts services at the Résidence Générale.[17]

The practical needs of a colonial empire could hardly be met inside the medinas, however. French architects went to their drawing boards to imagine new modern cities for Morocco. These modern cities rose next to the ancient medinas, producing these twin towns that are familiar to visitors in Morocco nowadays.

Politics, of course, remained just that. Lyautey, while he enshrined Morocco in a traditionalist vision, nominated the sultan's ministers and the high-level personnel. Those sovereign decrees, the *dahirs*, were prepared by the residence and submitted for approval by Yusef. The residence controlled the police, the armies, the diplomacy. Judicial and fiscal reforms that were the order of the day, and any legal matters pertaining to Europeans, became the prerogative of the residence. Already, the resident-general and his advisers spent days laying out plans for economic exploitation and development. Thus emerged a modern Morocco designed to enrich France.

Ironically, Lyautey's religious and monarchist inclinations lent credibility to the performance. Moroccans, speaking of French politicians, lamented, "How could they respect our sultan since they are republicans, and how could they respect our religion if they don't even respect theirs?"[18] Lyautey, however, convinced many that he respected the sovereignty of the sultan in earnest. While the idea of kingship had become alien to some European politicians, especially in the France of the Third Republic, Lyautey had long believed in the sacred, spiritual dimension of ancient monarchies; he understood the emotions of a subject who stands before his king or his queen. Thus he made a point of holding the sultan's stirrup when, during state ceremonies, Moulay Yusef mounted his horse.

No wonder that the resident-general, as the year passed, found supporters amongst the Moroccans, who appreciated his protection of Islam. On February 11, 1923, Lyautey fell sick while visiting Oujda. Transported immediately to Fes, his condition worsened and he hovered between life and death for ten days. Among those who did not give up hope were many Moroccans themselves. On February 23 the municipal council and the corporations gathered in the courtyard of his palace, by his room, to recite a great prayer. They asked that he visit the *zawiya* (shrine) of Moulay Idriss as soon as he was healed. Lyautey recovered, but declined to make a visit to the *zawiya* his priority. Explaining this to a friend, he said, "I consented, but I had to tell them that I would first stop at a Catholic church, which they perfectly understood and accepted. What a chic race next to our jerks."[19]

CHAPTER 11

Principles of War

The year 1914 began with a triumph, another demonstration of Lyautey's *baraka*. Legion troops from Morocco and Algeria joined in the town of Taza, one hundred and twenty kilometers east of Fes, establishing the long-awaited direct land connection between the two French colonies. From Tunisia to the Atlantic, North Africa was a continuous segment of the empire. The symbolic gesture required a tremendous effort from the troops. Securing the sector from Algeria to Taza was one year in the making under the orders of General Maurice Baumgarten. He commanded men from the First Regiment. To the west, Henri Gouraud left Fes on April 27 with soldiers from the Second Regiment, including Rollet's Third Mounted Company. Before reaching Taza, he encountered frightful resistance from the Tsoul tribes. Finally, on May 16, after a last attempt by the Moroccans to stop the French advance, Legionnaire Ehrhart could boast in his fine memoir, "Fanfare ahead playing the march of the Legion, we entered the kasbah, weapon on our shoulder, bayonet at the end of the barrel."

A military band sent from Sidi Bel Abbès played even louder the following day for a review of the troops under the eye of Lyautey, who had just arrived. There floated the flag of the Legion's First Regiment, especially delivered by airplane for the occasion. Ehrhart found the spectacle unforgettable:

> I sat at the top of the climb that leads to Taza. A light, pink cloud of dust stirred up by the horses' hoofs floated. The golden rays of a radiant sun ran across and through this cloud, like a mirage, I saw this imperial cohort: ahead, General Lyautey, followed by Generals Gouraud and Baumgarten. The golden leaves on their

kepis shimmered in the sun, creating an aura reminiscent of the
Thousand and One Nights.[1]

The two columns amounted to thirteen battalions, eight squadrons, and
seven pieces of artillery. The connection also took place in the air when
airplanes coming both from western and eastern Morocco flew over the
parade. Lyautey, ever the realist, recognized that the junction remained
purely military, and that it would take much more time before civilian travel
could be secured. On both sides of this "corridor" of Taza, the mountains of
the Rif and the Middle Atlas harbored determined enemies. Still, Lyautey let
slip rare words of imperial hubris from Taza: "Let us hope that the route
between the Atlantic and Carthage, which the Romans took for a moment
in history, will be reopened to civilization."[2]

Historical references to antiquity, no matter how seductive, were not
part of modern France's vocabulary. What the public needed was visual
communication, and the *Jonction de Taza* became the subject of a wide
campaign by means of postcards. Images of legionnaires standing proudly
before the crumbling walls of the city circulated. Ever since the conquest of
Morocco had begun, the public was asking for more and more information
about the idiosyncratic legionnaires of the French army. Covers of *Le Petit
Journal* proposed images of their combats, calling them "*troupes d'élite.*" In
1912, Georges d'Esparbès had published a new edition of a seminal book,
Les Mystères de la légion étrangère, in which he captured the particular ethos
of the legionnaire, including the challenges of the *cafard*. Nice drawings
enhanced a work that did much to solidify and, to a certain extent, create the
reputation of the corps beyond military circles.

By the beginning of July, the route that linked Morocco and Algeria
seemed calm enough. Legionnaire Ehrhart asked for a thirty-day leave to
travel to France for his engagement. He left carrying with him the flag of the
First Regiment, to get it embroidered at Sidi Bel Abbès with the letters
MAROC. "Heavy burden and huge responsibility," he sighed.

Ehrhart reached Oujda, however, to hear the stunning news that mobi-
lization for war had been declared: Forget the leave, return to the regiment.
"We crossed trains of troops, Zouaves, Skirmishers, and artillerymen who
were leaving for France."[3]

"Evacuate Morocco save for a few troops." The order that came on July 27,
1914, was undoubtedly the most challenging that Lyautey ever received. The

matter was simple for the military leadership in Paris: "The fate of Morocco shall be determined in Lorraine," that is, on the perennial theater to the east where French and German armies had collided for centuries. Lyautey had to send all his troops back to Europe, keeping just the necessary force to hold on to the major Atlantic ports.

Many of the legionnaires present in Morocco and Algeria before the war went to France, en route for remarkable exploits. Rollet had left Africa before war was formally declared to take a leave in France. He remained there to serve in and later lead the famed Marching Regiment of the Foreign Legion, constituted a year into the war, and in which the legionnaires sent from Morocco fought. They fought next to indigenous troops such as Moroccans and Senegalese who were previously enrolled in the colonial war theaters. Up to twenty-five thousand North Africans from the French colonies died in Europe during the conflict, which is twice as many victims as those counted in the ranks of Europeans from Algeria.[4]

Westerners who had little interest in fighting on behalf of French colonial imperialism joined the ranks of the Legion in Europe for the sake of the war effort, including a considerable number of Americans, such as the songwriter Cole Porter and the poet Alan Seeger; Seeger is also remembered for the poem "I Have a Rendezvous with Death," written based on his experience in the Legion. The Legion distinguished itself along the frontline in northeastern France, at great cost in human life, but it also found the more familiar backdrop of foreign lands in the Dardanelles Narrows, when Turkey entered the war against the Allies in the Spring of 1915.

Lyautey's *coup de génie*, meanwhile, was to take considerable liberty with the evacuation orders from the Chief-of-Staff's Office in Paris. The resident-general understood that abandoning the front around the Middle Atlas would irremediably ruin his accomplishments: Moroccans would waste no time in reclaiming their country. Lyautey positioned the few troops he had left at that very vanguard of the colonial front, in Boudenib, Taza, and Kenitra, wagering that the ports and plain regions would remain quiet and hardly need the bulk of the forces. The cities by the sea did remain quiet throughout the war. Such were the effects of what Lyautey called his "strategy of the lobster," leaving the emptied shell of his original military setup.

More than ever, the troops from the Legion formed an essential component of the contingents that remained. In exchange for sending to Europe the Moroccan fighters loyal to the sultan, Lyautey received Algerians and Senegalese who needed additional training, or metropolitan troops unlikely to last very long under the relentless North African sun.

What I need to operate in this rough country, with this heat, it's not white battalions made of fragile children, the stuff of hospitals, I have plenty of that and the acceptable proportion has already been reached. What I would need are battalions of strapping lads, legionnaires, Skirmishers, and black men.[5]

The influx of unreliable recruits meant the legionnaires had to be the perennial backbone of his scheme, with three battalions from the First Regiment based in Taza, and two battalions from the Second in Meknes; there were in addition three mounted companies in Boudenib and Fes. Of twenty thousand troops in Morocco, about a quarter were legionnaires. Since 1911 the proportion of indigenous elements in the Armée d'Afrique had grown remarkably, and this is why so many could be sent to fight in Europe when war was declared. The Legion, besides their superior training, provided the French with a safeguard against the treachery that they always feared in nonwhite troops. Which is ironic, given that in those particular circumstances, the Germans who formed the core of the Legion could not be sent to the European front and were themselves susceptible of less than stellar loyalty. True to their polyvalent capacities and tested mettle under fire, the remaining legionnaires built infrastructure, waiting to protect the mixed units that the Moroccans, emboldened by the weakening of the defense system, would soon attack.

Lyautey's hold on Morocco, even under the most optimistic assessment, remained considerably weakened. He had lost some of his favorite collaborators to the French front, the Gourauds and the Brulards that made up his *zawiya* of the faithful. Yet, ever the showman, he launched highly visible works of infrastructure to shore up public support for the colony and give the appearance of business as usual. Development at the harbor of Casablanca continued. The long wharf extended into the Atlantic, making the dreaded *barcasses* unnecessary, while a three-thousand-square-foot hangar, carriages on rails, and cranes equipped the port facilities.

Meanwhile, a new railway for passengers and merchandise connected Marrakech, Casablanca, Meknes, and Fes. Other works, perhaps less visible but of no less strategic importance, began as well. An extension of the narrow-gauge railway line from Taza to Fes and an airfield in Taza appeared. In the cities, water works, sewage systems, and road works improved sanitary conditions. Finally, in 1915, Lyautey organized a trade fair to showcase what import and export could bring to the kingdom. In his inauguration speech, he praised Sultan Moulay Yusef, certifying that under his watch ranks and hierarchies should "be kept and respected, that people and things remain to their ancient places, that those who are the natural chiefs command, and that the others obey."[6] All this cost a fortune, of course, and more than a few in Paris watched this effervescence, while the fatherland was at war, with bewilderment.

It did not escape the Germans that under the semblance of colonial peace and prosperity, Lyautey's Morocco was highly vulnerable. The loyalty of their brethren serving in the Legion might be, as it had been in the lead-up to the war, less than assured. Ehrhart, with his company deployed to the east, narrates how one day some German legionnaires contacted Moroccan dissidents, offering to let them in the fort where he served. One of those Germans then had a change of heart, and he informed his superiors of the plot. That night, Ehrhart and his comrades' task was to offer an appropriate reception for the intruders. They waited in hiding.

> When the Moroccans showed up, hundreds of them, it was midnight. They found the entrance door open, and German legionnaires to welcome them. They went through the networks of barbed wire, but when they were engaged, a flare went up in the moonless sky and the dance began. The wretched ones, where were they stuck? Guns, machine guns, the 75mm cannons, fire crackled from everywhere, and then, the bayonets. By daytime, more than two hundred cadavers were found in the wire and around the camp. The Seventh Company under the orders of Captain Kappler had had a good time. They sent the guilty Germans to the war tribunal, never to be seen again.[7]

Later attempts at shifting the loyalty of German-born legionnaires were successful, however, because they received support and money from the agencies that had operated in Spanish Morocco, all along the Rif mountain range and the Mediterranean coast, before the war. Cases of desertion multiplied, so much so that it became impossible to position legionnaire companies near the northern border. Some even went to the Moroccan enemy, fought against the French, and eventually blended into the population. Legionnaire Boulic, many years later, noted the remains of a stone house in the Amazigh hinterland that, given its features, could only have been built by European deserters.

Another German means to undermine the French was to foment and support revolt in the Moroccan population. "Rise, kill all the Frenchmen, especially the greatest enemy of Islam, General Lyautey—may God curse him! Your salvation will be obvious the day of his assassination," exhorted a German leaflet found in Larache, on the Northern Atlantic coast.[8] The Emir Abdelmalek—no less than a descendant of the Abdelkader who had challenged the French in Algeria—operated along the north side of the Taza corridor with an army of one thousand tribesmen. The French, when they captured their positions, found tools and radio equipment that unequivocally betrayed German backing—Abdelmalek's campaign collapsed when he lost his European support.

To the south, beyond the High Atlas in the Souss River Valley, German action was even bolder. Still relying of the powerful qaids of the region, Lyautey's man there was the pasha of Taroudant, Haida ou Mouis. The pasha faced remnants of El Hiba's army led by the chief Nadjem, while El Hiba remained at large farther south. German submarines delivered weapons to the dissidents, requiring French warships to patrol the coast incessantly, particularly toward the end of 1916. When Haida ou Mouis died, Lyautey had no choice but to send his troops in pursuit of El Hiba. Operations lasted well into the year 1917, until the leader of the great holy war, the man who had seized Marrakech in 1912 and almost terminated the newly established protectorate, died of natural causes.

The hardest blow sustained by the French did not come from resistance buttressed by the Germans but from the hardy Zayanes people, who dwelled in the center of the Middle Atlas slopes. Their leader, the qaid Mooha ou Hammou, was, by French own admission, a warrior they could only have respect for, and most likely the greatest they had to reckon with in Morocco. Intrepid, with a keen sense of justice and an aura of prestige, he was exactly the kind of man who could give some structure to the otherwise conflict-ridden tribes of the Middle Atlas. He also lived quite grandly as the lord that he was, traveling with his harem and imposing retinue, but at the same time he ate simply and slept in the most restricted comfort if the needs of his campaigns demanded it. In other words, he was the quintessential charismatic leader.

Led by this chief, the Zayanes held a central region that blocked direct passage from Fes to Taza and Marrakech, and even the old sultan trail along which caravans from sub-Saharan Africa passed over the Atlas, to bring their goods from the Tafilalet to the capital. The stakes were crucial indeed. Already they had inflicted a stinging blow to Charles Mangin at the battle of El Ksiba, in June 1913. After defying the efforts of French intelligence officers to separate them into factions and pit them against one another—thereby opting, thought Lyautey, for "the freedom of chaos"—the Zayanes attacked Khenifra, their capital city, which the French had controlled since June. The French response was so energetic this time that the Zayanes retreated to the mountains.

Success seemed close at hand until one officer, Colonel René Laverdure, pushed his luck too far. Having heard of the presence of a large *harka* at El Seghrouchen, he launched his mobile group from Khenifra. The attack was a success, but on his return on November 13, at El Herri, the column suffered a devastating counterattack that left more than six hundred men dead, including Laverdure. Lyautey could hardly put a brave face on the stunning losses:

> I do not believe there is such an example of the destruction of such an important force, of the disappearance of all of its officers (save for a few wounded who had been brought back at the beginning), of the loss of such supplies and such trophies, in our colonial history.[9]

This defeat highlighted the crucial dilemma faced by the French military higher officers who served in Morocco: They hardly had any opportunities to distinguish themselves while their colleagues fought on the German front. The nature of the colonial battle prohibited the kind of bravura that earned an officer a medal. One of Lyautey's most pressing preoccupations became the reckless disobedience of what he called the "*faiseurs de coups*," the chiefs who acted recklessly to earn a medal.

Lyautey, his military commanders, and the legionnaires had met the foe that would poison their lives for many years to come. Securing the plains where a majority Arab population lived a sedentary life had been relatively easy after the Chaouia campaign. But edging the coastal plains of the Chaouia and the Gharb, or framing the transversal Saïss conduit where Meknes and Fes sit, rose natural fortresses of mountains where the Imazighen who had attacked Fes cultivated an indomitable tradition.

The Imazighen were seminomadic people who often lived in tent encampments. The difference with the plains and city dwellers was not only linguistic and cultural, but political as well. Never had the sultan and his government, the Makhzen, been able to dominate them. The French who studied Morocco in colonial times neatly discerned two parts in the political topography of Morocco, the *bled el-Makhzen*, meaning the regions that remained under the authority of the sultan and his state, and the *bled el-Siba*, the regions where that power was less assured, in constant need of affirmation. This division was perceived as making the country a place rife with anarchy and needing Western pacification, but what constituted political authority eluded the French. Their military outposts became bases from which anthropologists could study the tribal mosaic of Morocco, its local saints, lineages, languages, and customs to better serve colonization. In any case, much Amazigh land was definitely the *bled el-Siba*, and its people surely were less keen on accepting the presence of the French in their land.

The Imazighen cultivated the art of war with dexterity and passion, partly because they often fought among themselves. A boy became an adolescent when he began to ride a horse, and an adolescent became a man when he bonded in horsemanship exercises, to learn how to raid sheep herds and fight. Their warrior culture elicited sober admiration, but also fear from the French. The Imazighen were, by all accounts, very brave.

French tacticians considered that one tribesman was worth many European-trained soldiers. First, the Amazigh traveled light, on foot, armed with his rifle, a knife, and a light satchel with a piece of bread, and moved about swiftly in the theaters of the Atlas, down its ravines and up its rocky outcrops. He knew the terrain perfectly. Hence Imazighen created the illusion that hordes were attacking, when there were just a few of them. They were fluid and fast enough to move about and appear on all sides of an ambush scene. Their tactics and codes of warfare appeared disconcerting. In the mountains, naturally, and given the superiority of the French armament, harassing the troops ("like a swarm of elusive wasps") and laying ambushes made the most sense for them.[10] They saw nothing dishonorable in withdrawing before a French party if an offensive did not turn out their way. They would scatter back to encampments, to reappear when French vigilance had let its guards down and a better occasion presented itself. Then, they excelled at finding the weakest elements in a withdrawing party. Confusion ensued, oftentimes followed by man-to-man struggle, knife against clumsy, heavy bayonet, where the European soldier was at another disadvantage.

Artillery fire, which was so central to the French power, could do little in that kind of terrain, and so the infantry remained central to the campaign. Amazigh people loved the *barud*, the brawl, where all senses are awakened and sensations are heightened. The Zayanes, as Lyautey's troops discovered to their bitter discontent, were emblematic of this warlike culture.

A colonial soldier always kept that last bullet, should he have the misfortune of finding himself at the mercy of his enemy. On the other hand, the Amazigh warrior who lay wounded did not accept help. Many a French soldier was killed by a wounded adversary as he tried to take him as a prisoner. A glorious death was a much better outcome than a life saved in the dishonor of defeat. A Legion officer put it bluntly: "We do not, then, make a practice of taking prisoners or of aiding the wounded, unless we are certain that they are unarmed."[11] The French lost their temper often. In March 1913, a scandal erupted when the Parisian newspaper *L'Humanité* published the pictures of severed heads, ghoulish trophies that the troops of Colonel Reibell had exacted as he fought tribes south of Meknes.

Once war was declared, the tribal council designated a leader, the *amghar*, who from then on would exert authority—if a charismatic chief such as Mouha ou Hammou had not already rallied the people. The outcome would depend on the warriors' skills, but mostly on what God's will decreed. Religious belief permeated every moment of the fight, which also explained why Amazigh fighters could easily seek a peace settlement and join the French in their fight against their brethren if they understood that, for the moment, that was God's will. They had to protect their own, and would readily seize an opportunity to switch their allegiances again.

Before this fascinating Amazigh enemy, Lyautey held on. He cordoned off the Zayanes in their mountains, knowing that traditionally they came to live in the plains when winter came. He could only hope that they would find the bitter months in the high altitudes too hard to bear. Meanwhile, the *Patron* crisscrossed Morocco in his big car equipped with a machine gun and loaded with enormous leather briefcases containing all the files needed to govern, and a typewriter. Lyautey tirelessly supervised his forces, or worked as the "salesman" of the protectorate, as he put it himself. As with many leaders of his kind, sleep came to him easily, and he did not need much of it anyway. Saint-Aulaire explains how, on their trips, Lyautey would rest his head on his shoulder and take a ten-minute nap, "to recharge his battery," oblivious of the car's jolts, or the dust. At halt, he lived in a lavish tent in the Arab style, topped with the golden globe emblem of the sultan's power, hosting guests draped in a black burnous with golden embroideries. In Rabat, Madame Lyautey performed admirably in her role of Morocco's first lady, while she remained busy setting up French health care in Morocco.

Lyautey bounced around Morocco trails and newly traced highways until a telegram written in clipped language arrived on December 10, 1916, from the Council of Minister's president, Aristide Briand: "In the eventuality of your being offered War Ministry under my presidency, could you accept without disadvantage to Morocco?"[12]

In the midst of an endless, disastrous war, having exhausted its resources in leadership, France considered turning to the veteran colonialist. The minister of war position had stayed empty since the death of its last occupant, who, ironically, was none other than Joseph Gallieni, the master in colonial philosophy of Lyautey's old days in Indochina and Madagascar. Public opinion, in an interesting turn, had come to see the ardent colonialist as the kind of man who could achieve his goals, a man who made decisions and acted.

In many ways, this was the kind of message that Lyautey had waited for all his life. At last, there was the opportunity to reverse what he saw as the inexorable decline of France. Those hapless politicians who squabbled in parliament, pretending to fight for progressive causes when all their efforts aimed at satisfying their narrow, selfish interests—these were the traitors who were directly responsible for the slaughter of France's youth at the front. He accepted the appointment, no matter how fragile and unsettled the situation remained in Morocco.

His trusted associate, Henri Gouraud, took charge upon Lyautey's anticipated leave. Certainly, there were many in France who expressed discomfort at the thought of elevating to head the Ministry of War a man who, as resident-general, united both military and civilian rule in what seemed like a combination verging on dictatorship. This suspicion might explain why Lyautey, having not left Morocco yet, learned that two important sections of his ministry had been removed from his portfolio. The War Committee was formed and given high prerogatives in the conduct of the war in Europe. This council included General Robert Nivelle, who ruled on war strategy. In other words, Lyautey's power and influence had been considerably diluted. Logistics were to be much more central to his responsibilities than he had bargained for.

Disappointed but still energized, Lyautey left on a submarine, landed at Marseilles, and arrived in Paris on December 22. Inès soon joined him. Quickly, his suspicions were confirmed: What the government wanted amounted to a political cover for the stunning casualties and poor leadership. A daily life of committee meetings, council meetings, and endless commissions before the Chamber of Deputies began—just what he abhorred. On February 1, he learned that Nivelle had devised a new plan to reverse the Allies' misfortunes against the Germans. He voiced his strong reservations at the initiative, while providing as much organizational support as he could. The Nivelle offensive—in which Legion troops of the Marching Regiment fought—is remembered as one of the most disastrous moves of the French during the war. At the battle of the Chemin des Dames alone, began on April 16, two hundred seventy-five thousand soldiers lost their lives. Nivelle resigned in disgrace, and a rising general, Philippe Pétain, was promoted to commander-in-chief of the French army.

Lyautey was not in France to live this catastrophe from up-close. His stint as minister of war had already ended in scandal. For a long time, the

French military leadership had known that some members at the Chamber of Deputies traded secret information to the enemy. On March 14, before a secret parliamentary committee, Lyautey refused to give full details on a new initiative, the reorganization of the French forces' aviation. His adversaries needed no more to accuse him of disdain toward the elected representative of the people. A verbal brawl erupted. Lyautey left the room wounded, his career as a politician who wanted to put France on a new path prematurely behind him. He handed in his resignation. The following day, supporters such as Eugène Etienne and Charles Jonnart paid him visits, trying to move him to reconsider his resignation, but to no avail. After two months spent at a spa town in France to soothe a strained liver—the consequence, most likely, of a life spent weathering the attacks of tropical diseases—he returned to Morocco as resident-general. Madame Lyautey, who led the Hôpital Complémentaire du Val-de-Grâce, returned to Morocco as well.

Morale improved when two generals, Joseph Poeymirau and Paul Doury, met in an area between the Middle and the High Atlas ranges, near what is now the town of Midelt, on June 6. Poeymirau's soldiers, including legionnaires from Meknes, had spent months establishing a French presence around the upper valley of the Moulouya River. Doury, also with legionnaires from Boudenib, had patrolled Atlas regions where no European had ever set foot. Lyautey could not contain his euphoria after the painful months spent in Paris:

> There is, certainly, the biggest step in Morocco since the meeting of the armies at Taza . . . as far as I am concerned, I swim in joy. I feel as if I had lived a four-month-long bad dream, as if I had lived a nightmare and, still, I wake up at night in anguish, thinking that I am again at a parliamentary commission.[13]

The French now controlled the age-old route taken by caravans traveling from the Tafilalet to the capital and Meknes. French military crews immediately set to work creating passable roads for an army. This way, Lyautey drove a wedge in the Middle Atlas, between the Zayanes to the left and the other, no less fierce, tribes of the mountains to the right, south of Taza—this sector became known, in military parlance, as the Tache de Taza, the "Taza Stain" on the military map where the rebels held out. The meeting of the armies at Taza and effective security security for the major roadways between Morocco and Algeria, both the Taza corridor and the old imperial path across the Atlas, shifted the French military center of gravity from Boudenib to Meknes as well. Boudenib might have been closer to the perennial pocket of resistance to the

French in the desert, but the bulk of the forces was by now concentrated in Morocco, and Lyautey had no intention of requesting support from Algeria. Morocco was his bailiwick. To show how much mobility he had acquired, he traveled to review Poeymirau's and Doury's troops, a combined force of seven thousand men.

Proof of the challenges to come in the mountains around Taza was given on July 8. Near Skoura, in a treacherous mountain pass and on a day when the sirocco made the use of artillery and machine guns impossible, the Aït Seghrouchen warriors killed more than one hundred soldiers from Taza and Fes troops that Poeymirau had led. The severe defeat might have turned to complete catastrophe had not the legionnaires of the Sixth Battalion of the Second Regiment been present to protect the other units during the retreat. Fifteen thousand cartridges later, "The two quarts of wine distributed in the evening were much appreciated," noted the company's *journal de marche*, its daily log.[14]

Concerning that nest of independence and rebelliousness, the Tafilalet, the outcomes were sorely mixed for the French forces. Colonel Doury, after the Middle Atlas passage was secured, moved to occupy a position in the oasis, in December 1917. He argued that the sultan's representative needed protection; there might have been yet more German foul play. Among the tribes, chiefly the Aït Atta, this move was nothing less than an attack. Doury's soldiers, including legionnaires from the Second Mounted Company, took on the resistance at Gaouz on August 9, 1918. If we believe the company's log, the encounter unquestionably merited distinction. "Under Captain Timm's vigorous impulse, the company threw itself with many bayonet charges, to save units that were fighting with an enemy ten times superior in number and animated with fanatical energy."[15] But by October, Lyautey realized that this front was a hornet's nest from which he needed to extract his companies.

On November 11, 1918, the Allies and Germany signed the Armistice that ended the Great War. For the legionnaires stationed in North Africa, of all stripes and nationalities, who knows what painful personal news had come during these four years. Lyautey lamented his own losses, both human and material. The husband of a niece he loved very much was killed on the field. The Germans who invaded the parts of Lorraine that had remained French after 1870—and where Lyautey's ancestral home was, in Crevic— carried out orders to douse the house with gas and set it on fire. The loss was overwhelming, given how all his personal archives and heirlooms went up in flames. "I am a living mummy," he wrote in the aftermath.

CHAPTER 12

A Quest for Redemption

P roud of its exploits in Morocco and in France during the Great War, the Foreign Legion regrouped in North Africa. A new organization plan renamed and redistributed the troops. The First Foreign Regiment stayed in Sidi Bel Abbès. The Second Regiment left Saïda in Algeria for Meknes, while the Marching Regiment, which had served in Europe, became the Third Foreign Infantry Regiment based in Fes. Lastly, the troops that had remained in Morocco formed the Fourth Foreign Infantry Regiment in Marrakech. A new cavalry regiment took its quarters in Tunisia. More than ever, the Foreign Legion served France throughout the Maghreb, and especially in Morocco.

Lyautey and his military officers, through the reconfiguration, faced a crisis. The Legion was in dire need of new recruits, hundreds of men. Many of the soldiers who had enlisted for the war in Europe had not reenlisted; for many, fighting for a nation in Europe appeared—rightly so—completely different from enlisting for service in the Armée d'Afrique. Other related factors contributed to the situation. Millions of civilians had died in France, and the remaining population experienced aversion to more fighting. "One cannot insist too much on the need to reconstitute as soon as possible the Foreign Legion, which is now completely disorganized," warned Lyautey.[1] He made sure his interlocutors understood how much he cared about the future of the force: "No one is more partisan toward the use of the Legion in Morocco than I am."[2] "The Legion is really the queen of the colonial battle, the incomparable troop, the one that never fails the chief who knows how to command it, how to employ it. It is the last resort reserve that holds when everything else fails."[3]

Over the next few years, a nervous Lyautey and his officers fought to recreate the force that had served France's colonial aims well. They ordered and wrote inquiries and reports on the current state of the Legion, and requested help from their government. French politics made their task difficult. The elections of 1919 brought to power a conservative cabinet, the Bloc National. Given the catastrophic consequence of the war for French demography—from 1915 to 1919, 1.75 million less children were born in France than in a comparable period before the war—they could hardly be interested in allocating the few precious men they had to Morocco and the colonies in general.[4] Then, in 1923, because Germany could not pay war financial compensation, France occupied the Ruhr region and required more contingents for that. Instead of help from Paris, Lyautey faced ever more pressing requests to downsize his forces.

One vital auxiliary in the general-resident's enterprise of renovating the Legion, if not saving it, was Paul-Frédéric Rollet. From the time he returned from Europe to Morocco to lead the Third Regiment in Fes, and well after he went to Sidi Bel Abbès in 1925 to take even higher responsibilities, the passion Rollet had for the Legion fueled an effort to improve the quality of the force. Covered with honors for his bravery during the war (notably as an officer of the Légion d'Honneur), Lieutenant-Colonel Rollet still carried with him the reputation of an all-too independent soldier prone to interpret the orders of his superiors the way it suited him. That, one can speculate, is what kept his bond with the Legion tight.

Typical in a flurry of documents that Lyautey and Rollet saw is a report filed by Commandant Auger in Meknes, on October 25, 1920.[5] The document highlighted both challenges and solutions for the future of the corps. The first order of business concerned recruiting practices and incentives. Too often, the Legion relied on less than reliable agents who pushed the homeless and aimless into a service that they did not really understand. The best spokespersons for the Legion were the legionnaires themselves, said Auger: Why not allow the men who finished a second enlistment to travel back to their country, giving them a chance to reconnect with their past once their loyalty to the Legion was ascertained, while asking them to recruit new volunteers? An enlistment bonus and the prospect, after six years of service, of a tour in the magical Tonkin surely could add to the persuasion. The legionnaire's spirit is at heart that of an adventurer, Auger reminded his readers in his report. Incidentally, Lyautey even floated the idea of granting legionnaires a *lot de colonisation*, a piece of land in the colonies, to give them an incentive to stay in Morocco, with the added advantage of "forming for later a population of colonials presenting good moral qualities and having absorbed from military service habits of order and discipline that could only help in the development of the country."[6] This, of course, was an idea straight out of Bugeaud's book, itself inspired by how Roman legionnaires had both conquered and settled in antiquity. Last but not least, and this came from Lyautey, too, the Legion still needed to contradict German obstruction by all means, "with images, and most especially with postcards."

Treating recruits respectfully once they enlisted appeared urgent. The old lore of traveling to Marseilles in one's old miserable clothes, to land at the gloomy, dirty Fort Saint-Jean, did not exactly foster loyalty from the start. At Sidi Bel Abbès, decent living conditions were paramount. Auger mentions how much the quality of food mattered in the ranks. Of course, training remained essential to the soldier. In Rollet's Third Regiment, new recruits received basic instruction over a period of about six to eight weeks. Then they moved to a base in the Atlas, where they learned the specific techniques necessary to serve in a post or a mobile group. Music, which had always been the pride of the Legion and an important remedy to the *cafard*, remained as a tradition. Rollet made sure that the new contingents that arrived at Fes were met outside of town, even at quite a distance, with a fanfare.

What kind of man made the best legionnaire? Auger, like many of his associates, had little trust in the French elements, finding "a few good ones; the rest are pariahs." Considering the demographic crisis that France faced after losing so many young men at war, depending solely on French recruits appeared unpatriotic. Here is an inventory of the clichés that emerged out of recruitment history at the Legion: Russians, for the most part former elements of the imperial army who came in droves after the Bolshevik Revolution, were good horsemen, one reads. Many served in the newly formed cavalry in Tunisia. As infantrymen they presented their own challenge: "Very intelligent or very stubborn, headstrong without really knowing why. With a sense of fatality rather than indifference. Takes long to instruct and educate. Becomes a remarkable soldier when he serves under the same chief for many years." Lyautey never hid his preference for enlisting Germans, who had a distinguished tradition of service. Still, Auger's report points to new, genuine difficulties:

> Germans: Less respectful of discipline than their prewar co-nationals. Seem to have felt the effects of Bolshevism. Were taken in hand again with great difficulties. Doubtful loyalties. German legionnaires were once capable of all devotion, in the

most difficult of circumstances. Once their officers had gained their trust.[7]

Perhaps more than Bolshevism, the harsh reparations demanded from Germany at the Treaty of Versailles that concluded World War I contributed to the same breakdown of loyalty than the war itself. Rashes of desertion continued to complicate the life of commanders. Nevertheless, while the proportion of Frenchmen who enlisted dropped dramatically after the war, the number of Germans increased in inverse proportion. In 1920, Lyautey signaled that their numbered reached a proportion of 60 percent.[8]

One consideration concerned the enrollments of indigenous elements in the Legion. In December 1924 there was a total of fifty-two North Africans legionnaires, or 0.6 percent of the force. The leadership estimated that a proportion of 2.5 percent represented the maximum the Legion could sustain. To the Ministry of War, Lyautey argued that mixing legionnaires, at a time when the number of German recruits had increased so dramatically, would be a dangerous game:

> It would be inopportune and impolitic to envisage any kind of mixing of foreign elements with indigenous ones, either North Africans or Senegalese. The legionnaire must remain a legion-naire, and it's only exceptionally, after a period of service long enough to prove his trustworthiness (through military instruc-tion and evidence of his loyalty), that he can be lent to another unit.[9]

The fear was of a cross-contamination between these foreign and indigenous elements, leading to desertion and sabotage.

Not much is related about the troops who might have balked at seeing soldiers of color join their own ranks. For sure, the legionnaires were hardly models of cultural empathy. In his memoirs, Legionnaire Maurice Magnus explains that one thing united the French and the German: "They dislike and despise the Arab."[10] Fighting against indigenous people is what consti-tuted the legionnaires as a corps. The Legion was a white, not to say often blond, troop. That racial element must have been indispensable to the cohe-sion of the corps. There are photographs showing happy visages of legion-naires of color, but the way the memoirs and the military archives tell the story, it's essentially a segregated affair. Vis-à-vis the other army soldiers drawn from the colonies, the Algerian Skirmishers, the Moroccan Goums, the Senegalese, they were kept at bay, and even when enrollments threatened its existence, the Legion rejected the idea of integrating soldiers of color. The French generals counted on the Legion as a guarantee in case the indigenous troops they used should revolt.

No matter how ambitious the plans to renovate the Legion were, and how eager the leadership was to realize them, there were many who harbored doubts concerning the restoration of the old Legion. An officer complained about his new recruits:

> They seem more malleable, less drunken, but also more thin-skinned, their mentality for the moment seems to be that of transplants, whereas before the war we had the "uprooted." Apart from the food, they are largely indifferent to their surroundings. The rather large number of letters that they write and receive shows that they have not broken with their old countries.[11]

Lyautey expressed similar doubts: "It will take many years before the new battalions may be comparable to the admirable instrument of colonial conquest that the old Legion formed, the way I got to know it and employ in the Tonkin, in Madagascar, in Algeria, and in Morocco even before the war."[12] Indeed, the publicity stunts that Lyautey envisioned to shore up the Legion, fueling the ever-growing public image of the Legion, would bring men that, by definition, could not re-form what the old Legion had been.

The good leader of legionnaires, had to show, above all, exemplary virtue under fire, he had to demonstrate "gallantry." Speaking of the legendary Russian captain Zinovy Peshkov, Adolphe Cooper wrote:

> When his company had to attack, [Peshkov] always showed the way with his revolver in his only hand. He would never dream of sending his men to battle unless he was leading them. If a man dropped wounded by a shot he would always stop. If the man was dead he would put his thumb and first two fingers together and cross himself three times in the Russian Orthodox way. Once in the thick of battle I saw him stop by a legionnaire who was lying on his back. It was one of his men. He had been wounded twice, and from his open stomach you could see the intestines escaping. The legionnaire looked at Peshkov and said, "*Êtes-vous content de moi?*" ["Are you happy with me?"][13]

Leadership bound the troop under fire, it performed an essential role, and that leadership was in trouble too when Lyautey launched his study of the Legion in 1919, after the effect of the war on the numbers and quality of recruitment became more obvious. The officers who knew the traditions were spread too thin by the reorganization. Many, as they rose in rank, were constrained by the ever-growing bureaucracy of the modern army, and less likely to directly impart that particular spirit of the Legion.

Yet Lyautey persisted categorically. It was the name of those legendary officers, still vivid in the stories of the corps, even twenty-five years after they had left, that held the Legion together: "What makes the Legion are its officers, whose names are still heard of twenty or thirty years later."[14] He highlighted the contribution of "those who have the sacred fire and who alone will be the administrators, the men of action, the leaders of the band and the psychologists. Let us place at the head of the regiments and the battalions men of this steel and who shine out, and the Legion will be reborn."[15] General Catroux put the role of the Legion officer almost in the same terms, but with interesting detail: "One would need to be a poet and a man of action, a leader of the band and a psychologist, all at the same time."[16] There were, indeed, many conditions to be a fine leader of legionnaires. The man needed to speak French, exert that subtle combination of courage under fire, through love, and human understanding. More than anyone else, the Legion officer gave his life to the corps, and that made it unlikely that he could have a family, even it stayed far away from the war theater. They did not call the Legion the "monastery of unbelievers" for nothing.

As far as he was concerned, Lyautey was a leader of the Legion both down to earth and living in high theatrics, and that, it seems, is what his men liked. At the age of fifty-eight, he still had an impressive physique. A biographer described hair "cropped short, visible when his kepi was not lowered on his eyes, a mustache that tobacco colored in reddish brown, the nose and the mouth askew, as if deformed by the constant howling at military drill sessions."[17] His silhouette was lean and straight, the hands sinewy, and he rode with elegance.

Lyautey viewed his own being as that of a warrior. That is why he believed in his own theater of an ancient monarchy when he set up the king of Morocco as a charismatic leader. The resident-general played the role of equerry to a king of Morocco as warrior with pedigree himself. He still held the sword that his grandfather had fought with in the army of Napoléon. Later, recalling a 1913 trip to Spain, he explained with deep emotion how King Alfonso XIII, upon seeing the weapon and learning of its august origins, had kissed it religiously. Lyautey was from a family of soldiers, and he recounted the exploits of his stepson at the ferocious battle of Sidi Bou Othman against the partisans of El Hiba, near Marrakech in early September of 1912, with fervor:

> The tales of fighting, the cavalrymen taking to me their swords covered in blood and bent, my stepson, Matthieu Fortoul, bringing the joy of his affection and his young heroism, still taken aback that he had participated in such a feast. Nothing can rival the stories of this beautiful charge on September 6, when four hundred horsemen, sabers shining, threw themselves at the multitude, crossing the camps, shoving everything, pointing at and cutting everyone they met, pursuing the Moroccans' distraught cavalry into the mountain. Fortoul has three of those of his conscience.[18]

In the letter to Albert de Mun written in October 10, 1912, in which he elaborated on the nature of sovereign power in Morocco, he speaks of his enduring pleasure of living amidst the riches of Morocco just as a warrior of Napoléon's army would have discovered Egypt:

> For the last ten days I've been living here a fairy tale, there is no orientalist painting that rivals the sparkle of my arriving in Marrakech on a splendid morning. The crowd of Arabs, the opulence of the cavalry, their standards fully deployed, the succession of parades, the joyous fanfares of our troops, victory and jubilation's perfume, the backdrop of the great Atlas. Then the encampments of the victorious military column in the sultan's garden, the officers' reception in a place drowning in greenery. That victory of the Armée d'Égypte led by Napoléon was on my mind.[19]

The resident-general identified with a code of honor, a romantic code of honor, that he projected onto the people he fought. No wonder he called his inner circle of officers his *zawiya*, like a Muslim religious fraternity. He treated his feudal cohort of manly, handsome officers with cozy familiarity and even affection, although, as the diplomat and fine memorialist Saint-Aulaire noted, this cozy side of him mostly represented the "coquetting of grandeur."[20]

At the heart of Lyautey's idea of the colonies was a firm belief in the virtues of elitism in a society of orders. He still lamented the consolidation of the French Third Republic and its low expectations, in the name of social justice, of what men could accomplish: "I feel utterly incompatible with egalitarian and collectivist society."[21] For him, the colonies were the space where great destinies could be accomplished. "It seems to me that all the vitality of our country concentrates in colonial life ... It's the only source of energy that is left."[22] Consequently, he staunchly advocated for a strict unity between military command and civil administration—or, rather, a military regime, the only one appropriate to colonization, in practical, political, and personal terms.[23]

The times when Lyautey had slept rolled in his old burnous, among his men, was long gone. Still, he remained close to the humble trooper, or at least he tried very much to give that impression. "*Je ne suis pas militaire, je suis soldat*," he maintained. Since writing his article "Du rôle social de l'officier," he saw it as his duty to provide decent living conditions for his troops. He created two rest houses for the legionnaires, one in Oran, the other one in Salé, so that they could recuperate between campaigns. Letters show him deeply concerned, after an inspection, by the sanitary conditions of the barracks: He ordered that they be equipped with adequate toilets. He might have been thinking of the beautiful British barracks he had seen in Singapore when he ordered that officers' quarters include rooms for recreation.[24] On the campaign, he still took time to talk to everyone, and explain his greater designs. One officer admiringly remembered, "Tonight, in one of those intimate chats, our favorite treat, the general expands on some of his ideas, as he sits before his tent, wrapped up in his brown burnous, facing the mountains of the Beni Snassen."[25]

Always verging on the histrionic, this high-ranking performer spoke to the legionnaires, imparting to them that, no matter how much hierarchy separated the resident-general from the simple private, they all formed a class of outcasts who had fled bourgeois society. Individuality and personal freedom had to reign supreme, because this is how, in his view, great things could be accomplished. "Marshal Lyautey was a legendary figure among the legionnaires," sums up Georges Manue.[26] Lieutenant Albert-Édouard Jaeglé (one whose career ended prematurely in 1908, in those columns of the upper Guir River), left this spirited portrait:

> Lovable by nature, he wishes to be liked, and is liked—with
> deplorable facility ... loved by his officers, by the soldiers, by

courtiers, scribes and functionaries, he himself loves women, pretty faces, flattery, workers because they serve him . . . A trifle deaf in one ear, tall and youthful appearance, he listens to one speaking without seeming to, and looks at things and men with a keen, clear eye, judging them quickly and often justly. He has no time to be modest.[27]

Lyautey related to his own soldiers, the legionnaires. What he saw in them motivated his confidence in the mission. What they saw in him as soldier in chief carried them, too. Legionnaire Ehrhart recalled seeing him arrive at a gallop in Talzaza, wearing a red and white burnous. *"Bonjour, mes légionnaires!"* saluted the chief.

> They were beautiful, those legionnaires of the Sahara, their faces tanned under the white kepi, their skin weathered by the wind and the sand. The collar of their tunic open and their waist wrapped in the blue cummerbund, with supple bodies trimmed and strenghthened by the long marches in the desert, a straight and direct gaze, they seemed to be saying: "Anything you'll like, my general, until death even." And he knew it. That is why he loved them so much.[28]

Good, efficient training for sure, a leader with the *baraka*. And something else. *"À moi! La Légion!"* was a rallying cry heard out not only on the battlefield, but out on leave, too, the validation of camaraderie in a culture of revelry, hard-drinking, and love-for-money that still defined the Legion after many decades.

As night fell over the Moroccan town, the legionnaires, returned from the *bled*, found many outlets to forget the fifteen days of their tour, the deaths, the sand in the cans of sardines, the foul water. There were no limits to what a legionnaire did when the much-awaited days of leave were upon him. "To fly out like a bomb" (*partir en bombe*), was to affirm, for a few hours or for a few days, that one had free will. At all ranks of the Legion, *la bombe* was intrinsic to the legionnaire's life and self-definition. Many years after the war in Morocco, a priest named Bruckberger found this placard in the mess at Aïn Sefra: "Alcohol kills. But the legionnaire does not fear death. Alcohol kills slowly. But the legionnaire is not in a hurry."[29]

Witness Rollet, who, in 1910, ended up under arrest for fifteen days because he spent eight days in Marrakech unbeknownst to anyone, instead of remaining, as his leave prescribed, in a tranquil post of the Chaouia. No doubt interaction with the fair sex was very much a priority for Rollet, and encounters of that sort in Morocco necessarily entailed mercenary love.

In those years of the French colony, drinking and prostitution played out endlessly throughout Morocco, in the cabarets and brothels of Khenifra, Kasba Tadla, Midelt, or Taza. Beyond the Atlas, in Béchar, in Aïn Sefra. Officers, depending on their ranks, might have preferred establishments a little less compromising, like the Eden-Concert or the Parisiana Bar in Casablanca, the lounge at the Sultan Hotel in Meknes, or the Hôtel du Ziz in Rich. The best-known in this chic category had to be the Hôtel du Maroc, in Fes, which stood in the heart of the native city:

> Each time a column returned, between two clashes or two deadly tours, the hotel offered us, each night, in an ambiance that hesitated between seedy joint [*beuglant*] and chic bar, between café-concert and grill room, between bistro and private coffee house, a haven where, little by little, rituals were created, a certain way of thinking, a freedom of being that was specific to the Legion, a stock of anecdotes that have nearly become legendary and that feed, even to this hour, that legionnaire humor that is unique in this world.[30]

Maurice Durosoy wrote about this legendary hotel in Fes. An officer freshly minted from Saint-Cyr who came to Morocco as an officer of the Office of Indigenous Affairs, Durosoy eventually became a close associate of Lyautey in Morocco, fought in World War II, and finished his career as a brigadier-general. He describes how, returned from the *bled*, with much money to spend, all ranks let loose: "Whoever never got to know the Maroc Hotel in Fes and its *beuglant* cannot imagine how much we had fun, and how little we needed to have fun."[31]

Time had passed since the first heyday of the colonization. Standing by the two long bars at the Hôtel du Maroc, the French officers now showed clean-shaven faces, with hair slicked back and shiny, and a wide cut for the suit. The pointy mustaches of the later nineteenth century were out of style. They danced to the fox trot, the dance *du jour*, with the demimondaines till dawn. One of these, La Paloma, a Casablanca lady who specialized in an updated version of the dance of the seven veils, ended up marrying a colonel.

No matter how upscale the beginning of the night, the officers often ended in the same brothels as their soldiers—they even had priority, or reserved days. Some of the more expensive houses promised quality, or at least the pretense of it. The legionnaire Jean Martin found that the women at La Maison Simone did not exactly match the promises of its signage:

> To justify the sign "Maison Européenne," Carmen, Louisette, Marinette, Mado, who were born in Essaouira, Meknes or Ksar El Souk [Errachidia], wore—depending of the hour—bathing suits or twenty-francs nightgowns. That got them some colorful allure, if not style! There were even two "authentic" Europeans, Nénette the Spaniard, who was rather taciturn in her normal state. But when she drank a little she became the life of the party, and that happened every day. Then there was Andrée, known as Dédée, a former neighbor of mine since she had lived on the same street as I used to, six numbers farther. That was in the old days, when "she did not live the life."[32]

Marrakech, in spite of its charms, offered Martin the same empty promises at "La Mère Marie." The resident matriarch "rented one of her boarders to me—'a very young one, a young one, you'll see!'—it was almost as if the girl was a virgin! She turned out to be a leathery piece of an old woman, but never mind, one is not to be picky upon returning from a column."[33]

Eventually the appeal of Morocco's bohemia gave way before the principles of organization and productivity. Visitors flooded Casablanca's infamous red-light district, Bousbir, a so-called "reserved district" built by the authorities in the Moorish style. In a complex of twenty-four thousand square meters, six hundred to nine hundred women worked in clouds of jasmine and rose perfumes. Moroccan women were available to all comers, but Moroccan men were strictly forbidden to hire prostitutes from Europe. Postcards sent throughout the world made Bousbir a coveted destination, for both gawkers and customers. To his credit, Martin found it "a historical monument of false historical color, built for the stupidly flabbergasted tourists."[34] Still, it satisfied the French authorities, who argued that the facility allowed them to control the spread of venereal disease. A military and a police detachment guarded the only entry to the complex. In Marrakech, the same type of quarters existed. The Glaoui, the qaid put in place by Lyautey, extracted most of his profits from it.

The same principles of efficiency also warranted the creation of the infamous *BMC*s, or *bordels militaires contrôlés*, that followed the troops during their campaigns, either military campaigns or for road construction. Some have suggested that they were meant to prevent a "certain drifting in sexual practices during those long months of isolation that cut the men from feminine intercourse," or to prevent the rape of Moroccan women after a military assaults.[35]

These traveling establishments consisted of a small group of women, most often assembled by the owner (called *la riffa*) of a brothel in a nearby garrison town. The military paid for both transportation and lodging. The women lined up after the soldiers, before departing on a campaign, to undergo a medical examination. Legionnaire Ehrhart describes the women's ordeal when, "every night, from five to eight, all were let loose from the barracks. Then, above the whirlwinds of the sirocco, rose the clamor of the soldier's crush to get into the cells. The moans of the women rose in the long wave of the sirocco."[36] Martin gives another idea of the reality of these women's lives:

> These females who followed the columns were in general Berber women. Once in a while a European got mixed in with the brunettes, she usually had reached the last stages of decay. In any case, they were the rejects of Morocco, the old stalwarts who, sensing that retirement was coming, were ready to earn some money at any cost. At Ou-Terbat, there were ten or twelve, handed to the fury of five thousand young solid males, boiling with vigor and vitality!!![37]

If becoming a legionnaire, and a soldier of the Armée d'Afrique in general, was to learn how to be a man, that education entailed a view on women and sexuality.

In Europe, World War I had profoundly altered women's role in society. During the war, European women had worked in jobs until then reserved to men, and had proved that they could aspire to more responsibility, at home, in the workplace, and in society in general. This affected gender norms, too. This was the heyday of the *garçonnes*, masculine women who wore their hair in a short bob, smoked cigarettes, and went out by themselves to dance the Charleston. Changes in women's role may have affected the mystique of the Legion in the interwar period, insofar as service abroad represented the attraction of fulfilling a traditional gender role. A photographic brochure heralding the exploits of the Legion in Morocco, published in 1937, presents the picture of a young prostitute, with the caption "Fed up with the women from Europe, I went there to have a taste of the soldier's girl [*fille à soldat*], not the sentimental type [*pas sentimenteuse*]."[38]

Homosexuality surely did exist in the Legion. It might even have prospered. Georges d'Esparbès mentions the presence of "inverts" and "sexual perverts" in the ranks, and considers homosexual attraction a manifestation of the *cafard*, although he also hints that these subjects might have had such disposition before joining.[39] The legionnaire Adolphe Cooper, upon arriving in Sidi Bel Abbès, quickly found out that a young recruit's warm welcome by elders might be a little more intimate than what he wished for: "The next thing I knew was that someone was lifting my blankets and was trying to get into bed with me."[40] Thanks to the knife that he had kept handy as a precaution, Cooper pushed back the inopportune visitor, but he could not find sleep for the rest of the night. At breakfast, a legionnaire came to congratulate him. Cooper also tells the story of a weathered legionnaire named Cabasso who, after meeting Charles de Foucauld in 1915, converted to more Catholic ways and eventually was ordained a priest. Having found this new path in life, he was discharged from the Legion, but had to come back to its ranks for another kind of redemption: "You see, Cooper, I am a born homosexual . . . I was soon in trouble with this perversion. I rejoined the Legion but managed to fight off all temptations with the help of my prayers."[41]

There are stories of male couples living together "like husband and wife," some erupting in domestic quarrels, of legionnaires with tattoos of male names, and of legionnaires who waltzed together.[42] Some anecdotes come from German anti-Legion propaganda. On the other hand, a report from the army's own services, written in the early 1900s, commented on how prison in the Legion was "an immoral thing." "Put the young soldier there; tomorrow the old one that . . . protects him will join him, sometimes the prey of sinful jealousy."[43] Observers often found love and sex among men inevitable, considering the long months they endured in seclusion, often in isolated posts. Colonel Weygand, when his columns rested in desert oasis, had to ignore the frolicking that took place between the legionnaires, and sometimes between the officers, too.[44] Gerald Ward Price, the *Times* correspondent who spent a good deal of time with the Legion in the early thirties, wrote:

> Boredom, the sense of being cut off from all ties of home and family, and the fact that some, undoubtedly, of the men in its ranks have criminal records and propensities, are not influences that make for virtue. There are, indeed, aspects of its private morals that are unsuitable for public comment. Nearly every legionnaire with whom I discussed conditions in the corps referred to these, sometimes with disapproval but generally with

indifference. But the Legion is probably no worse than any other haphazard collection of rather tough and hard-tried men, obliged often to live under conditions of isolation.[45]

Setting aside the tone of this passage, a corps renowned for harboring outcasts would naturally attract men who were shunned by their own societies in Europe. Besides, the ardent cult of military masculinity, as some legendary episodes of military history show, can find its origins, or conclusion, in love between men. Serge Gainsbourg's cover of "Mon Légionnaire" (1987) and Claire Denis's film *Beau Travail* (1999) both touch on the Legion's relationship to latent homoeroticism.

And so the scene of *la bombe* went on, as legionnaires entered those dark, narrow, twisted alleys of the medina, passing houses with the blue smoke of lamb grilling and, here and there, the singing of a group of soldiers, all reveling. Sitting on the ground, against the wall, some legionnaires are already drunk asleep, others hold the metal can of wine sold by the Greek *mercati*. Moroccans nod, inviting the soldiers in. You can hear the patrons howl some obscene song in the back room. Soon, there will undoubtedly be shouts and bangs, as soldiers from different corps finish the night properly, in a brawl. "*Oh! La Légion*" summons the comrades, no questions asked.

Far from this riffraff, Lyautey lived in his beautiful palaces, feasting on more refined splendors. In Marrakech he had declared that the Bahia Palace would be his official residence, an oasis of breezy courtyards where fountains murmured gently, leading to cooler, mysterious dark rooms. He had the house beautifully restored, to promote the crafts of Morocco. Edith Wharton, when she visited the palace after World War I, enjoyed "the scent of citron-blossom and jasmine, with sometimes a bird song before dawn, sometimes a flute's wail at sunset, and always the call of the muezzin at night."[46] Lyautey spoke of those houses "where he had established his sultanate" with exaltation.[47]

The resident-general's new residence and administrative complex in Rabat opened in 1923. Now monarchs, heads of state, ministers, writers, and celebrities flocked to celebrate the emergence of the new Morocco that one could traverse in a few hours on new highways and railways. Lyautey, who in 1921 had been made a marshal and then formally welcomed at the Académie Française, the keeper of French literary and linguistic tradition, was at the height of his prestige as he hosted the dignitaries, with Inès by his side. He can hardly have imagined that in the space of a few years, this entire dream would vanish like a mirage of that desert that held him so much in thrall.

CHAPTER 13

Middle Atlas

Not too far from the joints patronized by the French army, a war still went on. Now that the road connecting Meknes, Midelt, and eastern Morocco had been laid out and developed, the time had come to tackle both the Zayanes and the tribes of the Tache de Taza.

The Zayanes had shown signs of weakness since the end of the war. Three sons of the leader Mouha ou Hammou had submitted to the French, who waited for the father to surrender. Orders from Lyautey were to treat him with respect. Nevertheless, operations dragged on, to the point when dissenting voices in the army questioned whether the strategy of taking time to build roads and studding the mountains with forts was useful; didn't it allow the enemy to recoup its forces after a loss? But on March 27, 1921, news came that Mouha ou Hammou, the hero of El Herri, had died in an intertribal conflict. The Zayanes ceased to represent a significant threat to French occupation. The legionnaires of the Third Regiment, under Commandant Henri Nicolas, could then secure the Middle Atlas road axis.

Doubts remained about the Lyautey pacification methods, given how long it had taken even to begin effective control of the Atlas and the inconclusive results obtained so far. More and more, strategists spoke of the Moroccan plains under effective French control as "useful Morocco," which was a way to manage expectations in Paris about what could be realistically achieved in the hostile mountains.

The most stunning news of 1921 did not concern the French protectorate directly, or at least not yet. The Spanish had more and more difficulty holding on to their own Moroccan territory. In the Rif, a mountain range that runs parallel to the Mediterranean coast of Morocco, a new leader had attracted attention for a while. His name was Muhammad Abdelkrim El Khattabi. In the afternoon of July 22, 1921, at Annual, Abdelkrim's army preyed on the forces of a Spanish general, Manuel Fernández Silvestre, a staggering mass of sixty thousand soldiers, inaugurating the worst colonial disaster ever sustained by a European army. The battle raged for three weeks and left more than ten thousand Spanish soldiers dead. Lyautey summed up for a correspondent his interpretation:

> Briefly, the national character of this movement is what makes this [situation] new and severe. Its chief, Abdelkrim, is a very Europeanized *Monsieur* who knows what he's doing, holds his people, can rely on a real army, and declares the Rif's independence. I have messages from him where he calls himself "Delegate of the Council of Riffian Notables." You'll ponder the formula.[1]

For the moment the Riffians did not pose a direct threat to the French; they did not represent less a nagging, stinging concern. Abdelkrim could now count on thousands of guns, machine guns, and the cannons that he had captured from Spanish troops.

The fight for submission of the Amazigh fighters in the Atlas Mountains went on. Drawn from the four Legion regiments in Morocco, army commanders moved companies at will between detachments, from one subdivision to another. These *groupes mobiles* of the colonial army comprised elements drawn from different units, both European and indigenous ("Each race brings its own qualities," remarked a scholar of tactics in Morocco) and took on a range of functions, depending on the size and nature of the mission.[2] With appropriate backup and supply, they could also operate with autonomy. For the new recruits that slowly staffed the regiments decimated by World War I, the move from a training camp closer to the war theater was eagerly awaited: It marked the end of chores, of drilling, and, to a certain extent, of strict discipline. At last, with the first leave came an opportunity to explore that side of Morocco that veterans boasted of having taken by storm, too.

There were new weapons. If the "oil stain" strategy of Lyautey foundered, as demonstrated by the unresolved attempt at subduing the Zayanes, the instruments of death bequeathed by World War I would have to carry the mission. The shrapnel shells of the war were the first to make their appearance in the colonial war theaters. Around the same year, heavy artillery came to support attacks in the mountains. The seven-and-half-ton tanks built by

Renault, the ever-increasing use of air power, which would first be deployed extensively in the Middle Atlas campaigns of 1923 ("In Morocco, we cannot conceive of a mobile group or simple detachment operating without the help of aviation"), the armored lorries used to transport supplies—all of these were coordinated with advances in wireless radio equipment, under new powerful light projectors, that created new, efficient ways to subdue the people of Morocco's mountains.[3] Later in 1926, the troops received a new type of machine gun that was lighter, easier to carry, and more lethal.

Even more important, a new leadership rose. Two new officers stood out in the ranks of the Legion, and they were both destined for a great future: the Danish prince, Aage, and the Russian Zinovy Peshkov.

Aage, Count of Rosenborg, the grandson of King Christian IX of Denmark, had begun his career as an officer in the military forces of his country. He became acquainted with the Legion early. At the age of thirteen, he had met another famous compatriot, Christian Selchauhansen, who would die at the attack at El Moungar. Some suggest that when the lieutenant gave the adolescent a metal figurine of a legionnaire for his collection, Aage's fate was irrevocably determined. More prosaically, the bank that held Aage's fortune collapsed years later, so much so that his family was ruined. Aage then decided to join the Legion and was appointed on December 1922 to the Second Foreign Infantry Regiment in Meknes, leaving behind an Italian wife.

Financial distress had always been one of the reasons why men, including scions of wealthy families, joined the ranks. With his aristocratic extraction, Aage also fit perfectly the image of the legionnaire with a prestigious background, the sort that populates Legion lore. Louis II of Monaco, who served in the First Regiment at the end of the 1800s in Algeria, is a famous example. Less verifiable is Legionnaire Maurice Magnus's story that a certain John Smith in his regiment turned out to be a nephew of Kaiser Wilhelm. After Smith died, his body was taken back to Germany "on his Majesty's cruiser."[4] Aage of Denmark's notoriety, finally, benefitted from his cutting a striking figure. The prince was a tall, good-looking man, so much so that after serving for two years in Morocco in the early twenties, he went on a grand tour to promote the Legion in the United States, and remained an international celebrity who served the reputation of his corps. His memoirs, published in those years, were clearly part of a public relations effort.

Zinovy Peshkov also presents quite an unusual profile. Born in Nizhni Novgorod, Russia, and raised Jewish, Peshkov converted to the Orthodox religion and became the adoptive godson of the writer and political activist

Maxim Gorky. He traveled the world from Finland to Canada, and then the United States, joining the Legion at the onset of World War I. Much like Aage, he had parted with his family to join in the "monastery." Peshkov's rise in the ranks was fast, given his courage in combat and distinguished profile. In 1915, he lost his right arm during an assault near Arras. The following years saw him traveling even more, performing many services for the French government, until he rejoined the Legion in Meknes in the spring of 1923. His memoirs, another central document to understand the culture of the Legion in the interwar years, are, similar to Aage's, written in an effort to shore up the Legion's reputation for the larger public. One finds in them a resolute belief in the white man's civilizing mission: "Civilization is not only a privilege, it is a burden—an honorable burden for those who are conscious of the benefits that it brings."[5]

Thus, Aage's and Peshkov's profile and charisma contributed to enhancing the reputation of the Legion as the final attempt to master the people of Morocco's mountains began in 1923, chief among them the Aït Seghrouchen and Marmoucha people that the French called the "Prussians" of the Atlas, on account of their excellent fighting skills.

Indeed, the Aït Seghrouchen and Marmoucha tribesmen of Mount Tichkoukt in the Tache de Taza offered fierce opposition from the very first months of the 1922 campaign. About six to seven thousands of rifles of these Imazighen held the most impregnable redoubts of the Middle Atlas. On May 6, the Third Battalion of the Third Regiment approached the Tizi Adni pass, near Skoura, as part of a mobile group led by Commandant Henri Nicolas and Colonel Fernand Maire, a veteran of World War I—these two commanders, together with Henry de Corta, became known as the "Three Musketeers." Facing the impenetrable fire barrier shot by a maddeningly volatile enemy at Skoura, the troops had to pull back, but in a characteristic move the Imazighen rushed on to make the most of this vulnerable moment. Combat lasted almost eight hours, and cost almost one hundred men, many lost in body-to-body engagement. That won the Third Battalion a citation directly signed by Lyautey, enumerating the operations it had participated in, "while, faithful to the tradition of the Legion, it built outposts and executed many trail works."[6] The resident-general came to visit the survivors right after the battle, speaking "often in German" to the legionnaires, noted a witness.

Lyautey prepared his next campaign with more care. On December 22 he sent his orders to General Poeymirau, commander of the forces and their *groupes-mobile* at Meknes. Logistics were impeccably planned for a summer-long campaign. Since no map of the rocky, chaotic mountains they had to subdue existed, air reconnaissance spent weeks taking as much as two thousand pictures necessary to reconnoiter the region. Lieutenant-Colonel Huot, director of intelligence in Morocco, cooperated so that political action preceded and followed military force, according to Lyautey's colonial doctrine. The force gathered by Poeymirau numbered twenty thousand men, including six battalions from the Legion.

Pressure was intense. This was most likely the last time they could deploy such a large-scale effort, because the ministers in Paris had made significant cuts in the troops and funds allocated to the Moroccan war theater. Germany had defaulted on the reparations required by the Treaty of Versailles, prompting the French and the Belgians to occupy the Ruhr in 1923. The resident-general agreed with Minister of War Maginot on an exacting schedule to send colonial contingents of French-born soldiers back in Europe—naturally, the Legion could not serve in Germany, which explains once again how they remained so close to Lyautey during his residency.

Meanwhile, in the Rif Mountains north of the Middle Atlas, Abdelkrim's forces strengthened, and this demanded the presence of French forces in much larger numbers than Lyautey could have imagined. Rollet, fearful of the consequences, pondered that a catastrophe similar to that of Lang Son might "drag France into the abyss."[7] Also very much on the minds of Lyautey and Poeymirau was the frightening idea that the rebels led by Abdelkrim in the Rif might even join forces with their brethren of the Atlas. Despite earlier, optimistic plans for the full "pacification" of Morocco, realism prevailed concerning the goals and possible results of this campaign in the Atlas:

> The goal here is not necessarily to impose on those tribes an effective control nor to force them to submit to the general rules and modes of administration of the conquered regions. They live at the border of "useful Morocco" or at its extreme limit. What matters is to live peacefully with them and to reach a modus vivendi whereby they will leave us alone and reciprocally, frequenting our markets, leave the tribes that have submitted to us to go their own way.[8]

Effective sovereignty of the sultan, as the French could enforce it, was to be limited to the old *bled el-Makzhen*, leaving the *bled el-Siba* for all practical purposes what it had always been, the land of "free men."

Prince Aage found himself at the forefront of this campaign of 1923. He enrolled in the First Battalion of the Second Regiment, and integrated a mobile group from Fes, while Peshkov's assignment turned out to be relatively uneventful in this first year of his service, when he operated from Kasba Tadla near the quieter front with the Zayanes; he then served at a fort in the mountains over the winter months of 1923–24.

Aage's troops, after taking Recifa and Bou Khamouj, converged on the village of El Mers for a showdown. El Mers lies at high altitude, at the eastern foot of Mount Tichkoukt. Like Skoura, where the legionnaires had encountered uncommon resistance, the Amazigh settlement at El Mers guarded the natural fortress of the Tichkoukt and blocked one of the passages between the region of Fes and Meknes, the Moulouya Valley, and the southern oasis. Moreover, the Aït Seghrouchen considered El Mers their most important town, being both their ancestors' resting place and the village of their principal market.

On the twenty-fourth of June, the French army forces, including legionnaires from the Second and Third Regiments, left their base at Athia at dawn, traversing pastures and fields of grain, climbing rocky crests, descending down ravines in that rugged, austere mountain theater of the Middle Atlas. They marched on El Mers. Aage acted as liaison for Poeymirau. His battalion of the Second Regiment first found itself caught on a crest of the terrain, in perfect view of the enemy, who shot from their higher position. Buzzing over the scene, planes dropped messages to signal the presence of large contingents of Aït Seghrouchen warriors. Two men died trying to blast their enemies. Aage had the men move the gun a few yards aside. He then chose an old legionnaire for the second attempt at taking out the enemy's defense.

> He reached the gun and raised his body slowly, almost imperceptibly, in order to avoid attracting the enemy's attention by any sudden movement. He must have had an iron grip upon his nerves. It seemed, this time, as if we were going to succeed. The gunner was in position, he raised the sight leaf and adjusted his aim. In a moment, now, we should have been hearing the first burst, the staccato *ta-ta-ta-ta-ta* that would increase our firepower by fifty rifles. Then they got him.[9]

Aage ordered a fellow countryman, a young Danish man with a wide grin, to replace the dead legionnaire at the machine gun. Seeing the Dane's youth moved him, and Aage was about to reconsider this choice when "the boy moved up at once, however, and before we could restrain him, rose to his full height and walked calmly toward the gun, just as if there had not been at least a score of riflemen trying their level best to do him." But an explosion rocked the Moroccan position as the young daredevil prepared to shoot. The artillery finally brought much-needed relief to Aage's men. Twenty minutes later, the enemy had abandoned their position to retreat toward El Mers.

At ten o'clock, stomachs started to grumble, and General Poeymirau called for a pause to both recuperate and take positions for final assault. Poeymirau, "a short, squarely built man, gray-haired, gray-mustached, with a twinkling eye and extraordinarily cut uniforms," always ate his luncheon in style, no matter where he was. Indeed he was very French, and this was the way he chose to dissipate stress in stressful circumstances. That day, it was Aage's privilege to eat with the bon vivant.

> We lunched, then, on a delectable chicken stew, provided by the staff cook, washed down with some remarkable Burgundy supplied by the general. The troops, too, considering the circumstances, fared well, for the cooks had been left behind at the previous night's camp to prepare a hot meal. This was brought forward during a lull in the battle, and successive details of men were relieved from the firing line for a period long enough to have a decent luncheon. And so it was with something approaching equanimity that we faced the prospect of a hard afternoon fighting, after our strenuous efforts of the morning.[10]

El Mers waited in the hot hours of the Moroccan summer afternoon, its holy men's sacred tombs with green-tiled roofs shining in the middle of olive groves. A large kasbah, fronted by two deep trenches filled with defenders, protected it. Taking it was the key to victory. Inside the kasbah, more than one thousand fighters waited with machine guns.

Three companies of the Legion spearheaded the advance. The Moroccans repelled their charge three times from both the kasbah and the trenches that defended it. Aage, enraptured by the sight of this action, stood up imprudently, and felt a hit on his leg. It was a soldier using his rifle cannon to attract his attention and get him down, and not a bullet as Aage first thought. Two fresh battalions went in again with hopes of breaking the defense by overtaking the trenches. They did, but not without a bitter struggle at knife and bayonet point. Meanwhile, shooters inside the kasbah fired upon both legionnaires and their own, displaying such frenzy that they earned this high praise from a Dane that they had "the reckless bravery of the old Northern Berserkers."

At a crucial moment of the assault, a few legionnaires rallied around a lieutenant, who coordinated the final push.

> These men, some twenty in all, laid their rifles down, slung sacks of hand grenades about their necks, and crouched like sprinters awaiting the gun. At a given signal, they sprang toward the kasbah, those who survived the first volley covering the inconsiderable distance in a few seconds. These men, pulling the pins with their teeth, flattened themselves against the walls and hurled grenade after grenade through windows and loopholes.[11]

El Mers had fallen. A last fight occurred at the outskirts of the village, and many more men fell to sniper shots that night, but a few days later, the legionnaires could begin the construction of posts and roads. There were several more engagements in the Tichkoukt and in the Marmoucha territory until the end of the summer, when yet another passage through the Atlas could be considered opened by the French. A commander boasted that "the old Legion was *magnifique*, but the new one is about to surpass it."[12]

Legion heroics, unfortunately for the French, still could not mask that the Tache de Taza remained unsettled. Just a few dissident tribes offered their submission to the French, and the only strategy remaining consisted in blocking the Aït Seghrouchen high up in their mountain, with hopes that they would surrender after months spent in the bitter mountain winter. Three Legion battalions of the Third Regiment disseminated in a string of outposts along the mountain ranges.

Long months of living dangerously in isolated outposts of the Middle Atlas began for the troops, and for the Legion especially. The three battalions of the Third Regiment were spread across the periphery of the Tache de Taza, charged with watching over the Aït Seghrouchen. Given the fragility of French military control, and the possibility that open rebellion could always flare up, the task of the legionnaires remained mostly defensive.

The day began when the night watch was replaced: "The flag is being raised over the post, slowly rising above the white walls, and [is] taken by the morning wind into the blue sky . . . Perfect silence reigns."[13] The legionnaires went about their daily business. They fetched water at the nearest spring if the fort did not have a well; brought supplies to another, even more isolated, fort; tended to the fort's vegetable garden; or built a new oven to bake fresh bread. In the harsh climate of the mountains, the structure required constant repairs.[14]

At any time, a sniper could kill a sentinel too complacent, an ambush could destroy the group that went to fetch water. Sometimes, in the middle of the night, the Imazighen shot at the fort, just to keep the soldiers on edge. When the shots manifested something really serious, they took their positions at the turrets, and then went back to work as calmly as they had dropped their activities. Throughout the regularity of military life or the alerts, there was still plenty of time to meditate, up there in the Atlas Mountains.

Every fifteen days came payday. It was all spent right away on cigarettes and wine sold by the *mercatis* that showed up under the walls at this opportune moment. In the communal rooms thick with blue smoke, that's when the card games became more lively, and the singing rose in the night of the Atlas Mountains, nostalgic German Lieder mixed with French cabaret songs from Paris. That might be when a legionnaire would finally get that tattoo he had been thinking about. Legionnaires had always been infamous for their tattoos. Some of them were acquired during stays in the penal companies: "One had a big cat chasing a rat tattooed across his back—only the rear half of the rat could be seen on the buttock. Another had the battle of Camerone on his chest."[15] Peshkov says that he shuddered when he saw a man bearing the word FATALITÉ inked on his forehead.[16]

Maurice Durosoy also lived the winter months of 1923 and 1924 in the Atlas Mountains, to gather information and play the role of political mediator in the Oil Slick colonial method much vaunted among Lyautey's doctrinaires. He operated in El Mers by Mount Tichkoukt, which had just been taken. Still, no one could let their guard down at El Mers.[17] Two young telegraph operators were found with their throats slit open. Then, ten legionnaires died in ambush when they rode out to supply one of those outlying posts. High up in the mountains, the holdouts Sidi Raho and Saïd ou Mohand remained stubbornly indomitable.

Trying to ignore as much as they could the danger, Durosoy stuck to his mission. He found some encouraging signs: Slowly, "family by family," some Imazighen rallied to the French. He pictured Lyautey as working hard in Rabat, "bent under his two desk lamps, reading reports, preparing his orders. Step by step he follows our actions."[18] He marveled as he witnessed the succession of Amazigh festivals and rituals, the dances, the melancholic chants that were already memorializing the tragic chapter of their history, the French invasion. Dispensaries and schools went up, the villagers brought their crops at the markets. Once the hardest part of the job was accomplished, the legionnaires left.

By spring of 1924, Durosoy's work at El Mers got him a promotion: He became attaché to the resident-general, in charge of intelligence. Lyautey welcomed him in Fes, at his residence of Bou Jeloud, "a vast palace out of the Thousand and One Nights."[19] Entering the vast study ornamented in traditional Moroccan tile work and overlooking cool, lovely courtyards, Durosoy found an alert man, brilliant as usual. "Stand by, Lyautey ordered after explaining his new duties, we are leaving tomorrow for the Ouergha."

The Ouergha region, to the northwest of Fes, had very much supplanted the troubled Middle Atlas in the plans of the general-resident. After declaring armed conflict against Spain and inflicting the catastrophic and murderous defeat at Annual in the Rif, Abdelkrim had rallied other tribes—often with violence and coercion. By the end of that summer, he had secured allegiances north of Fes. When General Primo de Rivera came to power in Spain in the fall of 1923 and chose to disengage in Morocco, the Riffian chief's prestige reached new heights and he found it even easier to extend his reach throughout northern Morocco, from his city of Ajdir. To survive, however, an autonomous and prosperous republic of the Rif needed more land than those deeply etched valleys where most of the population lived. This is when he challenged those tribes who lived in the granary of the country, the Ouergha River plain.[20]

The French finally realized the very real danger that the Riffian chief represented for them. At the end of May 1924, twelve thousand of Lyautey's soldiers entered Spanish territory to establish a new line of fortifications. A multitude of small posts dotted the edge of the Rif, like a line of flower pots on the cornice of a wall. This is where Lyautey now wanted Durosoy to direct his intelligence gathering, and where he wanted to take him on a tour.

But before leaving for this new front, Lyautey took this convert to his *zawiya* on a walking tour of Fes. "Since [1912], you see, I wander alone without an escort, casually mingling with the crowd of my Fassi friends."[21] They went down the Talaa Sghira, which descends from the Bou Jeloud Gate into the intricate heart of Fes, toward the souks bursting with goods made by Fes's fine craftsmen and toward the Al Qarawiyyin school and mosque. They admired the Nejjarine Fountain, reputed to be Fes's finest.[22] Carried by the crowd, in a flow mingling simple woolen burnouses of the workers, the luxurious caftans of the merchants and notables, and the white dress of the women, Lyautey and Durosoy reached the shrine of Moulay Idriss II, the founder and patron saint of the city. This is where, a year earlier, the Fassis had invited Lyautey to pray after a near fatal illness. Standing outside the shrine's gate, Lyautey slipped an alm into an opening and respectfully bowed before the shrine. Since Lyautey had taken charge in Morocco, mosques were off-limits to non-Muslims by state decree. He took the opportunity to explain again how he had responded to the Moroccan well-wishers when he fell ill the year before.

> When thanks to their prayers I had found good health again, the Chorfas asked that my first visit be to Moulay Idriss and they had insisted that I enter the shrine. As I just did, I stopped before the door and just put a foot forward. Seeing their surprise and so touched by their gesture, I told them: I first went to thank god in the chapel of my religion, but believe me, if I entered the sacred mosque of Moulay Idriss, that would mean for me breaking a sacred tradition.[23]

Continuing their tour, Lyautey and Durosoy saw the tombs of the Marinid sovereigns who had ruled over Morocco from the thirteenth to the fifteenth centuries, on the mountain crest, right outside the city's northern gates, where the legionnaires had fought in 1912.

Sunset, to the west, brought a violet veil over the city. Between its crenellated, fiery red walls, Fes lit up as the call to the evening prayer, from one minaret to another, echoed throughout the town.

CHAPTER 14

The Rif on Fire

E ven by Morocco's scorching standards, the summer of 1925 was one of the hottest in memory. A fiery desert wind blew from the reddened horizon, parching the country as it howled by, the kind of wind that dries the sweat on one's skin right away, leaving one dizzy, with a thirst that no amount of water will quench.

The heat hardly spared the Rif Mountains in northern Morocco. The Rif chain, about three hundred and fifty kilometers long, arches along the Mediterranean coast from the northern tip of the kingdom to Algeria, to form a hermetic barrier against the sea. Its summit, the Jbel Tidirhine, peaks at twenty-five hundred meters (more than eight thousand feet), and there are barely any openings in the mountains. The valleys where the Rif Amazigh tribes live are deep, encased, isolated. To the north, it's a rampart of rock falling into the sea. To the south, high forests of pine and cedar give way to brush, and to the west, down toward the Ouergha River, the incline yields to undulating fields of wheat and barley. All this abundance, in the hot summer of 1925, had dulled to ochre.

Lyautey and his generals had reacted to the remarkable advances of Abdelkrim in Spanish Morocco, moving in 1924 across the Ouergha. They had not envisioned how the warrior of the Rif would eventually set his sights on French-controlled territory and chosen early action against this threat. Perhaps Lyautey, in assessing the political situation in Morocco, focused too narrowly on urban elites where new ideas from the Arab world spread.

Abdelkrim was not the kind of tribal chief the French had met in the Atlas—although those, as the contest at El Mers had just proved, could surely give them a run for their weapons. Born in 1882, the son of an Islamic judge, a qadi, Abdelkrim was educated and savvy. He belonged to the Beni Waryagher, one of the most important tribes of the Rif, centered south of Al Hoceima, in the center of the mountain range. He had attended a Spanish school, and then perfected his training at the famed Al Qarawiyyin school in Fes. Returned to the Spanish territory, he entered civil service, and eventually became a journalist. The Spanish put him in jail for a while, after he expressed resolutely anticolonial opinions. During his captivity he tried to escape and broke a leg, leaving him with a strong limp. Abdelkrim's presence never failed to make an impression; quite portly, he had a direct, sharp gaze that contemporary photographs render quite well. Abdelkrim, above all, showed superior intelligence and craft.

The Rif War raises further questions, notably on Abdelkrim's true objectives. How did he conclude that it made sense to take on the French, who had much better military leaders and troops than the Spanish? Did Abdelkrim's move actually mean that he had lost control of the uprising he had created, and somehow got drawn against his will in a cascade of events? In any case, a new war loomed, a war that would be fundamentally different from the recent conflicts that the French had waged. Lyautey faced a challenge as daunting as the rising of 1912.

The wider political context of this challenge differed very much, too. The Cartel des Gauches, an alliance of leftist parties, had taken power in 1924 in the Chamber of Deputies. These parties harbored deep suspicions toward the Moroccan pro-consul and his clinging to both civilian and military authority; they could, as well, hear the stronger anticolonial voices that came from the far left at the Chamber. It was not only Communism as an international movement that drew the world's attention on these tribesmen of northern Morocco. A larger political consciousness of what colonialism represented, for both subjugated peoples and their masters, had emerged. From the cover of *Time* magazine's August 17, 1925 issue, Abdelkrim stared back at the French and the Western powers with a cool, assured air.

Lyautey expected Abdelkrim eventually to play his hand. He did so on April 12, 1925, when he attacked the Beni Zeroual, who were pledged to the sultan, that is, to the French.

Legion buglers at the camp of Le Kreider in Algeria sounded "La Générale" the day after, on April 13. The Sixth Battalion of First Regiment of both Zinovy Peshkov and Adolphe Cooper had been stationed in this Algerian post to rest and train for the winter, but the time for action had come again and they looked forward to it. A legionnaire did not appreciate idleness, a sure trigger of the *cafard*. "Immediately the men assembled in the barracks and the roll was called. Every corporal and sergeant has a book in which the names of all the men who are to march with him are inscribed, and also a record of the armament and outfit that has been assigned to each man to carry with him."[1] The men received ammunitions and reserve food (two tins of corned beef and twelve biscuits, salt, and coffee). It all went with the rest of the equipment in the tightly packed sacks. Outside the sack hung extra shoes, a blanket roll on top, and collapsible tent poles. Standing by rank, at a resounding *"En avant! Marche!"* the Sixth began its journey to the Rif.

They passed through Sidi Bel Abbès, then Oujda. News came that the Riffians were attacking French posts and that tribes pledged to the French had defected. On April 25, they camped at Taza. "Notwithstanding that it was the month of April, there was great heat—distressing heat—and dust on the road."[2] As the legionnaires approached Fes they realized that this campaign would not resemble the previous ones, no matter how hard fought those had been. The sheer number of troops on the road betrayed that, and a disquieting air on the officers' faces. They marched. One-two . . . one-two . . . one-two. The songs of the Legion rose in the clouds of dust. They marched forward with little respite, because "useful Morocco" was not a safe country anymore. Then lorries appeared to take the battalion to Fes. Commanders feared that the very safety of Fes was at stake if the Atlas tribes joined the movement. "The Berber flies before victory," went the old French saying.

The Legion reached Fes at the end of April, just in time to celebrate the anniversary of Camarón. They had to reach the camp at Aïn Aicha, the base from which they could protect Fes, under the leadership of Henry Freydenberg. They were joined there by three companies of the Second Regiment. Other Legion contingents went to Fes-el-Bali, a small town not to be confused with the former capital.

As far as Lyautey was concerned, his strategy for engaging in colonial conflicts remained essentially the same, a tight balancing act between political and military forces. He considered the Rif a hornet's nest where one should never set foot, and always acted with this principle that military victories had to be obtained with minimum toll for the enemy, to avoid excessive resentment toward the French regime and create lasting submission to it. The posts had to be protected to manifest French supremacy, and concerning the troops' organization, he still favored those small mobile groups, created first and foremost to supply, cover, or rescue those posts.

"Before sunset all officers assembled at the tent of the commander of the detachment, then all went to a hill overlooking camp, from which one could see across the valley to the mountains—a succession of high peaks—on which were our posts," recalled Peshkov.[3]

Action at this point in May centered around the fort on the mountain of Bibane, the "prince" of the mountain towering over the plain leading to Fes, and which the Riffians surrounded, cutting off all channels to resupply the fort occupied by the French troops of Sergeant Bernis. Many smaller French posts, each with their own blockhouses, encircled this vital position and sustained vigorous assaults. On May 2 the French saved the posts of Aoudour and Achirkane but lost the one at Aoulai. May 4 was a day of starkly contrasting outcomes. Peshkov's men heroically rescued Taounat, while the enemy inflicted a devastating blow, repelling an attempt to break through the Moroccans's lines around Bibane and rescue the fort.

This war exceeded gloomy expectations right from the beginning. Up to sixteen thousand Riffian fighters from all corners of the north, supported by the regulars of Abdelkrim's army, inflicted painful setbacks. They mastered the use of their artillery and machine guns to pummel the small forts the French had built. These forts, built in dry-stone and surrounded by barbed wire, were a mistake. Set high up, they had no water; the strength of Abdelkrim made resupplying them almost impossible. Supply convoys traveled in difficult rocky terrain, climbing crests and ravines up and down, in a landscape of boulders and spiny brush, all that in eerie silence. The French found all the villages deserted. Lonely outposts sometimes had to survive on blocks of ice dropped by airplane; those did not take long to melt. Around the posts, the Riffians had built elaborate defensive works to ward off rescue operations, and even aerial drops. When the troops reached them, gory fights by hand grenade and bayonet took place. On May 15, the French took back Aoulai, which they chose to destroy rather than risk more lives to hold it.

In Bibane, where Abdelkrim had surrounded Sergeant Bernis and his Senegalese company, the centerpiece of the French plan to break the siege of this essential asset included Aage of Denmark. The prince was fighting his third Moroccan campaign under Colombat—a commander whom the soldiers called the "white rat" on account of his baldness and spiky mustache. On May 25, at dawn, Aage approached Bibane with the Twenty-Second Company of the Second Regiment, as a liaison officer of the advance guard. The temperature, noted another legionnaire, Ziegler, was already quite high. Since the last clash, the Riffians had reinforced their defense: Leaving the fort or approaching it appeared to be an impossible enterprise. "The Legion was in a blue funk, the nameless fear that precedes battle. I would not give a penny for soldiers who failed to act similarly in the event of an assault," commented Aage.[4]

On May 25 the legionnaires plunged forward under the cover of the 75mm artillery, in the haze of the morning mist and cannon fire. Bullets flew by with the sound of big bumblebees. In a moment, "The firing had grown so heavy now that one advanced in a sort of coma, the shattering din suspending all thought for the time." Bodies lay on the ground, and for the sprinters who reached the Riffian trenches isolating Bibane, a shocking realization: They were being fired upon by their own, so fast had they moved toward the enemy. Aage's duty was to put an end to this devastating error. To the left, more enemies fired from under the cover of a house. Several assaults only sowed death among the legionnaires. To the right, another battalion of the Legion desperately tried to take a similar firing spot. "Men went down like wheat before a scythe."

Rage, at long last, fired up Delande, the leader of this battalion. He gathered twelve officers, who, against all odds, were still standing:

> Serving each officer with a sack of grenades, the major distributed them at intervals along the line directly opposite the enemy trench and blockhouse. At a given signal they leaped the parapet as one man and advanced at a brisk run, hurling grenades as they came within the range of the Riffians. The trenches, at this point, were not more than fifty yards apart, so that it could not have taken the major and his daring party more than ten or twelve seconds to traverse it. Almost at once, it seemed, they came to close quarters. The enemy trench fairly spat fire, but the officers, instead of melting away, carried on. Then the grenades commenced to take effect. The grenadiers, every one of them experts, hurled their bombs with incredible speed and accuracy. The trench lip seemed, in spots, to rise up, only to crumble immediately into new and unfamiliar shapes. The major hurled bomb after bomb through a window at one side of the blockhouse. A wall bulged outward and then crashed. Nothing could have survived within.[5]

A mad dash crowned this feat of bravery. The twelve had the *baraka*—they all survived. This heroic charge described by Aage, however, brought more to the annals of the Legion than to the general outcomes of the fight for Bibane. Enemy fire cut down the next company. They all perished. Few men survived in the following one, and the fight went on with the same distress for hours.

At one thirty, Colombat ordered that all the artillery be aimed at the Riffian-controlled blockhouse that faced the main fort at Bibane. This charge stunned the occupants, so much so that after overcoming the resistance in the blockhouse Aage and his legionnaires finally made it to the fort that crowned the mountain. Inside were Sergeant Bernis, his French gunners, a French signalman, and forty-six Senegalese infantrymen—a force that still had to remain to guard the fort. The sergeant saluted the legionnaires after the supply mission ended: "Good-bye sir, I am afraid we are to be sacrificed."[6] According to Aage, this third relief mission at Bibane had cost five hundred men, including eighty officers—one out of four men in Colombat's force.

Saving Fes had to remain the priority. Since Abdelkrim had declared that he would be at Fes by the holiday of Eid al-Adha, which fell on July 2 that year, all efforts converged toward this goal of preserving the capital, and avoiding a disintegration of the entire French colony of Morocco. Given the number of Riffian soldiers that kept pouring in, saving all those posts, let alone maintaining them, was out of the question.

Just a few hours after the daring May 25 rescue, Bibane signaled that they were under yet another ferocious attack. There was nothing that the helpless onlookers could do. Two days later a large part of Sergeant Bernis's men in the fort were wounded. The message they received assured imminent relief. They knew all too well what to think of the promise.

Abdelkrim shifted his attacks to the east where Freydenberg defended the French line along the Rif. The post of Taounate assumed the importance that Bibane had had weeks earlier. Many smaller posts—Sker, Astar, Mezraoua—encircled it. Astar fell to the Rif's army. Peshkov's legionnaires, including Cooper, retook it on June 4. Upon entering the post, Cooper saw the body of a French officer: "His feet were burned away, his legs charred almost to the thighs and his eyes had been gouged out their sockets and hung down his cheeks."[7] On June 5, the Riffians, in numbers exceeding three thousand, approached Sker and Mezraoua.

The tragedy at Bibane concluded on that same day, the fifth of June. Aage described the Moroccans' surge toward the wall of the compound. The major inside was still communicating up to his last moments: "The heliograph flashed, despairingly, '*Poste fichu!*' Then came the final signal, never to be completed. We stood breathless, repeating every letter as it was flashed— 'S-E-R-G-E-A-N-T, Sergeant B—' and they scaled the walls, hundreds of them."[8] General Colombat, livid, weeping, ordered his artillery to be directed at Bibane. The cannons reduced the post to rubble, burying both defenders and attackers.

A few days later, on June 11, the tragedy at the post of Mediouna gave yet another grim trophy to the Foreign Legion. There had been two attempts at freeing the post, where a troop of Senegalese fighters also waited anxiously. They signaled that they considered blowing themselves up, and so forty legionnaires volunteered to try a last-ditch rescue. In the middle of the night they walked through the mountains, wearing softer shoes to avoid detection. The Riffians had surrounded Mediouna with two trenches, one facing out toward any attempt at breaking into the post, the other facing inward, to deter escape.

When they reached Mediouna, the legionnaires hurled themselves through those trenches, throwing grenades and firing rounds. Some made it to the fort, but there, they heard from the commander that they had to leave immediately—the entire structure, filled with mines by his order, was about to blow up. Only three legionnaires survived the ordeal. When they came back to their camp, Peshkov saw that "the expression on their faces was one of horror. The things they had seen were reflected there."[9] Later, a detachment of legionnaires reached Mediouna, which the Riffians had abandoned. Not one body of the French soldiers was found.

The Rif War, as it unfolded, emerged as a landmark episode in the French colonization of Morocco, for many reasons. As far as the Legion was concerned, General Durosoy called the harrowing weeks of the summer 1925 the "heroic phase" of the Rif War.[10] For Peshkov, the legionnaires' comportment was an astounding demonstration that there was no such thing as an "old" Legion that had faded after the war and now a "new" one—there was just the Legion, the legendary corps. Surely outstanding examples of bravery abounded, enough to inspire future legionnaires.

But the memoirs of the Rif campaign, for all their epic claims, have a desperate tone that reflects how violence had reached maximum intensity for the French. The Riffians fought brutally. Meanwhile, planes dropped a deluge of bombs on Abdelkrim's fighters, and sometimes on the population. To the ordinary soldiers, the laws of war had dissolved into the thin, burning air of the mountains. By the end of this ill-fated month of June, the troops offered the sad spectacle of a worn-out lot:

> All our kit was lost, our clothing was in shreds and we used to pin
> it together with thorns. Our shoes had gone and we used our putties
> round our feet. The really hard legionnaires discarded all footgear;
> the skin on their soles of their feet was a quarter of an inch thick.
> What really amazed me was that we all enjoyed life. The harder [it
> was], the more enjoyable it was, but there were also inhuman things
> perpetrated sometimes by us and condoned by officers.[11]

Cooper tells the story of how he and a few fellow combatants shot a prisoner in the back after telling him he could go away. Peshkov, who showed up at that very moment, asked them to reflect that the man might have had a wife and young children. They did not care; that was the stuff of war. Peshkov himself did not waste time over tender sentiments for a Moroccan who was caught in the camp after killing two soldiers. They dug his grave in front of him. "From time to time [the prisoner] would look at the sky and he would smile."[12]

The sirocco still blew from the depths of Africa, reaching the outposts built by the French in their haste to counter the most formidable enemy they had ever met in their colonial conquest, Abdelkrim. It was there, in those mountains of the Rif along which the hot sirocco climbed, in solitary forts perched on a rocky hilltop, that many a legionnaire's destiny was accomplished, where nothingness engulfed the forlorn lives, the labors, the deprivations. The Rif War occupies a very special place in the long gallery of heroic feats of the Foreign Legion. One often hears that the highest honor of war lies in sacrifice, sacrifice to the nation, to the corps, or to the comrades. But there comes a time when death is just death, even with the belief in redemption.

By the end of the month, startling events at the highest echelons of power in the French Protectorate of Morocco changed the course and nature of the Rif War and precipitated its denouement.

The president of the French Council of Ministers, Paul Painlevé, landed in Rabat on June 12 to see for himself the depth of French Morocco's predicament. Sixty-two-year-old Paul Painlevé, a mathematician with a round silhouette and a thick bushy mustache, did not exactly evoke images of a daring adventurer. To reach Morocco by plane was still quite an accomplishment in those days. And yet he arrived resolute, lifting aviator goggles from his face, having decided to have a good look on the war-torn colony of Marshal Lyautey.

In the Chamber of Deputies Painlevé faced steady pressure. To his political left, it appeared that the regime of the resident-general had reached its logical outcome: a dictatorship doomed to fail as it was mired in court flattery and solipsism. Further to the left, Communists questioned the very legitimacy of colonialism. Assemblyman Marcel Cachin saw the Rif uprising as a symptom of a larger pan-Islamic movement, in direct relation with Turkey's republicanism and Egyptian rejection of English rule. Indeed, many across the Arab world, and even farther east, in India, for example, observed the Moroccan quagmire with rapture.

Other international events elevated the significance of the Moroccan crisis. The French, who had obtained control over Syria following the dismemberment of the Ottoman Empire after the Great War, faced unrest among the Druze population, soon to become a bitter revolt as the summer of 1925 unfolded. Legionnaires from the First Regiment in Sidi Bel Abbès and the cavalry in Tunisia were sent out to Syria, where they played an active role in quashing the revolt. French public opinion, however, still adhered to the seductive image of Greater France, the exceptional nation that spread civilization across the world. Behind Abdelkrim's movement, which they could not fathom as a serious one, many French saw the hand of their perennial enemies the British.

Lyautey, the old lion in Rabat, welcomed the visit of Painlevé, thinking that his methods would be vindicated. But he had nearly exhausted his own physical and mental resources. In early June, he wrote a letter requesting the nomination of an army general to be at his side, with words unusual in how they conveyed weakness:

> I am well into my seventies and have had many health incidents over the last years, and yet I resist morally and physically before the heaviest effort I've ever had to endure. But I know very well that my strength could give way at any time, and the national interest that I am responsible for should not be at the mercy of an accident. Already, because of the surgeries I've had to endure, prolonged and hurried travel by car takes a heavy toll on me, and, as far as riding horseback is concerned, that's impossible.[13]

Lyautey was drained. By his own staff's admission, the septuagenarian marshal suffered from serious bouts of the *cafard*. But then, when he had to face distressing news, he would become agitated, torn by violent feelings. If this bipolar temperament might have served somehow in the past, leading him to act swiftly through deep introspection, at that advanced age it merely made Lyautey look indecisive and unpredictable.

Nevertheless, the marshal took Painlevé to Fes and near the front. They visited hospitals and reviewed the troops of the First Regiment. Painlevé awarded the three survivors of Mediouna the Médaille Militaire. One of them, Corporal Goulet of the Twenty-Second Company, was an old veteran who had fought at Fes, in France during World War I, and in Morocco.

After the ceremony, Lyautey took the man to his tent and served him coffee in person—a mundane gesture, perhaps, but one that the legionnaires appreciated and for which they granted the marshal both trust and reverence. One could still see smoking debris of the Rif's posts recently abandoned and destroyed in the distance.

Painlevé returned to Paris after a couple of days without offering much in terms of additional resources. Lyautey's grievance against the government, of course, concerned the meager reinforcement he had gotten in spite of several dramatic pleas transmitted over the previous year. Eventually reinforcements arrived, fourteen thousand in June alone.[14] But they were sorely inadequate for fighting a truly effective counteroffensive against Abdelkrim. Out of fifty-six battalions, three belonged to the Legion.

Fifteen days after the high-level visit, Abdelkrim once again shook the edifice of the French military protection to its foundations when he applied the force of his troops against Taza. In the first days of July he won over the Tsoul and Branes tribes who dwelled in the Taza corridor, blocking communications with Algeria and possibly planning to rally the Atlas Imazighen.

Lyautey, with this new threat, moved his headquarters to Fes on July 2, following Sultan Moulay Yusef. At least both men could celebrate Eid al-Adha with enough pageantry to remind Abdelkrim that he had not made it into Fes by the holiday. "Under an all-blue summer sky, airplanes and gracious storks flew over the city and the jubilant crowds, just as the powder of the mock-battle *fantasias* resounded. A brilliantly adorned and illuminated Fes lived all night the joys of the great celebration of Islam. Meanwhile, very serious events loomed."[15]

As the celebrations were ongoing, refugees poured into the city. "A true panic set in amongst the tribes of the Fes-Taza region, in the days of the second and third, one of those contagious panic waves that are suddenly set in motion in this country as I saw it twice, in 1912 and in 1919," wrote Lyautey with an almost palpable shiver.[16] Meanwhile, Aage had been ordered to reach Fes. There, he instructed recruits on how to man machine guns.

Louder voices among Lyautey's chiefs of staff called for abandoning Taza to save Fes. Locked in his headquarters at Bou Jeloud Palace, Lyautey and his staff reviewed all options. A secret envoy had met Abdelkrim on June 28. The war leader, quite in contradiction with the discourse he held before the tribes he brought into his confederation, denied that he was waging a holy war. He wanted recognition for a new Republic of the Rif.

Lyautey wavered at first, considered this as an option, but then he brushed it aside. Not only would it have encouraged sedition throughout the empire, but also the existence of a republic within Morocco squarely contradicted the sovereignty of the sultan he had cultivated with interest and passion. Other officers argued that Taza had to be evacuated, and the line of protection brought much closer to Fes.

On July 5, after spending a night pondering his options, Lyautey held steadfast, deciding that the front would remain. Lyautey might also have relied on a last-ditch option, one that very few knew about: He had requested stocks of chemical weapons, and the permission to use them—the Spanish had dropped such bombs against the civilian population of the Rif at least since 1923, if not 1921.

Three official requests from Lyautey to Painlevé are recorded for the month of May, urgently demanding chemical bombs. On May 11, following two earlier telegrams on this subject, presumably sensing reticence in Paris, Lyautey conceded that in past he had criticized the use of such weapons by the Spanish army. The sultan, understandably, had found it upsetting. But given the desperate state of the French defense before the Rif's forces, Lyautey needed the means to defend certain assets vital to the survival of the colony—presumably Fes itself. "These are shells that I would hold in reserve, with utmost discretion, to use them in the conditions that I have just described and in the last resort. So I ask you to speed up the shipment of these shells."[17]

President Painlevé balked. The memory of the terrible effects of mustard gas on the battlefields of the Great War was still too vivid, and so the weapons were never delivered. Lyautey argued again in June that the Riffians waged a savage war using modern weapons, and these special shells, the *obus* 20mm, were "indispensable." "Our adversaries operate with such savagery, with such cruelty, mutilating the wounded and prisoners, committing loot and burning, that all means appear justified to get ahead."[18] The Rif War came close to the very worst that war can be.

Paul Painlevé still needed informed opinions on the Moroccan situation after he returned from France. He appointed Philippe Pétain, the veteran of the Great War and a figure revered in the army, to investigate. Pétain, at that time, was widely regarded as the true hero, the stalwart of the Great War, having restored morale and tactical intelligence to the French army after the dreadful Nivelle offensive that Lyautey had had to support as minister of war in 1917.

Pétain went to Morocco from July 17 to 27. He visited the front and asked many questions in a tone that left little doubt as to a foregone conclusion. Both men's entourages observed, fascinated, this true clash of titans, the architect of colonial France and the savior of the battle at Verdun, the dandy aristocrat and the austere son of a farmer. Sure, there were protestations of goodwill and promises of collaboration. Tension peaked at a dinner hosted by the Lyauteys in the lavish gardens of Bou Jeloud Palace, in Fes. Durosoy and General Catroux, who attended, left striking descriptions of the scene in their memoirs.

> A well-set sirocco heated the temperature to unbearable levels, and any drafts had no other effect than to blow an even hotter breath of air. Lyautey naturally owned a luxurious stock of weather-appropriate uniforms, adorned with multicolored military orders under the Plaque Grand-Croix, all this opening onto soft and comfortable foulards. Marshal Pétain, who was on his first trip to North Africa, sported a simple uniform cut from a khaki cloth, with a tight collar; no doubt it had been cut in haste before leaving Paris and he wore it with the simple ribbon of the the Médaille Militaire.[19]

In the hot air weighed by the perfume of jasmine, attendants moved around slowly, their caftans brushing against the marble inlays of the patio. Lyautey, at ease in the heat, remained a model of affable and lively urbanity. When they hosted, the Lyauteys hired violinists who played old Andalusian songs from behind the rose bushes. Pétain, "enigmatic and marmoreal," indifferent to the refinements, responded tersely to his host's witticisms.[20] The visitor retired early, leaving Lyautey, well known to enjoy chats stretching well into the night, wondering whether his days in Fes were numbered.

Pétain returned to France with a report in his pocket and the fruits of an exchange with his Spanish counterpart, Primo de Rivera—he met him at a stopover in the Moroccan city of Tetouan. "What you do is politics; what I do is strategy," is how Pétain summed up the differences between the resident-general's views and his own.[21] The conflict had entered a new, decisive phase. There would be no talk of patient occupation of the terrain, no endless sipping of hot mint tea with chieftains of tribes that were the most susceptible to switch their loyalties and join the French against Abdelkrim.

Lyautey's military cabinet still argued for patient political action. One Lieutenant Vincent, for example, wrote this note on July 15, 1925: "We can see that in Morocco, any military action must remain inspired and conditioned, both in general and in its details, by indigenous politics, of which it is only an instrument."[22] From this principle followed the necessity of keeping both political and military command to one person, in the person of the resident-general.

But for thinkers of the Pétain school, this was a war, and it had to be waged like war. Although he could be blunt in person, Pétain softened his tone considerably when he spoke of the Moroccan commander in his correspondence with the government. The report he wrote after inspecting Morocco stated: "We can only bow before the Great Chef who, in spite of his age and the weight of his rough colonial career, directed and animated this defense and has been able to preserve before the rush of barbarians his civilizational achievement, which the entire world considers excellent."[23]

The die was cast in Paris. Back in Morocco on August 22, Pétain arrived as the newly nominated commander of the army. Lyautey was to remain only in his civilian leader capacity. He had learned of the decision earlier. The new commander wrote to Paris explaining how much the decision had affected Lyautey: "The July letter in which you withdrew his military command has affected him very much. You could have spared him this offensive blow since I was coming here to fix things."[24] To Lyautey and his close circle's frustration, the troops that could hardly be found early in the war now poured into Morocco, with additional resources for material and infrastructure, including heavy artillery, armored tanks, more airplanes. The number of soldiers grew to 160,000, including the Seventh Battalion of the First Regiment from Sidi Bel Abbès. Railways and new roads opened, built as if by magic. Army commanders brought in by Pétain coordinated with the Spanish.

From then on, a massive operation hammered the Rif. Abdelkrim's forces attacked ferociously in the last days of July, in a last effort to preserve their momentum, and the legionnaires waged merciless battles near Taza, notably on the twenty-fourth, when they rescued the fort at Bab Mouroudj. The Spanish reentered the conflict with a landing at Al Hoceima, on September 8, on the Riffian Mediterranean outlet. By mid-September, the enormous effort brought into place reestablished the French line of defense where it had had been drawn in 1924. The Rif, stunned silent by a deluge of bombs, smoldered in the late-summer heat.

The curtain was about to fall on Lyautey's reign in Morocco, an episode both tragic and fascinating in the long history of the kingdom. The marshal offered his resignation on September 24, 1925, and Painlevé accepted it promptly. Lyautey did not leave in haste the kingdom he had, for thirteen years, struggled to fashion into his own vision of a paradoxical alliance of tradition and modernity. He toured Morocco extensively with Madame Lyautey, visited his cherished palaces one last time, dived into the medinas.

On October 2, he bid adieu to Sultan Yusef. The sultan is said to have shown genuine emotion.

On October 10, in Casablanca, Monsieur and Madame Lyautey boarded the commercial liner *Anfa* bound for France. The French government had not seen fit to offer the honors of a military ship to him, a marshal. Was it the bad conscience of a Third Republic that had come to realize, perhaps, the contradiction inherent in its colonial credo, a wish not to offer a painful contrast with the brutal images of the war that reached the public in France, or just an oversight? On the piers of Casablanca's sprawling new port, a dense crowd of both Europeans and Moroccans waived good-bye. There were even qaids who had come from afar. Everyone sensed that an important page in Morocco's history was turning.

The *Anfa* sailed. After Tangiers, an unlikely, appreciated gesture of recognition came from the English: The governor of Gibraltar sent two destroyers, the *Whip* and the *Whitehead*, to escort Lyautey's passage through the strait. "Well, they, at least, know how to do it," commented Lyautey, who put on his best uniform and stood on the deck to acknowledge the salute.[25] The white ensign of the Royal Navy and the French tricolor flapped in the wind on the English warships. The sailors shouted a thunderous "Hurrah!" before they parted ways. In Marseilles, where the *Anfa* docked, Lyautey stepped onto French soil an ordinary citizen, without any fanfare or recognition.

Abdelkrim surrendered to the French in May 1926, marking the end of the Rif War. He was exiled to Réunion Island, to the east of Madagascar. Twenty years later, during a trip to Europe, he escaped to Egypt, where he spent the rest of his days. The rendition of Sidi Raho and Saïd ou Mohand, the irreducible Amazigh chiefs of the Middle Atlas, also took place that year.

Prince Aage left Fes in August of 1925 after an old wound reopened and the torrid temperature prevented it from healing. Once rested, he traveled to the United States on his promotional tour for the Legion. After eighteen years of service, Aage died of natural causes in Morocco. Peshkov remained in the campaign till a gunshot wound to his feet sent him to the hospital. During the Second World War, Peshkov took a post offered by General Douglas MacArthur. He died in Paris, a darling of high society.

CHAPTER 15

Beau Travail!

On April 30, 1931, large crowds gathered in Sidi Bel Abbès to celebrate a special anniversary. A century before, King Louis-Philippe of France had created the French Foreign Legion, allowing foreign-born soldiers to join the military and serve France. The centennial celebration took on added significance, since it was on that day that the men of Captain Danjou, in the Mexican hamlet of Camarón, had held out until they were almost all killed.

The future seemed bright for the Legion. Although the legionnaires who joined up in 1921 had not reenlisted as much Lyautey had wished, others had shown up, especially when the Great Depression befell Europe and America. The barracks were adequately filled with recruits, and the bleak years of 1919 to 1920 seemed like a bad memory. Those recruits benefitted from better attention from the moment they enlisted at a *bureau de recruitment*. They got new clothes for the trip that took them to the old fort of Saint-Jean in Marseilles.

Paul-Frédéric Rollet planned the centenary, which drew twenty thousand troops and guests from all corners of the empire. In 1925 he had been made commander of the First Regiment, stationed in the town, and in 1931 he took the newly created post of inspector of the Legion, which came with the rank of *général de brigade*. This inveterate womanizer had also chosen to marry in 1925. Actually, he did not have much choice. Once he returned to Sidi Bel Abbès, the civilian population of this very proper town found it a little beyond their tolerance for legionnaire eccentricity that they would have to host the commander of a major military force, Colonel Rollet, with his mistress, Alice Hébert, whom the colonel called Nénette. Perhaps in Fes, but in a proper French town, never.

Sidi Bel Abbès had not changed much; it was still that strange town that eerily evoked a provincial city in metropolitan France—if one set aside the palm trees and the population that mixed military personal, Europeans with a majority of Spaniards, and Algerians. The town was about to experience a burst of development. The headquarters of the First Regiment became the clearing point and training camp for all the regiments of the Legion two years after the centenary. Under Rollet, many new buildings went up, including a house for retired legionnaires. New establishments of this kind opened in Marseilles (1931) and in Auriol, too (1934).

There were speeches, a banquet, and concerts. Naturally, the troops paraded in perfect lockstep, and they did so before a brand-new monument centered in the barracks at the Quartier Viénot. A huge metal globe on which all the significant battles of the Legion shined in burnished letters topped a marble pedestal. Four statues of legionnaires guarded the structure. The march began with the ranks of the newly created *compagnies de sapeurs-pionniers* (sappers, or engineers), already displaying the axes, leather aprons, and square beards that would make them so popular in the parades of the Republic on the Champs-Élysées. They figuratively opened the road, marching to "Le Boudin." The legionnaires wore the kepi, owing to Rollet's keen sense of the cohesion symbols and practices could create and the way they cemented a sense of belonging to the Legion.

Until then, the soldier's head covering depended very much on the whims of the administration, or just what stock was available, but Rollet fought to make the kepi standard. In a report dated from March 1926, Rollet had deplored a lack of standards in the uniforms of the Legion. He explained that the legionnaire did not care at all for the colonial helmet, that he much preferred the kepi (he is "in love" with his uniform, specified Rollet), to such an extent that the Legion's First and Second Regiments had taken upon themselves to produce the kepis, which they gave to the soldiers. A few months after Rollet wrote this report, the army attributed to the Legion the use of the kepi cover, but in that light khaki fabric that the sun whitened to the legionnaires' content. At long last, in 1933, the white cover officially became part of the legionnaire's uniform. The detail had already caught the imagination of the larger public, and eventually became the most recognized and appreciated symbol of the Legion.[1] Rollet also established another outstanding feature of the uniform, the green and red epaulettes and the blue waistband, which the legionnaires wore for the centennial parade. Rollet had a flair not only for administering the Legion but also for reinventing its tradition, talents that amply warranted the sobriquet "father of the Legion."

But spectacle, a kind of spectacle well beyond the control of the brisk, slightly high-strung Rollet, already played a great role in defining what the Legion stood for. A year before the onset of the Rif War, in 1924, Percival C. Wren had published his famous novel *Beau Geste*. The first pages of the novel are striking. A rescue mission arrives at Fort Zinderneuf in the desert of French Sudan, only to make a gruesome discovery: All the legionnaires that are seen standing guard on the crenellated walls and fail to respond to the mission's salutations turn out to be cadavers riddled with bullets, set up to give the impression of a fully manned post during an attack by roaming Tuareg bands. A legionnaire of the rescue mission, Digby, then finds two bodies inside the fort who are his brothers, John and Michael "Beau" Geste. The latter holds a note claiming that he has stolen a precious gem, the "Blue Water."

The story flashes back to explain the dramatic mystery of these deaths. Raised in an opulent British country house by their aunt, Lady Brandon, whose husband lives overseas, the three brothers' lives are thrown into turmoil when that precious gem, the "Blue Water" sapphire, disappears. One evening, as Lady Brandon is showing the jewel, the lights go out, and when they come back on the stone has vanished. Beau leaves the house in secret to join the Foreign Legion, and so suspicion falls on him; his brothers, unable to accept their brother's guilt, successively join in the Legion, arriving at Sidi Bel Abbès. Eventually the two brothers Beau and Digby end up at Fort Zinderneuf, where they and the rest of the legionnaires are the victim of a noncommissioned officer, Lejaune, whose abject and sadistic behavior leads the soldiers to plot a mutiny; the Geste brothers would rather remain loyal to the flag. The fatal Tuareg attack renders the uprising's preparations moot. In the end, it is revealed that Beau had joined the Legion to protect the reputation of his aunt, after discovering that the real "Blue Water" was sold a while ago to cover debts incurred by her husband, a selfish man.

As interesting as this plot may seem, Wren's novel is far from a literary masterpiece. The central theme of honor, loyalty, and self-sacrifice are embodied by two-dimensional characters and some very wooden dialogue. Needless to say, colonialism, white racial superiority, and the peaceful virtues of French invasion are a given throughout, not only in the cartoonish description of the Tuaregs, but in the dialogue too: "I was glad to remember that these Tuaregs are human wolves, professional murderers whose livelihood is robbery with violence, which commonly takes the form of indescribable and unmentionable tortures," claims a character as he dispatches his attackers.[2] In all likelihood, Wren never joined the Legion, and he drew on the memoirs of George

Mannington and Frederic Martyn.[3] The novel did, however, capture well the romantic, self-abnegating ethos of the Legion. Sustained by many adaptations to the big screen and countless popular culture references, it popularized the image of the legionnaire's rugged face, below his white-flapped kepi, against a minimalist landscape of the sand ocean—not the edge of the Hamada, where legionnaires actually would most likely have been found—in the public's imagination. Postcards, memoirs, and popular-press articles were all readily available to that public. Rollet, even though he understood the powers of propaganda, and used them, found most of these works ridiculous, and called the 1926 adaptation of *Beau Geste* to the large screen a "*fantaisie abracadabrante.*"[4]

From then on, Hollywood would not dissociate the trope of the legionnaire from the hot sands of the Sahara, even though the Legion did not actually trample in the sand that much over its long history. In Joseph von Sternberg's 1930 film *Morocco*, the destiny of Marlene Dietrich, playing a cabaret singer, Amy Jolly, is sealed when she meets private Thom Brown (played by Gary Cooper) at one of her performances. The last images of the movie show her standing at the foot of a highly improbable sand dune outside Essaouira, in a glittery nightgown, torn between two lovers. Her decision made, she takes her high heels in her hands in a dramatic gesture, and heads straight for the desert with a cohort of other women, who, like moths drawn to a flame, have succumbed to the irresistible lure of the legionnaire, the weathered, brooding outcast who wears his emotions on the sleeve of his campaign coat. Nine years later, Gary Cooper again, mounted on a camel, tanned under his kepi complete with sun-flap, defied a backdrop of dunes in another adaptation of *Beau Geste*.

The image of the desert spoke to an ever-widening public. Raymond Asso composed "Mon Légionnaire" in 1936. The same year, Floyd Gottfredson drew the cartoon *Mickey Mouse in the Foreign Legion*. The memories of the lonesome legionnaires still resonated very much as news of their exploits emerged out of World War II, and then through the independence movements of Morocco, Algeria, and Vietnam.[5] After the success of films such as *Morocco* and *Beau Geste*, the public's taste for legionnaire stories reached a fevered pitch with countless pulp-fiction magazine stories and great movies. The Legion was also a popular theme on the television screen. From 1955 to 1957, NBC featured a series titled *Captain Gallant of the Foreign Legion*. Sinatra sang his own "French Foreign Legion" as a lively, romantic ballad.

Rollet died of natural causes in 1941, a legendary figure by that point. His wife, Nénette, wanted to preserve the memory of her husband and his outsize character. *La générale* Rollet installed a wax mannequin of the colonel, carefully crafted by the Musée Grévin, in a dedicated room in their private house. Any newly arrived officer had to come and salute the shrine in short order, lest by failing to do so he might ruin his budding career.

One man who could not make an appearance at the celebrations of the Legion's centennial in 1931 was Hubert Lyautey. No doubt he would have been a guest of honor. But the French government had named him commissar general of the 1931 International Colonial Exhibition, near Vincennes, right outside Paris's limits. The exhibition was set to open on May 6. In his regrets sent to Rollet, Lyautey explained that he would be at the Legion's centennial celebration in his thoughts:

> You know that I am legionnaire in body and soul. Since 1894, in the Tonkin, I have never ceased to march by the side of the Legion, in Madagascar, in the South Oranais, in the Algerian-Moroccan hinterlands, and after that in Morocco without respite, for thirty-three years uninterrupted. I was christened legionnaire in 1896 at the end of operations in the Upper Son Cau River. During my Oranais and Moroccan command, the Legion has been my troop, my most cherished troop, and during the war, from 1914 to 1919, it constituted my first force, my supreme reserve.[6]

No legionnaires were to be seen on the day the Colonial Exhibition opened, however. A four-car motorcade took President Gaston Doumergue and Lyautey around the grounds, to the acclaim of a dense and cheerful crowd. Saluting along the way were men of the Spahis and the Skirmishers, garbed in their finest and most exotic outfits. These soldiers made for much better visual attractions than the rugged, introverted, and weathered legionnaires, who were left to ponder their existential malaise in Algeria.

The president of France and his motorcade ended the tour at the Pavillon Permanent des Colonies, to hear speeches and formally open the exhibition. Lyautey welcomed the dignitaries in a private lounge built and decorated for him in the Art Deco style. Frescoes highlighted the wonders of Asia, while the furniture vaguely evoked faraway lands with inlays of exotic woods.[7] In the great hall, standing next to France's president in the middle, spectators saw the marshal, the emperor of Vietnam, the archbishop of Paris. "Each one of us must feel like a citizen of Greater France," proclaimed the politician Paul Reynaud in a soaring moment.[8]

The site of the exhibition, covering 275 acres, centered on Lake Daumesnil. Touring around, one could "travel the earth in one day," claimed the advertisement for the event. The organizers had built a gigantic replica of Angkor Wat to represent Cambodia.[9] Along the Grande Avenue des Colonies Françaises, visitors walked from the Houses of Catholic and Protestant Missions, to land at an enormous tower marking the triumph of the overseas armies. This theater became an exotic phantasmagoria at night. Powerful beams signaled the attractions from afar, and once there, a myriad of illuminations dazzled the families who came with their children. Waterworks that glistened during the day refracted multicolor lighting at night. Restaurants tempted the passerby with the perfume of exotic cuisines, and there were dances, displays of cultural artifacts and animals, and much more.[10] The organizers wished to stimulate commerce and industry, just as the effects of the Great Depression were being felt in France. Flanking the main entrance at the Porte Dorée, two huge constructions, evoking cruise ships and seemingly ready to sail to distant horizons, harbored the Cité des Informations, for trade councils, and the Section Métropolitaine, for domestic importers.

The colonies were eliciting wonder for their modernization. Teams of architects, urban planners, and financiers invented new models of modern living throughout old Morocco, from Fes to Marrakech.[11] Next to the medinas, their seedy joints, and heavenly palaces, sleek Art Deco buildings stretched their lines along vast avenues lined with palm trees. Casablanca was barely recognizable, now that it had become the economic showcase of the protectorate and handled 80 percent of Morocco's maritime traffic in its newly constructed harbor facilities. Between the late 1800s and 1926, the population of the city multiplied five times, to exceed one hundred thousand inhabitants.

A flow of civil servants fattened the bureaucracy of the residency.[12] Contrary to the other colonies in North Africa, in Morocco the majority of the settlers were of French origin. Numbering about one hundred thousand by 1926, they constituted the ranks of the modest class of workers and small merchants that lived mostly in coastal cities. As far as large-scale agriculture and mining were concerned, these remained in the hands of investors of much greater means. In the plains of "useful Morocco," one already observed signs of change in the traditional ways of life. Cattle raising diminished considerably, and some impoverished rural populations moved to form the first slums around those gleaming modern cities.

Meanwhile, the Legion accomplished Herculean works to break up the great barrier of the Atlas and allow the military to better control the Saharan areas. The Tunnel of Foum Zabel, also known as the Legionnaire's Tunnel, required high acrobatics to attach a road on the vertical rock-walls of the Ziz gorges, and then the digging of the tunnel itself. Trucks could do runs between Fes, Meknes, and Boudenib in just a few days after the tunnel was completed in March 1928. The legionnaires then carved a road from Marrakech to Ouarzazate, going over the Tichka Pass at an altitude of 2,260 meters (7,000 feet). Morocco was French colonialism's answer to that other mythical land of sunshine, California.[13]

Moroccans were more informed about the realities of colonialism than Lyautey would have wanted them to be. Those who had fought on the battle-fields of the Great War in Europe had seen wealth and modernity, and, on the same occasion, what the pretense of moral superiority amounted to. They had met Europeans, who, unlike most of the settlers, treated them with respect. Following the disintegration of the Ottoman Empire, a renewed awareness of identity emerged among Arab populations. Pilgrims to Mecca and students sent to study in Cairo brought back new ideas to the Maghreb. From the most remote regions of the French empire came news of revolts: the Yen Bai mutiny in Vietnam and the Kongo-Wara rebellion in French Equatorial Africa. Closer to Morocco, since 1920 the Destour party in Tunisia had provided an example of how people colonized by France should demand democratic reforms. Lyautey emphasized that the education of upper-class Moroccans would eventually make them, alongside their French mentors, stewards of their own country. But in 1925, following his efforts at creating a Moroccan elite, there were only twenty-five hundred Moroccans in the schools of the protectorate, absorbing a mere fifth of the education budget.

The secretary general of the Colonial Exhibition, Pierre Deloncle, made the case that one ought not to discredit the future of the civilizing mission in the colonies after the Great War. How could a proud French tradition of bringing good be extinct after so many centuries, he asked? On the walls of the main pavilion, carved in stone for posterity, was a list of colonizers beginning with the name of Middle Age crusaders such as Godfrey of Bouillon. Elaborating on the Near East, where the Allies had just carved out the spoils of the Ottoman Empire, which had fallen apart after the war, he asked: "Did those Crusaders lack dexterity with the indigenous populations? That is quite unlikely: How could their memory, in this early twentieth century, have such an aura of prestige if they had been harsh and disdainful?"[14] Communist critics of the exhibition, including writers such as André Breton, derided it as a colonial "Luna-Park" and highlighted the ills of what they called the "colonial robbery." They denounced the posters recruiting for the colonial army: "An easy life, colored women of ample bosom, the noncommissioned officer elegantly dressed in a light-cloth suit and roaming around in a rickshaw pulled by the man of the land—adventure, advancement."[15]

From his sleek Art Deco office at the exhibition, Lyautey surveyed the scene with satisfaction—eight million people visited the grounds until it closed in September. After his unceremonious ouster from Morocco, he had, predictably, dived periodically into serious bouts of depression. He and his wife split their time between a château in Lorraine and a Parisian apartment at number 5, Rue Bonaparte, on the Left Bank. At the house in Lorraine, he organized the collections of memorabilia he had brought back from the colonies—weapons, rugs, opium pipes—displaying them in specially conceived galleries. His two-story library reflected his wide taste and intellectual curiosity. He published more of his letters. When in Paris, he attended conferences and visited personalities from the world of politics and letters. He carefully refrained from commenting on Morocco, however. "Morocco? *Connais-pas!*"—"I don't know it!"—is how he abruptly dismissed impertinent inquires on the matter.

The official album put out by the periodical *L'Illustration* contained an opening text written by him. Lyautey avoided the kind of hubristic discourse displayed by the secretary general who spoke of medieval crusades. Somewhere in the notes he prepared for his speech on May 6 is this paragraph:

> Colonial action is a prime example of constructive and beneficial action, under the condition that we do not believe too firmly in the infallibility and perfection of our procedures. To always keep an eye open on what can be better than us in our different brothers, to adapt to their statutes, their traditions, their customs, their beliefs, in a word, to understand them.[16]

Lyautey remained consistently pragmatic throughout a life dedicated to expanding and consolidating the French empire. In his early years in Morocco, he stated, "I am firmly convinced that most of our colonial wars are misunderstanding," a laughable proposition, but in the worst moments of the Rif War, he also foresaw this "historical truth" that North Africa would eventually part ways with France.[17] Then again, he said he wanted this separation to be amicable, even "affectionate," and that would happen because by

then the merits and advantages of France's colonial action would have
become obvious.[18]

The truth of Lyautey, sadly, lay in the sobering fact that his ideal of a
peaceful colonial penetration, the method of the *tache d'huile*, the oil stain,
could already be deemed a failure by the time the exhibition opened. The
racial politics of playing Arabs against Imazighen in Morocco did not prevent
the latter from standing up to the French. In the south, expedient alliances
with the great qaids such as Thami El Glaoui hardly changed anything in
the lives of the humblest. "The Moroccan satrap estimates that the great
charter of the French bourgeoisie is subversive and dangerous," noted Ho
Chi Minh, as he learned that Lyautey forbid the publication of the Charter
of Human Rights in the protectorate.[19] The main pavilion of the exhibition
would remain as the Musée des Colonies after the closing of the exhibition.
Still a museum to this day, it is dedicated to French immigration history.

One year after the exhibition, in 1932, in the high mountains of the High
Atlas, in a chaos of deep gorges, sharp crests, and boulders, stained here and
there with a somber forest of majestic cedars, the last Amazigh holdouts still
defied the French colonial army, together with their families, resistants from
"pacified" regions pushed up there, and their herds. The sultans had never
dared to venture on those peaks. It fell on General Antoine Huré, trained
under the orders of Lyautey, to command the last phase of the French invasion aiming to subdue these holdouts and achieve complete domination over
Morocco. Things had been quiet since the end of the Rif War. As Huré
explained in his description of the campaign, Germany had begun to arm
herself again, and the unfinished business in Morocco had to be taken care
of, quickly. This campaign began in 1932. Political opinion in France might
have warmed up to colonialism at last, but it assumed that no more bad news
would come. Minister André Maginot, who traveled to Morocco, advised
Huré, "If you have an unfortunate fight, I'll hide your losses, I'll lie in the
face of evidence, but I'll do it only once. If you endure a second reversal, I'll
be forced to confess the truth, and then, all of those like you who want the
pacification of Morocco will be swept away like Ferry after Lang Son."[20]

Huré relied on the usual array of troops, a backbone of Legion companies, Algerian and Moroccan infantry, and thousands of auxiliaries from
those very Imazighen that a few years before still resisted the French,
including the Zayanes. Heavier weaponry gave these troops even better
chances to succeed. After the Rif War, the First Regiment had received a

battery of 80mm mountain artillery; in 1932, the Second and Fourth Regiments got their own artillery. Motorization of both transportation and attack vehicles strengthened the French forces. Aviators, tossed around by violent drafts and turbulence over the mountains, performed the dangerous and essential role of photographing the terrain and dropping bombs.

These last campaigns in Morocco were waged at vertiginous heights, sometimes under torrential summer storms. The Imazighen, surrounded in their high valleys, would not budge. As usual, they made the best use of a terrain they knew perfectly, using ravines as natural trenches and grottoes and caves as bunkers. Their determination to fight was inexorable, all the more so because prophecies spoke of them as the final, true victors in this last stage of Morocco's conquest. The French poured over these mountains a deluge of bombs and shells, and, when that still failed to provoke submission of the tribes, resorted to starve the fighters and prevent access to watering points. The women, who played an outstandingly tenacious role in this resistance, went to fetch water at night and were often shot. When the French cornered the fighters in their caves, they took them out with grenades. General Guillaume, who left the most detailed account of these fights, wrote that their intensity rivaled that on the front in France during World War I.[21]

Huré first neutralized the Tafilalet oasis, in February 1932, denying the fighters their usual base on which they could fall back to rearm. In August and September, the Second Regiment brought the raging battle to Mount Tazizaout against the holy man El Mekki Amhaouche and his three brothers. Legend had it that the mule of Muhammad had passed through the region, and so the Amazigh population held this corner of Morocco even more dearly. Aiming at one thousand combatants and their families, fire killed indiscriminately. On September 13, El Mekki Amhaouche offered his submission and that of twenty-three hundred families to Huré in person. Huré had special words of thanks for the legionnaires of the Meknes mobile group, who, despite having had fewer auxiliary troops and artillery to rely on, displayed great bravery.

Months later, in 1933, Huré tackled the resistance massed in the peaks of the Djbel Saghro below the Atlas range, at Bou Gafer, with the Second and Third Regiments. About a thousand Aït Atta men and their families withstood another deluge of bombs. On February 28, the Moroccans killed Henri de Bournazel, an officer of the Spahis whose swagger had since the Rif War produced a popular following in the news. Then Huré returned to the High Atlas, across the Dades River Valley, to subdue the fighters and their people massed on the Baddou mountain range at an altitude of 2,921 meters (almost 6,000 feet).

On May 1 the resistance inflicted some bitter losses on a company of legionnaires and Skirmishers they attacked at the post called Mserid, armed with grenades and daggers. The news was bad enough to reach Paris and alarm the French president, Édouard Daladier, who warned Huré, in the same vein as Maginot, that the government might fall if other news of this sort came.

The resistance's success at Mserid remained an isolated incident, and those in the Baddou Mountains faced artillery and aviation bombing. The testimonies of these campaigns are hard to collect, given their oral nature. Still, thanks to the work of the anthropologist Michaël Peyron, some songs have been collected and translated to give a measure of the resistance's character.

> It's the Baddou that take away the water,
> And even the pebbles made a mockery of me.

> I'd be content with plants and herbs
> if the grain of the Muslims is lacking,
> Eating dirt I prefer to the domination of the Christian.[22]

By the end of August the leader Ou Skounti presented his submission. He and his fighters had been the most stubborn and determined in a colonial invasion that had its share of indomitable, legendary resistants.

Legionnaire Jean Martin witnessed those last years of the grand French *geste* of conquering Morocco. He wrote candidly that fighting in Morocco was more than he had bargained for when he joined the fabled corps of the Foreign Legion, in those later years of the Moroccan conquest. After the full might of the French army, massive artillery, armored vehicles, and airplanes set the last redoubts of Amazigh resistance on fire in the Djbel Saghro, Martin emerged from a terrifying fight with striking disbelief:

> Death was not a new element in our legionnaires' existence. We had all accepted the risk of death, for the day it would come, *inch'Allah*! But there, that exciting and dangerous game played with chance was too uneven. The Saghro, an episode of European warfare in the center of Morocco, was not chasing adventure anymore, and we all had, more or less, the sensation that being in one piece was a miracle.[23]

The Moroccan enemy had a chance to win, and that, for Martin writing in the 1930s, changed the rules of the game: The symbolic meaning of the fight was no longer the same. Huré, after the Baddou, recalled passing by a column of legionnaires and Skirmishers: "Many walked barefoot . . . Their ripped coats and pants showed well what kind of climbing they had had to undergo. But what beautiful soldiers they were."[24]

By 1934, perhaps, the French could call the end of Morocco's "pacification," twenty-two years after the protectorate was declared. The same number of years remained before Morocco could gain independence and the son of Moulay Yusef could truly regain his sovereignty as King Mohammed V, in 1956. The most prominent historian of the protectorate, Daniel Rivet, estimates that at least one hundred thousand Moroccans lost their lives during the conquest of their country. Against that, the entire French forces are estimated to have lost eighty-six hundred men.[25]

Lyautey died in 1934 at his château in Thorey, Lorraine, still ruminating on dark thoughts. He had asked to be buried in Morocco, and so authorities built a mausoleum in Rabat, in the appropriate Moorish style. The remains of Inès Lyautey, whom the French government had made Commander of the Légion d'Honneur in 1946, joined his in 1953. After Moroccan independence, the French government feared depredation of the monument and transferred the marshal's remains to the pantheon of France's great military men, Les Invalides, in Paris, where he now lies a few yards away from Emperor Napoléon I (the remains of his wife were reinterred in Thorey). It is a fitting resting place for a man who cherished the sword that had belonged to a grandfather who fought with Napoléon in the Grande Armée. This time, a fleet of cruisers and full military honors were available in Rabat to give the marshal an appropriate farewell from Morocco.

Epilogue: *Mon Légionnaire*

In Lyautey's files at France's National Archives there is a manuscript written by the legionnaire named Eugène Boulic, who campaigned through the South Oranais with a company of the First Regiment and battled in the Middle Atlas.[1] The stories he tells unfold on lined paper in polished cursive handwriting, with a hint of the diligence that a good school of the French Republic imprinted on its young citizens at the turn of the century. Boulic's manuscript explains that he spent many years serving under Lyautey's orders, and he recalled that dedicated service with fondness and admiration. Boulic lived in Paris when he sent Lyautey his testimony, in which he asked for financial assistance. Lyautey responded in a note, remembering well those campaigns, if not Boulic's presence in particular, and gave him the name of a charity that would help.

A leader, high commander or modest noncommissioned officer, was an element essential to group solidarity. He set an example, especially in battle. He enforced the rules, but also knew when to close an eye to his men's behavior when that leniency secured even more trust. "I like this primitive life. I feel so strong and gay. I feel in communion with my men," declared Peshkov as he prepared to venture in the Middle Atlas in 1923.[2] The Legion admired Lyautey for his camaraderie with his men, and the sentiment was reciprocal.

The legionnaires best served Lyautey's colonial project. They fought with deadly force, they built with equal efficiency, and then fought again. How did the legionnaire fight so well? The legionnaires often showed a flamboyant lack of discipline. All agreed, however, that the "Legion under fire is always brilliant."[3] For those who have never fought, the question conjures up situations lived in the shocking, pressing awareness that one can die at any moment, that somebody will surely die in the midst of the advancing cohort under fire.

Legionnaire Boulic, who fought as a legionnaire during World War I as well, gives an honest assessment of that experience of the battle in the infamous, muddy, vermin-infested trenches of northern France. The core impulse of the legionnaire stems from his sense of responsibility for the group of other soldiers. After wondering what makes the soldier face situations where the odds of surviving are so slim, the legionnaire explained:

> The sentiment that animates me is not to complicate to understand: I walk because everybody walks and I am a man, damn! My comrades are not quitting, I will not quit either, the sergeant before the line of skirmishers sets the example and already he is wounded, I can see the blood dripping from his left hand. I walk like a man because I have my self-esteem; it dictates that running back would be cowardice.[4]

Colonel Fernand Maire, a World War I hero and veteran of the Legion in the interwar period, was revered by his soldiers, and readily confessed that his steadiness under fire was the result of constant effort to overcome his own fear.[5]

These soldiers were not always moved by a devotion to France. Actually, many of the German legionnaires that manned the corps did not like the French, sometimes to the point where the distaste compromised discipline. Evidence that legionnaires saw themselves as the soldiers of Europe's civilizing mission is also rather scarce. Surely Peshkov's memoirs display the staunchest confidence in France's colonial mission. However, Cooper records that he was left speechless in a conversation with a Moroccan qaid of the Draa Valley, as to why the French and the Legion had come over to kill his people:

> "To pacify your country," I answered, explaining to him that we brought over mechanical appliances to till the ground, built bridges for them, and gave them medical stores.
>
> "But," he answered, "we are quite satisfied to live as we have always done. We do not wish for your new ideas. We have never done you any harm and yet the more of us you kill, the more medals you get. Even your Mullah [meaning the priests] shake you by the hand for having killed us poor people who never harmed you."[6]

Remembering that he had already heard the same words elsewhere, Cooper readily admitted that he could not answer the qaid's indictment.

Legionnaires were driven to the Legion for a wide variety of practical and material reasons. Oftentimes enlisting was the only solution they faced, for manifold reasons. Enlisting allowed them to earn a modest pay with, luck permitting, the prospect of a decent retirement. The Legion, famously, did not ask too many questions concerning a troubled past, and living far away from home represented an attractive option for social outcasts. That the Legion offered many opportunities for drinking, sex with the indigenous population and prostitutes, or even sex with other soldiers, all that made it quite a desirable prospect.

The legionnaire's archetype emerged as a wounded character, a man with a melancholic, if not depressive, streak. The dreaded *cafard* clouded the sun that shone on the legionnaire's forehead, and this image is key to finding out who the mythical legionnaire was. "We're professional soldiers. We don't give a damn what we fight for. It's our job. We've nothing else in life. No families, no ideals, no loves."[7] These men not only wanted a solution to their problems, they also wanted to be cut off from their earlier existence. Hence, through hard work, physical hardships, and a highly structured life, the legionnaire forgot the burdens that life had placed on him. "One often hears of the need to respect human dignity. Well, I am sorry I have to say that I've encountered the great respect for human dignity at the Foreign Legion," certifies Legionnaire Flutsch.[8]

But the mission of the Legion was at its heart military, and fighting is an ugly reality. Legionnaires' memoirs, as much as they hardly profess trust in the civilizing mission, say little about the true horrors of armed combat. Here and there evidence of what constituted a legionnaire core reality peeks out.[9] Maimed, scarred bodies were constant reminders that war exacts its toll on bodies. The Legion's *salle d'honneur* in Sidi Bel Abbès featured the wooden hand of Danjou, whose gallantry was intrinsic to the Legion's infamous fight at Camarón, and Peshkov had lost an arm in combat. So what lifted the body of a legionnaire off the ground, and pushed him through a hail of bullets, running toward a row of armed, ferocious men who defended their ancestral lands, their families, and their possessions?

Fighting is life affirming, it is a manifestation of a will to power, as Ernst Jünger wrote.[10] It offers moments of exhilaration. The legionnaires, time and time again, are described as itching to fight. Boulic evoked those times when the soldiers "fully enjoyed the brutal inebriation of fighting, till victory of death, because in the Army of Africa, and especially in the Legion, one did not know what retreat meant. This was the true Legion."[11] Fighting is existential. It's a rush, an addictive rush.[12]

The legionnaire lived this excitement with sheer esprit the corps, the tightest bonds of solidarity that held the Legion, and only that. This is the ideal that stories, customs and rituals, and training instilled in the new recruit from day one in Sidi Bel Abbès. Unyielding dedication was the legionnaire's redemption, not sacrifice for the nation, nor hatred for the enemy, but esprit de corps in a white European troop, used by France to build an empire.[13] Paradoxically, it is because they formed an army of outcasts, and often outlaws with its own idiosyncratic culture that they remained together. Warfare is now approached as an activity that not only wounds body, but the psyche as well. One can say, then, that legionnaires came to the fight already wounded, or at least that's what their writings suggest.

This Legion's model of the outcast warrior has to be viewed in historical circumstances: a disenchanted modernity in Europe and colonialism, a cultural mood felt even more vividly after World War I. Ernst Jünger saw it clearly: Europe's young left were, in many ways, victims of *ennui*, "those young persons who, in the foggy dark of night, left their parental home to pursue danger in America, on the sea, or in the French Foreign Legion. It is a sign of the domination of bourgeois values that danger slips into the distance."[14] In the Legion you acquired character, the evidence of your inalienable volition. To be a soldier in the Tonkin or in the Moroccan *bled*, no matter who you were, a private or a marshal, was to seek remediation toward a lost unity, even transcendence.

All the same, the legionnaires killed civilian populations to build a colonial apparatus. Profound ambivalence lay underneath the image. Hence Boulic, as he contemplates a Moroccan family trotting along a path in the calm countryside: "Those ones, my God, they've never heard of the wireless telegraph and Mistinguett [a popular singer], but they are no less happy for it."[15] Another page in Boulic's memoir is striking. A piece of stone in the walls of his fort in the Middle Atlas becomes the subject of meditation. In the hard limestone he observes distinct fossil traces of seashells, just like those he has seen on France's beaches: how intriguing, given that he stands hundreds of kilometers from the sea, and at more than one thousand meters in altitude. Boulic is thrown back in time, many millennia back, to the very appearance of what we called "life," when those basic cell organisms swam in a primitive, murky sea.

He pictures combinations of more complicated organisms, lands rising slowly, producing conditions that require further adaptation, volcanoes surging, in the shadow of which strange ferns, huge plants thrive and decompose, forming a rich humus where reptilian creatures crawl, already showing stumps of what will be the wings of our birds' ancestors. Life complicates even more. Oviparous creatures yield to mammals, and those adapt to the seasons that now mark the earth's revolutions. The sea is now the one we know, less extended, but of clear blue depth:

> Here stops the primitive dream suggested to me by the sight of these fossil shells. These ancestors are worthy of many other ones that have succeeded them since the birth of those so-called civilizations, because the obscure conscience of those primary organisms only urged them to ensure the life and reproduction of the species. However, this conscience now developed has, under the name of intelligence, the notion of Good and Evil, and yet, in spite of its almost miraculous ascent, it does not seem to have progressed as much in the realm of Goodness as in scientific knowledge. As we have seen recently, the civilized men that we pretend to be, put this marvelous domain in service of brutal force and methodical destruction.[16]

What cruel irony, this colonial adventure of the legionnaires. Self-loathing gave it meaning. The thrust was so strong that it killed.

The legionnaires were dreamers. "They make up stories," explained Auger, who wrote one of the reports commissioned at the height of the Legion's crisis in 1919–1920.[17] Georges Manue, with more flair, evoked "these splendid stories of the legionnaire in which truth and dreams mix seamlessly."[18]

It's this dream that Legionnaire Boulic couched in his memoirs with his fine handwriting, on those pages written in his small *chambre de bonne* in the Fifth Arrondissement and destined to end up in Marshal Lyautey's papers. On a rainy afternoon, under a gray, leaden sky, the old legionnaire thinks of the *bled*, of his African days. "I vegetate," he sighs. From his window he sees dirty, wet roofs, while from the narrow courtyard a fetid smell rises. Screechy jazz notes come from a speaker somewhere on the building's floor. The horns of taxis and buses echo from the Parisian street. He cannot shake off that powerful spell of Africa. He dreams of it again and again: "And in spite of myself my thoughts bring me back over there, in the silent and calm country where I lived so many years, in that landscape of endless plains or tormented mountains, in that dry land of endless, luminous horizons." The forlorn legionnaire concludes: "Oh! Paris, Queen of the World! Yes, maybe for those who have not seen anything else."[19]

Afterword

Memories of the colonial period are in a political contest, and they remain up for grabs. The statue of Lyautey that once guarded the center of Casablanca's main square has been prudently moved to the confines of the French consulate nearby, but in 2005, the French National Assembly passed a law requiring French teachers to emphasize the positive role of imperialism, especially in North Africa.

Seen that way, the Foreign Legion and the images that surround the corps constitute a *lieu de mémoire*, a "place of memory." Every Fourteenth of July, on Bastille Day, when the French army corps parades down the Champs-Élysées in Paris to much applause, the legionnaires who walk down the iconic avenue to the notes of "Le Boudin" march, with their slow pace of eighty-eight steps per minute, claim the loudest applause. Bearded engineers of the Sappers section, wearing the characteristic leather apron, open the parade. Rather than evoking brutal conquest, these soldiers from all over the world make a case for universal values as embodied by France.

But the history of the Legion in the 1950s and 1960s, involved as they were in the movement for independence of French colonies and decoloniza-tion, also informs perceptions of the Legion. Throughout Vietnam, Legion troops faced the Communist and nationalist armies of the Viet Minh led by Ho Chi Minh starting in 1947. The struggle intensified until the landmark battle of Dien Bien Phu was fought from March 13 to May 7, 1954. The French defensive forces at Dien Bien Phu, a large base in a wide valley of the western Tonkin mountains, including two airfields, featured the Legion prominently, as well as Vietnamese and North African Skirmishers. They aimed at preventing the Viet Minh from using neighboring Laos as a rear base. Under the command of General Vo Nguyen Giap, the Viet Minh's thirty-five thousand fighters submerged the French forces and inflicted terrible losses while tightening their stranglehold over Dien Bien Phu. The legionnaires fought till the bitter end and lost six battalions, so beleaguered that they spoke of yet another Camarón, but eventually General Christian de Castries had to surrender. Ongoing negotiations in Geneva between France and her former colonies took a decisive turn, and Indochina gained its independence that same year.

Still reeling from the bitter defeat they had suffered at Dien Bien Phu, those Legion troops and officers who came back from Indochina, tired, found themselves fighting in Algeria's struggle for independence, from 1954 to 1962. Against the forces of the National Liberation Front, they served in the Battle of Algiers in 1957, and then conducted anti-guerrilla operations across the country. General Charles de Gaulle, who had launched negotiations with the NLF, faced stiff opposition in the army against abandoning France's most significant colony, and, obviously, not the least from the Legion, given how closely the corps was attached to Algeria. Hence, Legion officers played a prime role in the Generals' Putsch that sought to overthrow General de Gaulle in April 1961, leading to the dissolution of the First Foreign Parachute Regiment. Then, more Legion officers joined the Organisation Armée Secrète (OAS) fighting to maintain French hold over Algeria after the failed coup—whether the rest of the corps itself would have followed these renegades remains the object of speculation. After France reached the Évian Accords with the NLF and a referendum was held in France, Algeria became an independent country.

On October 24, 1962, the last legionnaires left the Quartier Viénot in Sidi Bel Abbès and transferred to France. The monument at Quartier Viénot was carefully dismantled and transported to the Legion's new headquarters in Aubagne, near Marseilles, where it still stands. Along with the monument came caskets holding the remains of Aage of Denmark and Paul-Frédéric Rollet. All the other precious artifacts of the museum were also transferred at independence, save for one: the flag commemorating Tuyen Quang. The captain who had taken it from the Chinese, de Borelli, had declared that it should stay in Sidi Bel Abbès forever, or else it should be burned. The flag went up in flames on the eve of the Legion's formal departure.

Through this postcolonial prism, the Legion becomes another kind of emblem. One of the most ardent fighters against the Algerians was a former legionnaire called Jean-Marie Le Pen, who, as the founder and leader of the Front National with a former OAS member, Jacques Bompard, has reminded the public of how his three years spent in the Legion determined his existence. Recently, in the Calais crisis, when thousands of refugees and migrants, unable to reach the United Kingdom, accumulated in makeshift camps on the French side of the Channel, a former commander of the Legion, Christian Piquemal, was arrested by the French authorities at an anti-Islam protest in the streets of Calais, causing outrage in some quarters of the Legion's aficionados.

Nothing can be forgotten, contrary to what Piaf sings in "Mon Légionnaire," nor should it be. Hence, it seems appropriate to revisit some essential decades in the history of the Legion and delineate the figure of the legionnaire. Finding the sources of resistance to colonization represented a hard challenge in the context of people with oral traditions, and distinguishing and isolating the actions of the Legion in military operations where other colonial corps such as the Tirailleurs and the Spahis operated with equal brio was just as daunting. Concerning the writing style of this portrait, I noted that some historians describe the invasion of a foreign land as a "conquest," followed by a phase called "pacification." The indigenous enemies who resist pacification are viewed as "insurgents," "rebels," and "pirates." That linguistic breakdown of colonization must have a powerful effect, because it creates the illusion of benign power and uncontested authority. But in the end, I chose to inhabit the contradiction, or ambivalence, between a certain feel for the exiled, the brazen, and the louche, while trying to remain attentive to the stark facts and realities of history. Myth has its roots in historical reality. I wanted to show not only a complex military history, but also, and more to the point, a complicated history of feelings about and perceptions of the Legion.

This history and portrait of the Legion's dream world provides context to the Legion's memory. Would it also explain why, despite its reputation for still imposing on its recruits a grueling physical training and assigning them the riskiest missions in hard terrain, the Legion continues to attract men from every possible corner of the world, who enlist in a fabled corps to fight on behalf of France?

The command of the force of about seven thousand men, together with its First Regiment, has been established in Aubagne near Marseilles since Algeria won its independence in 1962. The other main corps, the Fourth Regiment, is based in Castelnaudary, a site that also serves as the main training camp. Their missions still take legionnaires to faraway lands. During the first Gulf War, twenty-four hundred legionnaires from a variety of regiments deployed in Iraq. The legionnaires also operate in countries that were once part of that very empire conquered by their predecessors in the Legion. In December 2012, the United Nations' Security Council allowed a military intervention in Mali to repel Islamic militants: Opération Serval, led by the French, featured Legion parachute and infantry troops.

From its founding year in 1831 until 1962, more than six hundred thousand recruits saluted the tricolor flag of France floating over the austere defense walls of the Fort Saint-Jean in Marseilles, the Legion's transit center for Algeria, to contemplate a new existence. Since 1962, an additional fifty thousand have joined under the insignia of the seven-flame grenade.

Acknowledgments

I want to acknowledge first George Gibson, true gentleman of publishing in New York, and Will Lippincott, always the *agent extraordinaire*. My gratitude then goes to Rob McQuilkin at LMQLIT and Jacqueline Johnson and the team at Bloomsbury Publishing.

Many people in libraries and archives made writing this book possible. It was an honor to visit the Foreign Legion's base, museum, and archive at the Quartier Viénot in Aubagne. I thank Capitaine Géraud Seznec and Lieutenant Christophe Lafaye for their courteous and professional welcome, Commandant Jean-Michel Guimard for invaluable information concerning the legionnaires. Thanks also for the research assistance at McCabe Library (especially Sandra Vermeychuk) and for the general support provided by Swarthmore College.

Friends have, since the beginning of this project, been extraordinarily helpful and encouraging: colleagues Carina Yervasi and Tim Burke; brilliant students Josh Cohen and Danny Hirschel-Burns; friends such as Michelle Hartel. In Paris, I salute affectionately Bertrand and Hortense Creiser, and in Copenhagen Lotte Folke-Karsholm. Finally, I want to say thank you to Bruce Grant, who always reads everything twice.

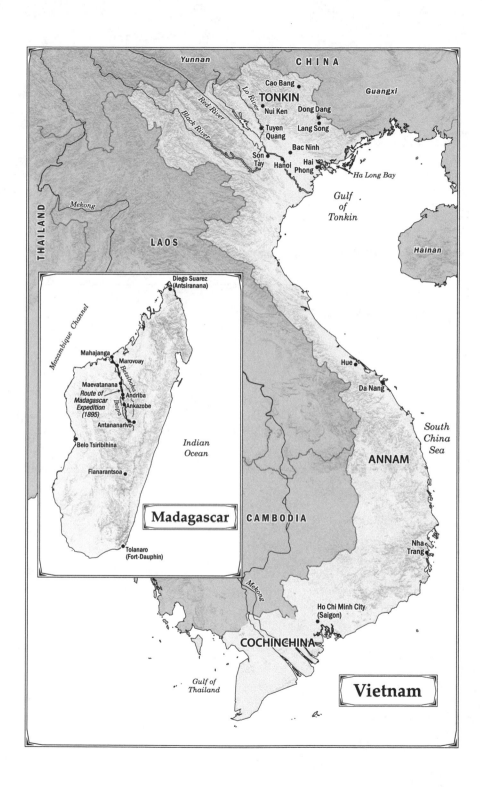

Yunnan   CHINA
                                              Guangxi
                    Cao Bang
              Red River   TONKIN
        Lo River
        Black River Nui Ken   Dong Dang
                    Tuyen   Lang Song
                    Quang
                         Bac Ninh
              Son   Hai
              Tay Hanoi Phong
                              Ha Long Bay
                         Gulf
Mekong   of
                         Tonkin
THAILAND
        LAOS   Hainan

                 Diego Suarez
                 (Antsiranana)

Mozambique Channel

        Mahajanga
              Marovoay
                              Hue
        Maevatanana
        Route of   Andriba   Da Nang
        Madagascar
        Expedition Ankazobe
        (1895)
        Antananarivo
                         Indian   South
                         Ocean   China
        Belo Tsiribihina   Sea

        Fianarantsoa
                                    ANNAM

                    Madagascar   CAMBODIA

                                       Nha
                                       Trang

                         Mekong

                              Ho Chi Minh City
                              (Saigon)

                    COCHINCHINA

              Gulf of
              Thailand   Vietnam

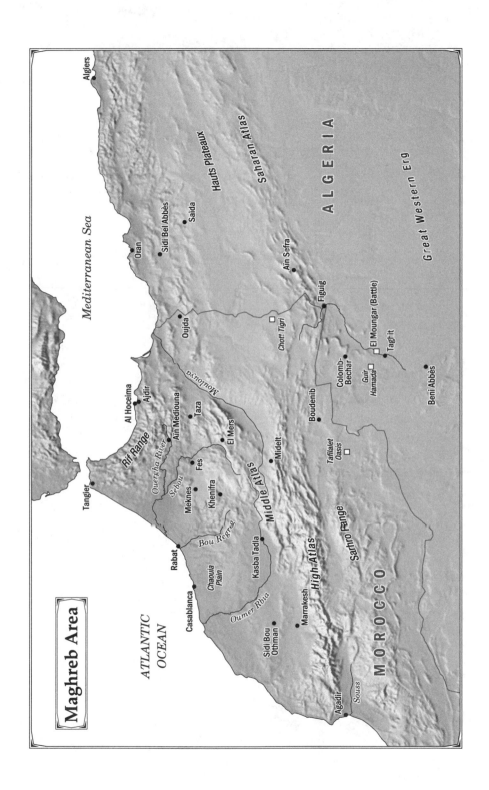

Maghreb Area

ATLANTIC OCEAN

Mediterranean Sea

ALGERIA

MOROCCO

Hauts Plateaux

Saharan Atlas

Great Western Erg

Rif Range

Middle Atlas

High Atlas

Sarhro Range

Ouergha River

Moulouya

Sebou

Bou Regreg

Oumer Rbia

Chaouia Plain

Souss

Tafilalet Oasis

Algiers
Oran
Sidi Bel Abbès
Saïda
Aïn Sefra
Figuig
El Moungar (Battle)
Taghit
Chott Tigri
Oujda
Colomb-Bechar
Guir Hamada
Beni Abbès
Boudenib
Al Hoceïma
Ajdir
Aïn Mediouna
Taza
El Mers
Midelt
Fes
Meknes
Khenifra
Tangier
Rabat
Kasba Tadla
Casablanca
Sidi Bou Othman
Marrakesh
Agadir

Notes

INTRODUCTION

1 Lyautey, quoted in Soulié, pp. 507–8.
2 Le Révérend, pp. 259–60.
3 Aage of Denmark, p. 140.
4 Catroux, p. 86.
5 Stuart, p. 18.
6 A singer named Marie Dubas first interpreted "Mon Légionnaire" in 1936. Piaf recorded the song for the first time a year later.
7 D'Esparbès, p. 62. A second edition of *Les Mystères* appeared in 1912.
8 Aage of Denmark, pp. 61–62.
9 Aage, quoted in Porch, *French Foreign Legion*, p. 426.
10 Martyn, p. 114.
11 Sylvère, p. 155–56.
12 D'Esparbès, p. 181.
13 *Livre d'Or*, p. 421.
14 Maurois, p. 146.
15 Pechkoff (author's name as published), p. 34.

CHAPTER I: AN EARLY HISTORY OF THE LEGION

1 Jünger, p. 42.
2 *Légion*, p. 491.
3 Mannington, pp. 10–11. See also Martyn, who, facing his own recruiting officer, heard: "'Monsieur has no doubt reflected over this step, and knows that the life will not appeal to anyone who does not love the soldiering trade for its own sake. There are many, too many who join the Legion with no sort of qualification for a soldier's life, and these men do no good to themselves or to France by enlisting. I always try to impress upon every candidate that it is a step that should not be taken without much reflection.'" (pp. 14–15).
4 *Légion*, p. 322.
5 Lamping, p. 36.

6   Bugeaud, quoted in Porch, "Bugeaud," p. 378.
7   Lamping, p. 70.
8   Inevitably, the French conquest of Algeria degenerated into a string of atrocities. There was little interest in taking prisoners. An infamous massacre happened in June 1845, in the Darha mountain range. While attempting to dislodge hundreds of fighters and villagers who had sought refuge in caves, the French commander ordered his soldiers to light fires at the entrance of the caves: up to eight hundred people, including women and children, were asphyxiated.
9   Tocqueville, p. 111.
10   Lamping, p. 23.
11   Ibid., p. 77.
12   Lamborelle, p. 37.
13   Baumgart, p. 215.
14   Bazaine, quoted in Dabbs, p. 230.
15   In 1767, Monseigneur Pigneau de Behaine landed in the south of Vietnam, close to today's border with Cambodia, with a mission to evangelize. In a context of civil disturbance, Pigneau de Behaine gained the trust of the future emperor Gia Long and was able to launch a broad campaign of conversions to Catholicism. That was also an advantage in the game of influence that already existed between the French and the English. He was not the first Frenchman to set foot in that part of Asia. The Jesuits had been there before, among them Alexandre de Rhodes, who left a lasting legacy to the Vietnamese: a transliteration of their language in romanized characters, the Quoc Ngu that, together with an elaborate system of diacritical signs, successfully replaced ideograms. Hence Vietnam became the rare Southeast Asian language that can be deciphered with relative ease by the Western eye.
16   *Légion*, pp. 101 and 647.

CHAPTER 2: ALGERIA!

1   Le Révérend, p. 53.
2   Ibid., p. 59.
3   Ibid., p. 75.
4   Lyautey, quoted in Teyssier, p. 33.
5   Maurois, p. 21.
6   Lyautey, quoted in Teyssier, p. 58.
7   Le Révérend, p. 60.
8   Ibid., p. 59.
9   Ibid., p. 107.
10   Gallieni, quoted in Michel, p. 42.
11   Ibid., p. 53. See also Ellie, pp. 16–17.
12   Chartrand, p. 251.
13   Ibid., p. 318.
14   Ibid., p. 431.
15   Armengaud, p. 89.
16   Ibid., p. 71.
17   Le Révérend, p. 106.
18   Ibid., p. 98.
19   Lyautey, quoted in Teyssier, pp. 86–87.

CHAPTER 3: 1885

1 Leroy-Beaulieu, quoted in Girardet, p. 27.

2 Lyautey, *Lettres du Tonkin*, vol. 1, p. 48.

3 Bonnetain, p. 32.

4 Martyn, p. 122.

5 Bolis, p. 14.

6 Martyn, p. 124. See also Rosen: "When the transports sail from Oran or Marseilles with relief companies of the Legion on board, the Suez Canal is a favorite means of deserting. According to the Canal regulations the steamers must slacken speed in the narrow straights of Suez, and the legionnaire takes the opportunity to jump overboard. He swims the short stretch to land and [safety]. The sentries on the transport may not use firearms in the international waters of the Suez Canal, and therefore cannot fire on the deserter as he swims. Neither is extradition from the English or Egyptians authorities to be feared" (p. 221).

7 Mannington, p. 63.

8 By the end of the century Singapore had become the largest trading place of Southeast Asia. Paul Bonnetain, the author of the geographical exploration tome *Le Monde pittoresque et monumental*, upon discovering a sleepy Saigon that stretched its afternoon nap as long as it could, lamented, "At the same time, though, Hong Kong and Singapore—and it must be as hot in these ports—are bustling with activity. Banks, offices, the stock-exchanges, the common citizens are doing business, and at the club, between two cocktails drunk while standing up before the bar, the pencils of the brokers run over their transaction logs. We definitely lack those qualities that, when found in excess, make the Englishman unbearable to us!" (p. 126).

9 Pfirmann, *Képi Blanc*, 345 (August 1976), p. 44.

10 Mannington, p. 89.

11 Brocheux and Hémery, p. 4.

12 Mannington, p. 68.

13 Hocquard, p. 213–14.

14 Martyn, p. 202.

15 Service Historique de la Défense (henceforth cited as SHD), Algérie (henceforth cited as 1H), 1015.

16 Camps, p. 37.

17 Ibid., p. 22.

18 Lonlay, p. 104.

19 Camps, p. 48.

20 On March 3, lore has it that Legionnaire Streibler took a fatal bullet for Officer de Borelli as both men were inspecting Chinese camps and barracks largely evacuated, save for a few holdouts. Borelli spoke of the suffering of his men in a poem "To My Men Who Died," surely the better known, albeit not the finest, in a surprisingly wide range of legionnaire-written poetry (*Légion*, pp. 1033–35).

> *Compagnons, j'ai voulu vous parler de ces choses,*
> *Et dire en quatre mots pourquoi je vous aimais:*
> *Lorsque l'oubli se creuse au long des tombes closes,*
> *Je veillerai du moins et n'oublierai jamais.*

> Companions, I wanted to tell you about these things,
> And say in a few words why I loved you:

When oblivion casts its shadows along the tombs,
I'll stand by and will never forget.

21 Verdier, pp. 185–86.
22 Fourniau, p. 12.
23 *1885: Le Tournant*, pp. 60–61, 78.

CHAPTER 4: *LE CAFARD*

1   Le Révérend, p. 114.
2   Ibid., p. 148.
3   Ibid., p. 165.
4   Lyautey, quoted in Teyssier, p. 117.
5   Ibid., p. 165.
6   Verdier, p. 298.
7   Pfirmann, *Képi Blanc*, 347 (June 1976), p. 43.
8   Sylvère, p. 64.
9   Quoted in Fourniau, p. 23.
10 Dreyfus, p. 177.
11 Pfirmann, *Képi Blanc*, 347 (June 1976), p. 43.
12 Dreyfus, p. 68.
13 Pfirmann, quoted in Porch, *French Foreign Legion*, p. 236.
14 Lyautey, quoted in Bodin, p. 38.
15 Martyn, p. 11.
16 Ibid., p. 26.
17 Ibid., pp. 114–15.
18 Mannington, pp. 232–33, 234.
19 *Légion*, pp. 583–84.
20 Pfirmann, *Képi Blanc*, 346 (May 1976), p. 39.
21 Des Écorres, p. 149.
22 Girod, pp. 244–48.
23 Quoted in Fourniau, *Vietnam*, p. 25.
24 See Bodin, p. 52.
25 Mannington, p. 237.
26 Pfirmann, *Képi Blanc*, 347 (June 1976), p. 43.
27 Mannington, p. 285.
28 Bôn Mat, p. 34.
29 "La Légion étrangère en Extrême-Orient 1898–1946," p. 7.
30 Carpeaux, pp. 112–15.
31 Martyn, p. 176.
32 Le Révérend, p. 192.
33 Clemenceau, quoted in Gury, p. 86.
34 Kohn, quoted in Randau, p. 208.
35 Le Révérend, p. 43.

CHAPTER 5: OIL SLICK

1   Lyautey, *Lettres du Tonkin*, vol. 1, p. 83.
2   Ibid., pp. 280, 294, 296.
3   Ibid., pp. 286, 175.
4   Archives d'Outre-Mer (henceforth cited as AOM), Microfilm Series 129, 77.

5 Bolis, pp. 26–27; see also Bôn Mat, pp. 25–26.
6 Menditte, p. 91.
7 Lyautey, *Lettres du Tonkin*, vol. 1, p. 321.
8 Ellie, p. 322.
9 Quoted in Bodin, pp. 202–3.
10 Menditte, p. 139.
11 Sylvère, p. 263.
12 Mannington, pp. 325–26.
13 Sylvère, p. 213.
14 Magnus, p. 119.
15 Menditte, p. 136.
16 Lyautey, *Lettres du Tonkin*, vol. 1, pp. 77, 105, 152.
17 See Fourniau, pp. 141, 188.
18 Le Révérend, p. 207.
19 Ibid., p. 254.
20 Ibid., p. 102.

CHAPTER 6: GRIM MARCH

1 Darricarrère, p. 244.
2 Langlois, p. 59.
3 Ibid., p. 59.
4 Cooper, p. 79.
5 Langlois, p. 71.
6 Cooper, p. 79.
7 Hocquard, p. 87.
8 Darricarrère, p. 136.
9 Langlois, p. 103.
10 Reibell, p. 123.
11 Langlois, p. 116.
12 Reibell, p. 104.
13 Langlois, p. 140.
14 Ibid., p. 189.
15 SHD, Madagascar (henceforth cited as 8H), 35.
16 *Légion*, p. 403.
17 Ellis, p. 130.
18 Gallieni, quoted in Michel, p. 161.
19 Lyautey, *Lettres du Tonkin*, vol. 2, p. 242.
20 Lyautey, *Correspondance*, p. 298. See also Le Révérend, p. 213.
21 Lyautey, quoted in Teyssier, p. 190.
22 Ibid., p. 169.
23 Lyautey, *Lettres du Sud*, p. 126.
24 Ibid., p. 135.
25 Lyautey, *Lettres du Tonkin*, vol. 1, p. 340.
26 Soulié, p. 12.
27 Ibid., pp. 98, 106.

CHAPTER 7: IN THE LEGION

1 Sowerwine, p. 89.
2 Jünger, "On Danger," p. 29.

3   Martin, p. 13.
4   Jünger, *African Diversions*, p. 63.
5   Ibid., p. 63.
6   *Légion*, pp. 98, 101, 646.
7   Soulié, p. 61.
8   Magnus, p. 141.
9   Cooper, p. 63.
10 Archives Nationales (henceforth cited as AN), Papiers Lyautey (henceforth cited as 475 AP), 256.
11 Rosen, p. 38.
12 See *Légion*, p. 176–78. The music of Le Boudin was composed by François-Nicolas Wilhem, probably during the Crimean campaign. The lyrics, however, mention the Siege of Tuyen Quang, so they must have been written after 1885. Specialists struggle to figure out what *le boudin* means: it could be a type of blood sausage, or the rolled-up tent that the legionnaires put over their knapsacks when marching.
13 Rosen, p. 55.
14 "Men who can converse [in] three tongues are to be found in almost every barrack room," wrote Frederic Martyn in the mid-1890s (p. 106). He speaks of many officers knowing at least six languages, and then of the extraordinary case of a Swiss sergeant, a former professor "credited with knowing no fewer than twelve languages." Petrovski assured Martyn that the officer spoke the best Russian he had ever heard from the mouth of a foreigner.
15 Sylvère, pp. 84–85. The famous episode of the Green Hill took place in Crimea, in 1855.
16 Soulié, p. 54.
17 Ibid., p. 12.
18 Rollet, quoted in ibid., pp. 23, 20, 55.
19 Cooper, pp. 158, 161.
20 Archives Diplomatiques, Correspondance Politique et Commerciale (henceforth cited as AD, CPC), Nouvelle Série (henceforth cited as ns) Algérie, 26.
21 Sylvère, p. 115.
22 Cooper, p. 18.
23 Sylvère, p. 68.

CHAPTER 8: BEYOND THE DESERT

1   Guillaume, p. 106.
2   Ibid., p. 109.
3   Cooper, p. 75.
4   Martin, p. 48.
5   Ehrhart, *Képi Blanc*, 520 (February 1992), p. 30.
6   *Légion*, p. 838.
7   Foucauld, quoted in Gandini, p. 117.
8   Lyautey, *Paroles d'action*, p. 381.
9   Gandini, p. 117.
10 Foucauld, *Lettres et Carnets*, p. 202.
11 Lyautey, *Vers le Maroc*, p. 38.
12 Lefebvre, *Képi Blanc*, 111 (July 1956), p. 45.
13 Lyautey, *Vers le Maroc*, p. 39.
14 Ibid., p. 32.

15 Ibid., p. 278.
16 *Légion*, p. 1004.
17 Eberhardt, quoted in Brower, p. 206.
18 Eberhardt, vol. 1, p. 128.
19 Ibid., p. 129.
20 Randau, p. 208.
21 Ibid., p. 203.
22 Lyautey, *Vers le Maroc*, pp. 179–80.

CHAPTER 9: MOROCCO THAT WAS

1 Lyautey, quoted in Abitbol, p. 415.
2 SHD, Morocco (henceforth cited as 3H), 23.
3 Kuntz, p. 405.
4 The French used the latest military equipment, including a balloon that allowed them to survey their surroundings. The snitch, as the soldiers nicknamed it, served mostly to signal the French presence to the enemy (hence the nickname).
5 On February 2, Boutegourd's troops suffered one of their most stinging reversals at Dar Ksibat, as they went out to seize a herd of sheep that would have fed them for many days, the Oulad Saïd warriors killed eleven of the troops, including four legionnaires. Pushing east where the rising, mountainous terrain provided safe harbor for the Hafidians, the columns reached a large camp of the M'Dakra, on March 8, near Sidi Aceïla. The camp sat at the edge of a ravine five or six hundred meters deep, down which the Moroccans sought to escape. From a vantage point, the French aimed the fire of their machine guns at the crowd below: "The bullets fell on the mass of fugitives, covering with bodies the path and slopes of the pass that the Moroccans tried in vain to climb under the artillery's and the infantry's gusts of fire." Echoing through the valley, "the noise was terrifying, the carnage atrocious." See Grasset, p. 123; Kann, p. 38.
6 Grasset, p. 136.
7 Scenes of horror alternated with moments of laughter. The English observer Reginald Rankin explains the ruse that the legionnaires used to herd sheep they brought back from fighting: "The sheep were troublesome; they refused to follow the track; and the legionnaires found running after them a course with many a fall in the mud. So with their usual genius they devised a labor-saving plan. If the sheep strayed a little from the track, the corporal cried, '*Bellez!*'—'Bleat!'—and a perfect tornado of 'baas' issued from the bearded throats of the escort, so marvelously and unutterably sheeplike that the errant muttons were momentarily convinced of the presence on the road of a large party of their species, and so thither, with their gregarious instincts, they at once returned." See Rankin, p. 129.
8 Kann, p. 45.
9 SHD, 3H, 259 (citing from a French translation of Premschitz's work commissioned by the French army).
10 AD, CPC, ns Algérie, 26.
11 Sylvère, pp. 250–51.
12 The problems posed by German propaganda and desertion were far from over after this dispute was settled. Just a month later, in December 1908, a group of German legionnaires from the Second Regiment, led by Legionnaire Pal, tried to escape: they mutinied at their garrison in Aïn el Hadjar and hijacked a train to escape. Subsequent interrogation revealed that Pal had indeed been prodded by a representative of a pan-German league in Algiers. There was great suspicion that their agents had infiltrated

the ranks of the Legion as well. Another soldier named Moppert had been arrested in Germany for molesting a child in a public bathhouse before escaping his country's police and joining the ranks in Algeria. Some questioned whether German authorities did not strike a deal with such outlaws, letting them go if they agreed to serve in the Legion as spies. Lyautey, as head of the Oran division, downplayed the severity of the case in a report dated on December 17. He noted that all the recruits that had joined Pal were younger recruits who had not yet acquired "the cohesion or the esprit de corps of the older ones at the Legion, for whom cases of desertion happen only singularly." That, remarked Lyautey, could hardly make the need for better recruitment of officers less urgent: there were so few possibilities of advancement for the NCOs, and a dearth of candidates for the higher-rank officers, that a revision of the statutes might be in order. See AD, CPC, ns Algérie, 26.

13   Centre de Documentation Historique de la Légion Étrangère (henceforth cited as CDHLE), *Journal de marche*, pp. 91–93.
14   AN, 475 AP, 256.
15   Lefebvre, *Képi Blanc*, 121 (May 1957), p. 50.
16   SHD, 3H, 565.
17   Lefebvre, *Képi Blanc*, 121 (May 1957), p. 51.
18   Lyautey, *Vers le Maroc*, p. 68.
19   Le Révérend, p. 241.
20   Gury, p. 102.

CHAPTER 10: *BARAKA*

1   AN, 475 AP, 256.
2   *Traité.*
3   AD, CPC, ns Maroc, 223.
4   Lyautey, quoted in Rivet, vol. 1, p. 160.
5   Hubert, pp. 155–56.
6   Ibid., p. 192.
7   Saint-Aulaire, p. 262.
8   Lyautey, quoted in Rivet, vol. 1, p. 144.
9   Ibid., p. 138.
10   Lyautey, *Lyautey L'Africain*, vol. 1, p. 60.
11   Inside Marrakech, Mangin found a population that quickly had grown disenchanted of the new sultan's puritanism. El Hiba had ordered that all celibate women, including widows, divorcees, and *femmes galantes*, marry one of his mujahideen, many of whom had already looted and sacked many of Marrakech's finer townhouses. In the sultan's old palace where the holy chief had taken his residence, delightful marble courtyards were ruined after serving as stables.
12   Cornet, p. 174.
13   Lyautey, *Lyautey L'Africain*, vol. 1, p. 43.
14   Harris, p. 124.
15   Incidentally, Lyautey made sure that the ceremonial parasol seized from Hiba was sent to the Army Museum in Paris.
16   Lyautey, *Correspondance*, p. 193.
17   Lyautey, *Lyautey L'Africain*, vol. 1, p. 264.
18   Saint-Aulaire, p. 263.
19   Le Révérend, p. 309.

CHAPTER 11: PRINCIPLES OF WAR

1 Ehrhart, *Képi Blanc*, 538 (October 1993), p. 57.
2 Lyautey, *Lyautey l'Africain*, vol. 2, p. 171.
3 Ehrhart, *Képi Blanc*, 539 (November 1993), p. 47.
4 *Légion*, p. 115.
5 Lyautey, *Correspondance*, p. 164.
6 Lyautey, quoted in Teyssier, p. 388.
7 Ehrhart, *Képi Blanc*, 539 (November 1993), p. 48.
8 Lyautey, *Lyautey l'Africain*, vol. 3, p. 303.
9 Ibid., vol. 2, p. 300.
10 Fabre, p. 26.
11 Aage of Denmark, p. 81.
12 Briand, quoted in Maurois, p. 272.
13 Lyautey, *Lyautey l'Africain*, vol. 3, p. 237.
14 Mahuault, p. 91.
15 Ibid., p. 93.

CHAPTER 12: A QUEST FOR REDEMPTION

1 Lyautey, *Lyautey l'Africain*, vol. 3, p. 345.
2 SHD, 3H, 697.
3 AN, 475 AP, 138 (Lyautey to the Ministre de la Guerre, July 22, 1920).
4 Sowerwine, p. 117.
5 AN, 475 AP, 138.
6 SHD, 3H, 697.
7 AN, 475 AP, 138.
8 AN, 475 AP, 138.
9 AN, 475 AP, 138.
10 Magnus, p. 170.
11 Lyautey, quoted in Porch, *French Foreign Legion*, p. 384.
12 AN, 475 AP, 138.
13 Cooper, p. 121.
14 AN, 475 AP, 138.
15 Lyautey, quoted in Porch, *French Foreign Legion*, p. 409.
16 AN, 475 AP, 138.
17 De Tarde, p. 167.
18 Lyautey, *Correspondance*, p. 194.
19 Ibid., p. 194.
20 Saint-Aulaire, p. 271.
21 Lyautey, *Vers le Maroc*, p. 279.
22 Le Révérend, p. 229.
23 Ibid., pp. 245–46.
24 Lyautey, *Lyautey L'Africain*, vol. 3, pp. 111, 254.
25 Kuntz, pp. 86-87.
26 Manue, p. 14.
27 Maurois, pp. 117, 130.
28 Ehrhart, *Képi Blanc*, 519 (January 1992), pp. 30–31.
29 *Légion*, p. 696.
30 Dorian, p. 203.

31 Durosoy, p. 46.
32 Martin, p. 250.
33 Ibid., p. 192.
34 Ibid., p. 218.
35 *Légion*, p. 696.
36 Ehrhart, *Képi Blanc*, 536 (July 1993), p. 56.
37 Martin, p. 104.
38 *Revue Voilà*, September 17, 1937.
39 D'Esparbès, p. 270.
40 Cooper, p. 14.
41 Ibid., p. 140.
42 SHD, 3H, 259.
43 SHD, 1H, 1015. Ehrhart, in *Képi Blanc*, 518 (December 1991), p. 30–31, tells the story of a legionnaire who committed a crime so that he would be able to join his male lover in prison.
44 Peyrefitte, *Propos*, p. 27.
45 Ward Price, p. 21.
46 Wharton, p. 109.
47 Le Révérend, p. 364.

CHAPTER 13: MIDDLE ATLAS

 1 Le Révérend, p. 303.
 2 Fabre, p. 33.
 3 Ibid., p. 193.
 4 Magnus, p. 141.
 5 Pechkoff, p. 96.
 6 Soulié, p. 358.
 7 Ibid., p. 364.
 8 SHD, 3H, 917.
 9 Aage of Denmark, p. 89.
10 Ibid., pp. 89, 92.
11 Ibid., p. 98.
12 Soulié, p. 360.
13 Pechkoff, p. 78.
14 The forts were simple structures, built by the legionnaires with the material they excavated or produced—stones, bricks, lime. Around the stonewalls ran barriers of barbed wire to which the soldiers attached tin cans, so that any attempt at trespass could be detected.
15 Cooper, p. 43.
16 Peshkov again: "I cannot sleep at night. I go out on the terrace and give myself up to the wind that blows from the open spaces, and I have vague impressions of things that happened long ago . . . echoes from another life . . . murmurs and sighs of a world invisible and yet real, that is all encompassing. I ask myself whether in a former existence I have not lived in Africa" (Pechkoff, p. 4). If there is one theme that runs through Peshkov's memoirs, it's the notion of an alchemy, of a transmutation of matter through a synthesis of opposites in the great cosmic spectacle in Africa.
17 Right after arriving, Durosoy witnessed a tragedy: the rivulet that flowed near El Mers village burst its banks during a sudden rainstorm and took away twenty men and a hundred horses. Weeks later, once the larger part of the troops left, Durosoy had to

endure another kind of calamity, less tragic, but altogether maddening: the myriad of flies that, lacking as targets the hundreds of horses and mules of the attack forces, were now finding in the remaining humans the only subjects left to torment.

18 Durosoy, p. 40.

19 Ibid., p. 58.

20 Abdelkrim built infrastructure, including telephone lines. He benefitted, it seems, from the support of a legionnaire named Joseph Peter Klems who had deserted from the Legion in August 1922 and converted to Islam while still in Algeria fighting against the French, to then operate in the Middle Atlas. Eventually he joined the cause of the Riffians. Caught by the French after the war, he was sent to the penal colony in Guyana.

21 Durosoy, p. 64.

22 One extraordinary feature of Fes was its age-old water system, a network of underground canals that tamed the natural rivulets on which Fes was built and circulated the water everywhere, feeding into fountains, public baths, and houses. The French who visited always marveled upon hearing the rushing sound of water nearby, even as their walks through Fes progressed toward the dense center.

23 Lyautey, quoted in Durosoy, p. 66.

CHAPTER 14: THE RIF ON FIRE

1 Pechkoff, p. 159.

2 Ibid., p. 180.

3 Ibid., p. 192.

4 Aage of Denmark, p. 163.

5 Ibid., pp. 167–68.

6 Ibid., p. 172.

7 Cooper, p. 119.

8 Aage of Denmark, p. 175.

9 Pechkoff, p. 266.

10 Durosoy, p. 136.

11 Cooper, p. 119.

12 Pechkoff, p. 210.

13 Lyautey, *Lyautey L'Africain*, vol. 4, p. 322.

14 Courcelle-Labrousse and Marmié, p. 211.

15 Durosoy, p. 166.

16 Lyautey, *Lyautey L'Africain*, p. 354.

17 SHD, 3H, 602.

18 Courcelle-Labrousse and Marmié, p. 202–3.

19 Durosoy, pp. 189–90.

20 Catroux, p. 229.

21 Durosoy, p. 190.

22 SHD, 3H, 917.

23 SHD, 3H, 917.

24 Pétain, quoted in Bourget, "La Rivalité," p. 130.

25 Durosoy, p. 208.

CHAPTER 15: *BEAU TRAVAIL!*

1 SDH, 3H, 697. In 1947, the official magazine of the corps took its name, *Képi Blanc*, from the white cap. Nowadays, the kepi does not include a cover, since it is directly

manufactured from white material. Officers wear a black kepi adorned with the seven-flame grenade.

2   Wren, p. 256.

3   This information on P. C. Wren's *Beau Geste* and its sources comes from Legion historian Martin Windrow. See his careful explanations in *Our Friends*, pp. 622–27.

4   *Légion*, p. 150.

5   The Legion took the town of Narvik in Norway at the end of May 1940, thus interrupting the "Iron Route" along which the Germans transported the Norwegian ore essential to their military industries. At Bir Hakeim in the middle of the Libyan desert, from May 26 to June 11, 1942, the Thirteenth Demi-Brigade of the Legion resisted Italo-German forces led by General Erwin Rommel in person. Winston Churchill might have fallen into hyperbolic rhetoric when he said that without Bir Hakeim, World War II would have lasted two more years, yet the unyielding resistance of the legionnaires under an astoundingly heavy bombardment does appear heroic. See *Légion*, p. 164.

6   Lyautey, quoted in Soulié, pp. 507–8.

7   The exotic was fashionable in 1930s France, influencing both luxury markets and mass consumerism. The chocolate brand Banania put the jovial face of a Senegalese Skirmisher on its boxes, to great commercial success. One wouldn't have been surprised to see the kepi of the legionnaire on a cereal box.

8   Ageron, p. 573.

9   There were pavilions for all the French colonies of the Indochina Union, Madagascar, Algeria, Morocco, and many more. Other countries present were Italy, the Netherlands, and the United States, the latter offering a visit to a replica of George Washington's plantation mansion, Mount Vernon.

10   The two thousand native people that the organizers brought from abroad populated the exhibition as sales persons, guides, or as beneficiaries of French civilization in schools. Unlike the previous show in 1900, Lyautey forbade the exhibition of native people in degrading conditions. It was, for the times, considered a great step in humanitarian sensibilities.

11   The true mastermind of this planning and building effort was Henri Prost, who worked in close collaboration with the resident-general.

12   Lyautey remained adamant that he would not allow Morocco to be "Algerianized," by which he meant becoming a real French department, as opposed to a protectorate. He held the Algerian settlers in rather poor regard: they "have a pure *Boche* [derogatory word for Germans] state of mind, with the same theories on inferior races that warrants exploiting them without mercy. There is no humanity and intelligence in those settlers" (Abitbol, p. 434). In 1919 he had had to weather a severe political crisis when renewed attacks in the press called for a direct administration and a parliamentary regime in Morocco that would have deprived the sultan of whatever sovereign powers he had left.

13   Georges Manue, a legionnaire, extolled upon his arrival "the true beauty of Casablanca, isn't it this tableau drawn in lines so neat? The pure sky frames houses with flat roofs; the sun playfully reflects on the steel of the machinery, it even animates the coldness of metals, it even assorts the tints of that metal with those, more mobile, that the sea brings between the piers" (Manue, *Sur les marches*, p. 15).

14   *Album*, np.

15   "*Ne visitez pas l'Exposition Coloniale,*" np.

16   AN, 475 AP, 208.

17   Kuntz, p. 89.

18 Ageron, p. 218.
19 Ho Chi Minh, quoted in Rivet, vol. 3, p. 320.
20 Maginot, quoted in Huré, p. 45.
21 Guillaume, p. 384.
22 Peyron, "Tazizaout," np.
23 Martin, p. 153–54.
24 Huré, p. 159.
25 Singer and Langdon, p. 223.

EPILOGUE: *MON LÉGIONNAIRE*

1 Eugène Boulic, born on November 11, 1879, joined the Second Foreign Regiment on December 19, 1905. He came from the French army and its reserve contingents with a spotty record stating "*absences illégales*" as the cause for a demotion from the rank of corporal to simple private, at the end of the year 1900. Following more trouble with the authorities at the Legion, he transferred to the First Regiment in 1907 and remained there as a *soldat de 2ème classe*. His "État signalétique et des services" record at the Legion lists campaigns in Algeria (1905-1908), in the Algero-Moroccan borderlands (1908), in the Saharan regions (1908-1909) and in Algeria again (1909).

2 Pechkoff, p. 28.

3 Kuntz, p. 404.

4 AN, 475 AP, 256.

5 *Légion*, p. 583.

6 Cooper, pp. 137–38.

7 Quoted in Porch, *French Foreign Legion*, pp. 342–43.

8 Sylvère, p. 117.

9 Martyn speaks of the "sickening thud" he heard as he skewered the soldiers of King Behanzin of Dahomey with his bayonet. Or take Ehrhart's recollection of the time he went out on a mission to castigate the Beni Ouaraïn people in 1914, some days after taking the gateway city of Taza. A captain, Baudoin, falls near him in the middle of firefight. Ehrhart rushes to help: "The bullet hit him right in the middle of the fore-head, one of those big lead bullets that Moroccan guns shoot. I dropped my bag and put it under his head. I spoke to him; he was not answering. He groaned, bloody dribble oozed at the corner of his mouth. He had a hiccup that squirted brain matter through the gaping wound on his head. It dripped on my hand as I held him. I tried to give him some water with a mint cordial when the physician came with Colonel Boyer. I raised my eyes saying, 'Colonel Baudoin.' He answered, 'What a tragedy for France.' The doctor saw my hand full of his brain and said, 'It's useless to give him some water, it's over'" (Ehrhart, *Képi Blanc*, 539 [November 1993], p. 46).

10 Ernst Jünger, the former legionnaire and veteran of World War I, aptly described war as a "storm of steel." He wrote that war offered the man who fights a unique opportunity. Transcending the horrors of the battlefield, he can realize himself fully. See Jünger, *Der Kampf*.

11 AN, 475 AP, 256.

12 See Cendrars, *J'ai tué*.

13 True, a report in Lyautey's papers (AN, 475 AP, 73) states that the legionnaires appreciated the Tirailleurs Sénégalais with whom they fought, but the way the memoirs and the military archive tell their story, it's essentially a segregated affair. Did the Legion draw its motivation to fight from racial and religious prejudice, then? A lesser-known song of Edith Piaf composed by Raymond Asso, "Le Fanion de la Légion" ("The

Pennant of the Legion") is about a company of legionnaires who, held up in the iconic fort isolated in the *bled*, take a last stand against what the song refers to as *les salopards* ("bastards").

Just as night blankets the plain,	*Comme la nuit couvre la plaine,*
The bastards, toward the small fort	*Les salopards, vers le fortin*
They have slipped like hyenas	*Se sont glissés comme des hyènes*
They fought till morning,	*Ils ont lutté jusqu'au matin:*
Howls of rage,	*Hurlements de rage,*
Body to body, savage,	*Corps à corps sauvages,*
The dogs were scared of the lions.	*Les chiens ont eu peur des lions.*
They did not take the position.	*Ils n'ont pas pris la position.*

This word *salopard* is often used by the legionnaires to describe their North African adversaries. Clearly, the legionnaires were hardly models of cultural empathy. In his memoirs, Maurice Magnus explains that one thing united the French and the German: "They dislike and despise the Arab" (Magnus, p. 170). See Rivet, vol. 2, pp. 16–18.

14   Jünger, "Danger," p. 29.
15   AN, 475 AP, 256. Lyautey, expressing his early distress that the southern Algeria that he had fallen for will be destroyed by the armed forces that he had brought, exclaimed, "Ah! The implacable civilization. Here is a happy people, honest, believing in religion, patriarchal, around which the desert has put a defensive belt that saved its oases from any agitation. After ten years of railways and an infusion of European ideas, what will be left of it? Where is truth, where is progress?" See Le Révérend, pp. 80–81. See also Kuntz, p. 514: "I glance one last time at this quiet and unknown corner, and I think of the civilization of these brave people, sweet and simple, that we are going to destroy and replace with our own civilization, tumultuous, complicated, busy. I wonder if the man who will come by this same place in half a century will find the same honest, sound population, as perfectly happy."
16   AN, 475 AP, 256.
17   AN, 475 AP, 138.
18   Manue, *Sur les marches*, p. 12.
19   AN, 475 AP, 256.

Bibliography

ARCHIVES AND MANUSCRIPT COLLECTIONS

Archives Diplomatiques, La Courneuve
Correspondance Politique et Commerciale
Ancienne Série—Madagascar: Dossiers 58, 59.
Nouvelle Série—Algérie: Dossiers 24, 26; Maroc: Dossier 223

Archives Nationales, Pierrefitte-sur-Seine
Papiers Lyautey 475 AP (Dossier 256 includes the memoirs of Legionnaire E. Boulic)

Archives d'Outre-Mer, Aix-en-Provence
Fonds territoriaux
Algérie, Gouvernement Général, Affaires Indigènes
Territoires du sud—22H: Dossiers 44, 63

Indochine, Fonds de l'État-Major de l'Indochine
Microfilms 77, 78.

Dons et acquisitions
Dossier 13X

Centre de Documentation Historique de la Légion Étrangère, Quartier Viénot, Aubagne
Historique de la 24ème Compagnie Montée du 1er Régiment

Service Historique de la Défense, Vincennes
Algérie—1H: Dossier 1015
Indochine—10H: Dossiers 3, 5, 57, 61, 62
Madagascar—8H: Dossiers 35, 51, 69, 98, 100

Maroc—3H: Dossiers 23, 76, 77, 90, 148, 259, 308, 312, 314, 479, 565, 576, 602, 697, 900, 916, 917

PRINTED DOCUMENTS

Sources
By Louis Hubert Gonzalve Lyautey
Correspondance 1891–1914 (with Albert de Mun). Paris: Société de l'Histoire de France, 2011.
Du rôle social de l'officier dans le service militaire universel. Paris: Perrin et Cie, 1891.
Du rôle colonial de l'armée. Paris: A. Colin, 1900.
Lettres du Tonkin et de Madagascar, 1894–1899. 2 vols. Paris: A. Colin, 1920.
Lettres de jeunesse; Italie—1883; Danube—Grèce—Italie—1893. Paris: Grasset, 1931.
Lettres du Sud de Madagascar, 1900–1902. Paris: A. Colin, 1935.
Lyautey l'Africain: textes et lettres. 4 vols. Paris: Plon, 1954–1957.
Paroles d'action—Madagascar—Sud-Oranais—Oran—Maroc (1900–1926). Paris: A. Colin, 1927.
Vers le Maroc: lettres du Sud Oranais, 1903–1906. Paris: A. Colin, 1937.
Le Révérend, André, ed. *Un Lyautey inconnu: correspondance et journal inédits, 1874–1934.* Paris: Perrin, 1980.

Foreign Legion
Aage of Denmark. *My Life in the French Foreign Legion.* London: Nash and Grayson, 1928.
Armengaud, Jean-Louis. *Le Sud-Oranais: journal d'un légionnaire, 1881–1882.* Paris: Charles-Lavauzelle, 1893.
Bolis, Ernest. *Mes campagnes en Afrique et en Asie, 1889–1899: Légion étrangère, Infanterie de marine, Algérie, Soudan, Tonkin.* Strasbourg: C. Gassmann, 2001.
Bôn Mat. *Souvenirs d'un légionnaire.* Paris: Messein, 1914.
Cendrars, Blaise. *J'ai tué.* Saint-Clément: Fata Morgana, 2013.
Cooper, Adolphe R. *March or Bust: Adventures in the Foreign Legion.* London: Hale, 1972.
Doty, Bennett J. *The Legion of the Damned.* New York and London: The Century Co., 1928.
Écorres, Chartrand des. *Au pays des étapes: notes d'un légionnaire.* Paris and Limoges: Charles-Lavauzelle, 1892.
Ehrhart, Joseph. "Mes treize années de Légion étrangère." *Képi Blanc,* 516 (October 1991)–546 (June 1994).
Erlande, Albert [Brandenbourg, Albert-Jacques]. *C'est nous: la Légion!* Paris: Les Éditions de France, 1930.
Jünger, Ernst. *African Diversions.* London: John Lehmann, 1954.
———. *Der Kampf als inneres Erlebnis.* Berlin: E. S. Mittler & Sohn, 1926.
———. "On Danger." *New German Critique* 59 (1993).
Lamping, Clemens. *The French in Algiers: I. The Soldier of the French Foreign Legion.* New York: Wiley & Putnam, 1845.
Lasvigne, Henri. *Monsieur Siwisky Soda: nouvelles sur la Légion Étrangère.* 1932.
Lefebvre, G. "Carnets." *Képi Blanc,* 107 (March 1956)–125 (September 1957).

Le Poer, John Patrick. *A Modern Legionary*. New York: Dutton, 1905.

Magnus, Maurice. *Memoirs of the Foreign Legion*. London: Secker, 1924.

Mannington, George. *A Soldier of the Legion*. London: J. Murray, 1907.

Manue, Georges. *Têtes brûlées: cinq ans de Légion*. Paris: Nouvelle Société d'Éditions, 1929.

———. *Sur les marches du Maroc insoumis*. Paris: Gallimard, 1930.

Martin, Jean. *Je suis un légionnaire*. Paris: Librairie Arthème Fayard, 1938.

Martyn, Frederic. *Life in the Legion*. New York: Charles Scribner's Sons, 1911.

Menditte, Charles de. *Vie militaire dans le Haut-Tonkin, 1895–1897*. Vincennes: Service Historique de l'Armée de Terre, 2003.

Pechkoff [Peshkov], Zinovy. *The Bugle Sounds*. New York and London: D. Appleton and Co., 1926.

Pfirmann, Jean. "Les Carnets du Sergent Pfirmann." *Képi Blanc*, 341 (December 1975)–354 (February 1977).

Premschitz, Raimund Anton. *Meine Erlebnisse als Fremdenlegionär in Algerien*. Metz: P. Müler, 1904.

Rosen, Erwin. *In the Foreign Legion*. London: Duckworth, 1910.

Sablotny, Richard. *Legionnaire in Morocco*. Los Angeles: Wetzel, 1940.

Silbermann, Léon. *Cinq ans à la Légion Étrangère, 10 ans dans l'infanterie de marine; souvenirs de campagne*. Paris: Plon, 1910.

Stuart, Brian. *Adventures in Algeria*. London: H. Jenkins, 1936.

Sylvère, Antoine. *Le Légionnaire Flutsch*. Paris: Plon, 1982.

Weygand, Jacques. *Légionnaire*. Paris: Flammarion, 1951.

Ziegler, Charles. "Souvenirs du Rif." *Képi Blanc*, 232 (August 1966)–233 (September 1966).

Other Documents

Abdelkrim. *Mémoires*. Paris: Librairie des Champs Élysées, 1927.

Album de l'Exposition Coloniale de Paris – 1931. Special issue of *L'Illustration*, 1931.

Les Armées françaises d'outre-mer. Paris: Ministère de la Guerre, 1931.

Augagneur, Jean-Victor. *Erreurs et brutalités coloniales*. Paris: Éditions Montaigne, 1927.

Azan, Paul. *L'Expédition de Fez: avec 114 photographies et deux cartes hors texte*. Paris: Berger-Levrault, 1924.

Bidou, Henry. "Nouveaux Problèmes marocains." *Revue des Deux Mondes*, February 1 1925, pp. 538–54.

Bonnetain, Paul. *Le Monde pittoresque et monumental*. Paris: Quantin, 1887.

Borde, Félix. *Dix ans de Tonkin, 1888–1898*. Paris: F. Carbonnel, 1913.

Bordes, Pierre. *Dans le Rif: carnet de route d'un marsouin*. Lyon: E. Vitte, 1929.

Capperon, Louis. *Au secours de Fès*. Paris: Charles-Lavauzelle, 1912.

Campagnes d'Afrique, 1835–1848: lettres adressées au maréchal de Castellane. Paris: Plon, 1898.

Campagnes de Crimée, d'Italie, d'Afrique, de Chine et de Syrie, 1849–1862: lettres adressées au maréchal de Castellane. Paris: Plon, 1898.

Camps, Capitaine. *Le Siège de Tuyen Quan*. Verdun: V. Freschard, 1902.

Catroux, Georges. *Lyautey le Marocain*. Paris: Hachette, 1952.

Carpeaux, Louis. *La Chasse au pirates: Tonkin*. Paris: B. Grasset, 1913.

Caussin, E. *Vers Taza: souvenirs de deux ans de campagne au Maroc.* Paris: Fournier: 1922.

Chabrol, Emmanuel-Pierre-Gabriel. *Opérations militaires au Tonkin.* Paris: Charles-Lavauzelle, 1897.

Challan de Belval, Albert. *Au Tonkin.* Paris: Delahaye et Lecrosnier, 1886.

Chatinières, Paul. *Dans le Grand Atlas marocain: extraits du carnet de route d'un médecin d'assistance médicale indigène, 1912–1916.* Paris: Plon-Nourrit, 1911.

Corhumel, Édouard. *Journal de marche.* Mesnil-sur-l'Estrée: Firmin-Didot, 1896.

Cornet, Charles. *A la conquête du Maroc Sud avec la colonne Mangin, 1912–1913.* Paris: Plon-Nourrit, 1914.

Darricarrère, Jean. *Au pays de la fièvre: impressions de la campagne de Madagascar.* Paris: A. Michel, 1906.

Dreyfus, Gaston. *Lettres du Tonkin, 1884–1886.* Paris: Harmattan, 2001.

Duchesne, Jacques. *L'Expédition de Madagascar: rapport d'ensemble fait au Ministre de la guerre le 25 avril 1896.* Paris: Charles-Lavauzelle, 1896.

Durand, A. *Les Derniers Jours de la cour Hova.* Paris: Société de l'Histoire des Colonies Françaises, 1933.

Durosoy, Maurice. *Avec Lyautey: homme de guerre, homme de paix.* Paris: Nouvelles Éditions Latines, 1976.

Eberhardt, Isabelle. *Œuvres complètes: écrits sur le sable.* 2 vols. Paris: B. Grasset, 1988–1990.

Ellie, Paul. *Le Général Gallieni: le Tonkin, Madagascar.* Paris: F. Juven, 1900.

Esparbès, Georges d'. *La Légion étrangère.* Paris: Flammarion, 1901.

Fabre. *La Tactique au Maroc.* Paris: Charles-Lavauzelle, 1931.

Forbes, Rosita. *El Raisuni: The Sultan of the Mountains.* London: T. Butterworth, 1924.

Foucauld, Charles de. *Lettres et carnets.* Paris: Seuil, 1966.

——. *Reconnaissance au Maroc, 1883–1884.* Paris: Challamel, 1888.

Frichet, Henry. *À Madagascar: journal d'un sous-officier.* Paris: Boivin, 1901.

Gallieni, Joseph-Simon. *Gallieni pacificateur: écrits coloniaux.* Paris: Presses Universitaires de France, 1949.

——. *Gallieni au Tonkin (1892–1896).* Paris: Berger-Levrault, 1941.

——. *Lettres de Madagascar: 1896–1905.* Paris: Société d'Éditions Géographiques, Maritimes et Coloniales, 1928.

——. *Rapport d'ensemble sur la pacification, l'organisation et la colonisation de Madagascar (octobre 1896 à mars 1899).* Paris: Charles-Lavauzelle, 1900.

——. *Trois colonnes au Tonkin, 1894–1895.* Paris: R. Chapelot, 1933.

Girod, Léon-Xavier. *Dix ans de Haut-Tonkin.* Tours: A. Mame et fils, 1899.

Gouraud, Henri. *Au Maroc, 1911–1914, souvenirs d'un Africain.* Paris: Plon, 1949.

Grandmaison, Louis de. *En territoire militaire: l'expansion française au Tonkin.* Paris: E. Plon, Nourrit et Cie, 1898.

Grasset, Henri-Joseph. *À travers la Chaouia avec le corps de débarquement de Casablanca 1907–1908.* Paris: Hachette, 1912.

Guillaume, Achille-Jean. *Conquête du Sud-Oranais: la colonne d'Igli en 1900.* Paris: Charles-Lavauzelle, 1900.

Guillaume, Augustin. *Les Berbères marocains et la pacification de l'Atlas Central (1912–1933).* Paris: Julliard, 1946.

Harris, Walter. *Morocco That Was*. Edinburgh and London: Blackwood, 1921.

Hellot, Frédéric. *La Pacification de Madagascar: opérations d'octobre 1896 à mars 1899*. Paris: R. Chapelot, 1900.

Hocquard, Édouard. *L'Expédition de Madagascar*. Paris: Hachette, 1897.

Hubert, Jacques. *Les Journées sanglantes de Fez, 17-18-19 avril 1912*. Paris: Chapelot, 1913.

Huré, Antoine. *La Pacification du Maroc*. Paris: Berger-Levrault, 1952.

Jaurès, Jean. *Contre la guerre au Maroc*. Paris: Bureau d'Éditions, nd.

Kann, Reginald. *Impressions de campagnes et de manœuvres, 1907–1908*. Paris: Charles-Lavauzelle, 1909.

Khorat, Pierre [Ibos]. *En colonne au Maroc*. Paris: Perrin, 1913.

Kuntz, Charles-A. *Souvenirs de campagne au Maroc*. Paris: Charles-Lavauzelle, 1913.

Lamborelle, Louis. *Cinq ans en Afrique*. Bruxelles: 1863.

Langlois, Gustave-Léon. *Souvenirs de Madagascar*. Paris: Charles-Lavauzelle, 1900.

Leconte, Jean-François. *Marche de Lang Son à Tuyen Quan, 1ère brigade, Giovanninelli: combat de Hoa Moc, déblocus de Tuyen Quan, 13 février–3 mars 1885*. Paris: Berger-Levrault, 1888.

Lentonnet, Jean-Louis. *Expédition de Madagascar: carnet de campagne*. Paris: Plon, 1897.

Lonlay, Dick de. *Le Siège de Tuyen Quan*. Paris: Garnier, 1886.

Loti, Pierre. *Au Maroc*. Paris: Calmann-Lévy, 1898.

Ne visitez pas l'Exposition coloniale. 1931.

Mangin, Charles. *Souvenirs d'Afrique: lettres et carnets de route*. Paris: Denoël et Steele, 1936.

Maurois, André. *Marshall Lyautey*. London: J. Lane, 1931.

Mordaccq, "Pacification du Haut-Tonkin." *Journal des Sciences Militaires* (1901): 237–74.

Poirmeur, Henri. *Notre vieille Légion*. Paris: Berger-Levrault, 1931.

Rankin, Reginald. *In Morocco with General d'Amade*. London: Longmans, Green and Co, 1908.

Reibell, Émile. *Le Calvaire de Madagascar*. Paris: Berger-Levrault, 1935.

Revue Voilà. September 17, 1937.

Saint-Aulaire, Auguste de. *Confessions d'un vieux diplomate*. Paris: Flammarion, 1953.

Sarrat, Louis. *Journal d'un marsouin au Tonkin, 1883–1886*. Paris: France-Empire, 1987.

Segonds, Marie. *La Chaouia et sa pacification*. Paris: Charles-Lavauzelle, 1909.

Tocqueville, Alexis de. *Writings on Empire and Slavery*. Baltimore: Johns Hopkins University Press, 2001.

Traité conclu entre la France et le Maroc le 30 mars 1912, pour l'organisation du Protectorat français dans l'Empire Chérifien. Bulletin Officiel de l'Empire Chérifien, 1 (November 1, 1912): 1–2.

Vanlande, René. *Au Maroc, sous les ordres de Lyautey*. Paris: Peyronnet, 1926.

Verdier, Armand. *La Vérité sur la retraite de Lang Son*. Paris: A. Savine, 1892.

Ward Price, George. *In Morocco with the Legion*. London: Jarrolds, 1934.

Wharton, Edith. *In Morocco*. London and New York: Tauris Parke, 2004.

Wren, Percival Christopher. *Beau Geste*. Philadelphia and New York: J. B. Lippincott Company, 1925.

Selected Secondary Sources

Abd el Krim et la République du Rif. Paris: Maspéro, 1967.

Abitbol, Michel. *Histoire du Maroc.* Paris: Perrin, 2009.

Ageron, Charles-Robert. "L'Exposition coloniale de 1931." *Les Lieux de mémoire,* vol. 1, pp. 561–91. Paris: Gallimard, 1984.

Aldrich, Robert. *Greater France: A History of French Overseas Expansion.* New York: Macmillan, 1996.

Allain, Jean-Claude. *Agadir 1911.* Paris: Publications de la Sorbonne, 1976.

Amouroux, Henri. *Pétain avant Vichy.* Paris: Fayard, 1967.

Atlas des empires coloniaux, XIXe–XXe siècles. Paris: Autrement, 2012.

Audoin-Rouzeau, Stéphane. *Combattre.* Paris: Seuil, 2008.

Baumgart, Winfried. *The Crimean War, 1853–1856.* London: Arnold, 1999

Berenson, Edward. *Heroes of Empire: Five Charismatic Men and the Conquest of Africa.* Berkeley: University of California Press, 2010.

Bernard, Augustin. *Les Confins Algéro-Marocains.* Paris: Laroze, 1911.

Bodin, Michel. *Les Français au Tonkin, 1870–1902: une conquête difficile.* Saint-Cloud: SOTECA, 2012.

Boniface, Xavier. *L'Armée, l'Église, et la République, 1871–1914.* Paris: Nouveau Monde Éditions, 2012.

Bouchène, Abderrahmane. *Histoire de l'Algérie à la période coloniale, 1830–1962.* Paris and Alger: Éditions de la Découverte, 2012.

Bourachot, André. *De Sedan à Sedan: une histoire de l'armée française. Vol. 1, 1870–1918.* Paris: Bernard Giovanangeli Éditeur, 2011.

Bourget, Pierre. "La Rivalité Pétain-Lyautey de 1925 au Maroc: un nouvel éclairage." *Guerres Mondiales et Conflits Contemporains* 181 (1996): 125–33.

Brocheux, Pierre, and Daniel Hémery. *Indochine, la colonisation ambiguë, 1858–1954.* Paris: Éditions de la Découverte, 1995.

Brouste, Judith. *L'Appel du Sahara.* Paris: Éditions Place des Victoires, 2011.

Brower, Benjamin C. *A Desert Named Peace: The Violence of France's Empire in the Algerian Sahara, 1844–1902.* New York: Columbia University Press, 2009.

Brunon, Jean, et al. *Le Livre d'or de la Légion étrangère.* Paris: Charles-Lavauzelle, 1958.

Charles-Roux, Edmonde. *Un désir d'orient: jeunesse d'Isabelle Eberhardt, 1877–1899.* Paris: Grasset, 1988.

Chavenon, Marie-José. *Inès Lyautey: l'infirmière, la maréchale.* Paris: Gérard Louis, 2010.

Clerisse, Henry. *La Guerre du Rif et la tache de Taza, 1925–1926.* Paris, 1927.

Conklin, Alice L., et al. *France and Its Empire Since 1870.* Oxford: Oxford University Press, 2011.

Cooke, James. *New French Imperialism, 1880–1910: The Third Republic and Colonial Expansion.* Hamden, Conn.: Archon Books, 1973.

Cunningham, Michele. *Mexico and the Foreign Policy of Napoléon III.* New York: Palgrave, 2001.

Curtis, Michael. *Three Against the Third Republic: Sorel, Barrès, and Maurras.* Princeton: Princeton University Press, 1959.

Dabbs, Jack Autrey. *The French Army in Mexico, 1861–1867: A Study in Military Government.* The Hague: Mouton & Co., 1963.

Daughton, James Patrick. *An Empire Divided: Religion, Republicanism, and the Making of French Colonialism, 1880–1914.* Oxford: Oxford University Press, 2006.

Deroo, Eric. *La Vie militaire aux colonies.* Paris: Gallimard, 2009.

———. *Histoire des tirailleurs.* Paris: Seuil, 2010.

Despierres, Jean. *L'Indochine d'antan: Tonkin, Annam, Cochinchine, Cambodge et Laos à travers la carte postale ancienne.* Paris: HC Éditions, 2008.

Dictionnaire de la colonisation française. Paris: Larousse, 2007.

Dorian, Jean-Pierre. *Le Colonel Maire: un héros de la Légion.* Paris: Albin Michel, 1981.

Doury, Paul. *Un échec occulté de Lyautey.* Paris: L'Harmattan, 2008.

Dunn, Ross E. *Resistance in the Desert: Moroccan Responses to French Imperialism 1881–1912.* London: Croom Helm, 1977.

Ellis, Stephen. *The Rising of the Red Shawls: A Revolt in Madagascar, 1895–1899.* Cambridge: Cambridge University Press, 1985.

Finch, Michael. *A Progressive Occupation? The Gallieni-Lyautey Method and Colonial Pacification in Tonkin and Madagascar, 1885–1900.* Oxford: Oxford University Press, 2013.

Fogarty, Richard. *Race and War in France: Colonial Subjects in the French Army, 1914–1918.* Baltimore: Johns Hopkins University Press, 2008.

Franchini, Philippe. *Les Guerres d'Indochine.* Vol. 1. Paris: Pygmalion, 2008.

Frémeaux, Jacques. *De quoi fut fait l'Empire.* Paris: CNRS Éditions, 2010.

———. "Troupes blanches et troupes de couleur." *Revue Historique des Armées* 218 (2000): 19–30.

Fourniau, Charles. *Vietnam: domination coloniale et résistance nationale (1858–1914).* Paris: Les Indes savantes, 2002.

———. *Annam-Tonkin, 1885–1896: lettrés et paysans vietnamiens face à la conquête coloniale.* Paris: L'Harmattan, 1989.

Gandini, Jacques. *El Moungar: les combats de la Légion dans le Sud Oranais: 1900–1903.* Extrem-Sud, 2000.

Gendre, Claude. *Le Dê Thám (1858–1913): un résistant vietnamien à la colonisation française.* Paris: L'Harmattan, 2007.

Gershovich, Moshe. *French Military Rule in Morocco: Colonialism and Its Consequences.* London: Routledge, 2000.

Girardet, Raoul. *L'Idée coloniale en France de 1871 à 1962.* Paris: La Table Ronde, 1970.

Glaoui, Abdessadeq El. *Le Ralliement. Le Glaoui, mon père: récit et témoignage.* Rabat: Marsam, 2004.

Courcelle-Labrousse, Vincent, and Nicolas Marmié. *La Guerre du Rif.* Paris: Tallandier, 2008.

Guinle, Pierre, and Giuseppe Ricci. *Filmographie de la Légion étrangère.* Rimini: Riminicinéma, 1992.

Gury, Christian. *Lyautey-Charlus.* Paris: Non Lieu Éditions, 2010.

Hefferman, Michael. "The French Right and Overseas Empire, 1870–1920." In *The Right in France: From Revolution to Le Pen,* ed. N. Atkin et al. New York: I. B. Tauris, 2003.

Histoire de la France coloniale. 2 vols. Paris: A. Colin, 1990–1991.

Hoisington, William A. *Lyautey and the French Conquest of Morocco.* New York: Palgrave, 1995.

————. "Designing Morocco's Future." *Journal of North African Studies* 5 (2000): 63–108.

Hortes, Jacques. *Historique et combats des compagnies montées de la Légion étrangère: du Mexique au Maroc, 1866–1950.* Nice: Gandini, 2001.

Huré, Patrice. *Portraits de Pechkoff.* Paris: Éditions de Fallois, 2006.

Jobin, Guillaume. *Lyautey: le Résident.* Casablanca: Casa Express Éditions, 2014.

Katz, Jonathan. *Murder in Marrakesh: Émile Mauchamp and the French Colonial Adventure.* Bloomington: Indiana University Press, 2006.

Kobak, Annette. *The Life of Isabelle Eberhardt.* New York: Knopf, 1988.

Lafaye, Christophe. *5ᵉ Étranger: historique du Régiment du Tonkin.* Paris: Lavauzelle, 2000.

Laine, Serge. "L'Aéronautique militaire française au Maroc, 1911–1939." *Revue Historique des Armées* 133 (1978): 107–120.

Laroui, Abdallah. *L'Histoire du Maghreb.* Paris: Maspéro, 1970.

La Légion étrangère: histoire et dictionnaire. Paris: Robert Laffont, 2013.

"La Légion étrangère en Extrême-Orient, 1898–1946." *Bulletin de L'A. N. A. I.* (Association Nationale des Anciens et amis de l'Indochine et du souvenir indochinois) 2 (2005): 7–14.

Lejeune, Dominique. *Les Sociétés de géographie en France et l'expansion coloniale au XIXᵉ siècle.* Paris: Albin Michel, 2015.

Marseille, Jacques. *Empire colonial et capitalisme français: histoire d'un divorce.* Paris: Albin Michel, 1989.

Mahuault, Jean-Paul. *L'Épopée marocaine de la Légion étrangère, 1903–1934.* Paris: L'Harmattan, 2005.

Maxwell, Gavin. *Lords of the Atlas: The Rise and Fall of the House of Glaoua, 1893–1956.* New York: Dutton, 1996.

McAleavy, Henry. *Black Flags in Vietnam.* London: George Allen and Unwin, 1968.

1885: Le Tournant colonial de la République. Paris: La Découverte, 2007.

Michel, Marc. *Gallieni.* Paris: Fayard, 1989.

Mounier-Kuhn, Alain. *Les Services de santé militaires français pendant la conquête du Tonkin et de l'Annam, 1882–1896.* Paris: NEP, 2005.

Munholland, Kim. "Rival Approaches to Morocco: Delcassé, Lyautey, and the Algerian-Moroccan Border, 1903–1905." *French Historical Studies* 5 (1968): 328–43.

Neviaski, Alexis. "Le Recrutement des légionnaires allemands." *Guerres Mondiales et Conflits Contemporains,* no. 237: Dossier: "La Légion étrangère" (2010): 39–61.

Nguyen, Khac Vien. *Vietnam, une longue histoire.* Hanoi: 1987.

Peyrefitte, Roger. *Propos secrets.* Paris: Albin Michel, 1977.

Peyron, Michael. "Tazizaout et Baddou: note de recherche sur des hauts lieux de la résistance amazighe. Haut-Atlas marocain (1932–1933)." michaelpeyron.unblog.fr/category/non-classe (accessed September 15, 2016).

Porch, Douglas. "Bugeaud, Gallieni, Lyautey." In *Makers of Modern Strategy.* Princeton: Princeton University Press, 1986.

————. *The Conquest of Morocco.* New York: Farrar, Straus and Giroux, 2005.

————. *The French Foreign Legion: A Complete History of the Legendary Fighting Force.* New York: HarperCollins, 1991.

Randau, Robert. *Isabelle Eberhardt: notes et souvenirs.* Paris: La Boîte à Documents, 1989.

Randrianja, Solofo. *Madagascar: A Short History*. Chicago: University of Chicago Press, 2009.

Randriamamonjy, Frédéric. *Histoire de Madagascar, 1895–2002*. 2009.

Remond, René. *The Right Wing in France: From 1815 to de Gaulle*. Philadelphia, University of Pennsylvania Press, 1966.

Rivet, Daniel. *Lyautey et l'institution du Protectorat français au Maroc, 1912–1925*. 3 vols. Paris: L'Harmattan, 1988.

Sheean, Vincent. *Adventures Among the Riffi*. London: George Allen, 1926.

Singer, Barnett, and John Langdon. *Makers and Defenders of the French Colonial Empire*. Madison: University of Wisconsin Press, 2004.

Slavin, David H. "The French Left and the Rif War, 1924–1925: Racism and the Limits of Internationalism." *Journal of Contemporary History* 26 (1991): 5–32.

Soulié, Pierre. *Le Général Paul-Frédéric Rollet*. Triel-sur-Seine: Éditions Italiques, 2001.

Sowerwine, Charles. *France Since 1870: Culture, Society, and the Making of the Republic*. New York: Palgrave McMillan, 2009.

Taraud, Christelle. *La Prostitution coloniale: Algérie, Tunisie, Maroc (1830–1962)*. Paris: Payot et Rivages, 2009.

Tarde, Guillaume de. *Lyautey, le chef en action*. Paris: Gallimard, 1959.

Taylor, K. W. *A History of the Vietnamese*. Cambridge: Cambridge University Press, 2013.

Teyssier, Arnaud. *Lyautey*. Paris: Perrin, 2004.

Thomas, Martin. *The French Empire Between the Wars: Imperialism, Politics, and Society*. Manchester, UK: Manchester University Press, 2005.

Trout, Frank E. *Morocco's Saharan Frontiers*. Geneva: Droz, 1969.

Venier, Pascal. *Lyautey avant Lyautey*. Paris: L'Harmattan, 1997.

———. "Lyautey et la soumission du Rabezavana." *Australes*, 1996.

———. "Lyautey et l'idée de Protectorat de 1894 à 1902." *Revue Française d'Histoire d'Outre-Mer* 78 (1991): 499–517.

Price, G. Ward. *Giraud and the African Scene*. New York: Macmillan, 1944.

Wawro, Geoffrey. *The Franco-Prussian War: The German Conquest of France in 1870–1871*. Cambridge: Cambridge University Press, 2003.

Wesseling, Henk. "Imperialism and the Roots of the Great War." *Daedalus* 134 (2005): 100–107.

Windrow, Martin. *French Foreign Légionnaire, 1890–1914*. Oxford: Osprey Publishing, 2011.

———. *Our Friends Beneath the Sands: The Foreign Legion in France's Colonial Conquests, 1870–1935*. London: Weidenfield and Nicholson, 2010.

Image Credits

Index

A Note on the Author

Jean-Vincent Blanchard is Professor of French Studies at Swarthmore College, Swarthmore, Pennsylvania. Born in Canada and raised in Europe, he earned his Ph.D. from Yale University. Blanchard has published on a broad range of subjects in politics, history, religion, philosophy, and the arts. He traveled extensively while researching *At the Edge of the World*, retracing the steps of many of the Foreign Legionnaires and translating original source material. Blanchard is the author of several books published in Canada and France; his first book published in the United States was *Éminence: Cardinal Richelieu and the Rise of France*.